Remembrance and Reconciliation

Remembrance and Reconciliation

Encounters between Young Jews and Germans

Björn Krondorfer

Yale University Press   New Haven and London

Designed by Sonia L. Scanlon.
Set in Baskerville type by Marathon Typography
Service, Inc., Durham, North Carolina.
Printed in the United States of America by Vail-
Ballou Press, Binghamton, New York.

Library of Congress Cataloging-in-Publication-
Data
Krondorfer, Björn.
    Remembrance and reconciliation : encounters
between young Jews and Germans / Björn
Krondorfer.
        p.   cm.
    Includes bibliographical references and index.
    ISBN 0-300-05959-0
    1. Holocaust, Jewish (1939–1945)—
Germany—Influence.   2. Holocaust, Jewish
(1939–1945)—Germany—Public opinion.
3. Public opinion—Germany.   4. Reconciliation.   5. Germany—Ethnic relations.   I. Title.
DS135.G332K76   1995
940.53'18—dc20   94-28747
                        CIP

A catalogue record for this book is available from
the British Library.

The paper in this book meets the guidelines for
permanence and durability of the Committee on
Production Guidelines for Book Longevity of the
Council on Library Resources.

10   9   8   7   6   5   4   3   2   1

to Edith Millman and Ed Gastfriend
for their courage to reach out to the children and
grandchildren of their victimizers

to my parents
for their efforts to learn from the past

to our daughter, Zadekia—
for her, the Holocaust will be the memory of a different
millennium—that she may enjoy life without forgetting

Contents

Preface

For the past ten years, the relationships between Jews and Germans after the Holocaust have occupied much of my thinking and work on both a personal and a professional level. To organize the different experiences and ideas has been a challenging project. Writing about Jewish/German relations after the Holocaust as a non-Jewish German often felt like walking a tightrope. In my head, I heard the voices of some Germans charging me with catering to a particular Jewish view and of some Jews suspecting me of wanting to exonerate Germans. But there are also many Jews and Germans who have taken the risk to meet one another and together confront the Holocaust. Their voices and actions encouraged me to write this book.

My wife, Katharina, is one of those who struggle with Germany's past as she studies the Holocaust in relation to contemporary sexism and antisemitism. She has encouraged me in making sense of my particular struggles and has read different versions of the manuscript with a critical eye. Our discussions about German identity never cease to be stimulating; now that our daughter is a citizen of two countries, they take on a new challenge. I want to thank my parents, brother, and sister for their patience in listening to my stories and thoughts. That we continue talking despite many disagreements shows our willingness to learn from each other.

My love and respect go especially to Lisa Green, Brigitte Heusinger, Erica Kaufman, Sheila Zagar, and Martin Zeidler. We have shared unforgettable years in the Jewish-German Dance Theatre. Without our dance and work, this book could not have been written. I also thank Ruth Laibson, who, as executive director of the Philadelphia Interfaith Council on the Holocaust, has tirelessly worked to organize the summer programs for American and German students. My gratitude goes also to Christian Staffa, for his friendship and his efforts in organizing the German half of the summer programs on the Holocaust. I cannot imagine a better person with whom to share

the task of facilitating these programs. I wish to thank the Berlin Evan-
gelische Akademie, the Washington bureau of the Friedrich Nauman
Foundation, and the board of directors of the Interfaith Council on the
Holocaust, Philadelphia, in particular Leon Bass, Sister Gloria Coleman,
Dorothy Freedman, Ed Gastfriend, Mina Kalter, Ben Loewenstein, John
Raines, and Louis Temme. They all helped in different ways to create a
rare educational opportunity for American and German students to
study the Shoah.

Special thanks go to Josey Fisher, who read the entire manuscript
and offered many good suggestions. For reading parts of the manuscript, I am indebted to Michael Glaser, Ruth Zöe Ost, and the faculty
writing group at St. Mary's College, Maryland (Robin Bates, Ann
Leblans, Jorge Rogachevsky, and Katharina Von Kellenbach). I am also
grateful to Adena Potok for her encouragement. I was able to test my
ideas on the ties between Holocaust memory and creative rituals in various academic settings, such as the Ritual Studies Group of the American
Academy of Religion, the international Holocaust conferences in Oxford
and Berlin (Remembering for the Future, 1988 and 1994), the Conference on Nontraditional/Interdisciplinary Programs (1992), and the Conference on Christianity and the Holocaust at Rider College (1994).

There are many other individuals who helped to shape my thinking
on post-Shoah Jewish/German relations over the years. To mention them
all is impossible, but my thoughts are especially with the American, German, Jewish, and Christian students of the 1989, 1991, and 1993 summer programs. They have had the courage to confront one another as
the third generation after the Holocaust. I want to thank those who sent
me additional material and granted permission to use it.

Most quotations and sources used in the book can be documented.
However, since I am also relying on journal entries, conversations, and
stories as I remember them, I ask the reader to trust my conscientious
effort to report as accurately as possible. At the same time, I realize that
my observations and interpretations are my own. The book mentions
many individuals who have been and still are a part of my life. Some
have consciously accompanied me on the journey of exploring Jew-
ish/German relations, others were incidental to it, albeit important in
their views and opinions. It is my hope that even readers who dissent
from my conclusions will be inspired by this book to pursue and refine
the work toward reconciliation.

Remembrance and Reconciliation

Introduction

My relationships with Jews got off to a heart-wrenching,
alienating start. Jews were introduced to me dead.
  —Sabine Reichel, a German writer living in New York

Germans devoted to working through the past seem bound
to succumb to blind pathos or morbid fascination.
  —Susan Neiman, a Jewish-American writer who lived in Berlin

This book is about young American Jews and non-Jewish Germans and their efforts to come to terms with the history, memory, and memorialization of the Holocaust. These "young" Jews and Germans, who are today mostly in their twenties, belong to the third generation born since the extermination of European Jews by the Nazis during World War II. They are, in general, the grandchildren of the generation that lived during the years 1933–1945.

Third-generation American Jews and non-Jewish Germans are divided by their national, cultural, and religious identities and the history of the Holocaust, or Shoah. But the Holocaust memory also unites them: both groups are tied to a past that has defined them as the descendants of victims or victimizers. Some Jews and Germans of the third generation have begun to work together to understand the effects of this traumatic past, struggling against the mistrust and suspicion that characterize their interactions to this day. To transform their strained relations, they must learn to trust each other and allow their long-stored anger, guilt, grief, and pain to emerge. Reconciliation demands a willingness to become vulnerable and honest in the presence of another.

Because honesty and trust are central to reconciliatory efforts, I begin this book by talking about my own, as yet uncompleted journey into the rugged territory of post-Shoah Jewish/German relations.[1]

1

My Discovery of Jews

When I arrived in the United States, at the age of twenty-four, I was entirely unprepared for my encounter with Jews. My wife, Katharina, and I had scholarships to study Jewish-Christian dialogue[2] at Temple University in Philadelphia, but we somehow did not reckon with the likelihood of actually meeting Jews. I had experienced Jewish-Christian dialogue at German universities as a probing of biblical texts in the light of what was presented as the Jewish tradition. But Jews were absent from our discussions as they were generally absent from postwar German society. And I had not even noticed their absence.

I was born and raised in postwar Germany in a fairly liberal home in which education was more valued than religion. My parents had spent their childhood years in territories that no longer belong to Germany. My mother lived near Königsberg in East Prussia (today, Kaliningrad in Russia) until she fled from the advancing Soviet army at the end of the war. My father grew up in Czechoslovakia, was drafted into the German Wehrmacht at the age of seventeen, and was put into a Czechoslovakian prisoner-of-war camp at the end of the war. My parents met after the war in a small town in West Germany. They liked to travel to other countries, and in the mid–1960s the family (which by then included myself and my brother and sister) moved to Afghanistan for three years. In Germany, our home was always open to visitors of various national and ethnic backgrounds. People came and went, but I don't remember ever meeting a Jewish person in our home. Perhaps I met Jews without knowing it.

As I grew out of my child's world, I slowly became familiar with the fact that something terrible had happened to Jews, something that I later learned was called the Holocaust. *Jude* was a term my generation had learned to avoid, for whenever it was mentioned, the adults reacted in inexplicably strange ways. I remember one family reunion—I might have been twelve at the time—in which my mother yelled at her brother because he spoke contemptuously of Jews. It all happened so fast and with such ferocity that I got frightened. Nothing was explained to us children. This is how we learned to avoid the issue. For all practical purposes, Jews did not exist.

I had met Israelis twice—first, as a child, when my family returned to Germany from Afghanistan via Iran and Israel. Israelis were just as exotic as the Iranians, Indians, and Afghans with whom I had come into contact. There was no special connection between them and us. Years later, when I returned to Israel to tour its Christian holy places with a group of Germans, I missed the chance to correct my perception. By then, as a university student, I was operating on the peculiar assumption that Israelis were somehow not Jews. Israelis, I must have believed, were a nation; *Juden,* on the other hand, I associated with either biblical figures or pictures of corpses from the camps. I understood that Jews had been killed in the course of the "Final Solution," but I did not know why and how they happened to be in Germany before 1933. Nor was I worried about my ignorance. "Since Jews were an abstract race for me," Sabine Reichel wrote of her experience of being brought up German, "they remained mythological for a very long time. Even the word 'Jew' . . . couldn't be formed by German lips" (1989:134).

I remember well my first encounters with Jews, that is, my first conscious encounters with Jews, in 1983. I was so dumbfounded by the fact that I was sitting among young Jews in a classroom that I did not even know how to start a conversation. I did not understand why they were studying religion. I was startled when they announced that they would celebrate the New Year in September. I had never before heard of women studying for the rabbinate. I did not know that Jews could be religious or secular; nor did I understand why modern Jews were attracted to Judaism, which at the time I viewed as an "obsolete" religion. In fact, I was surprised to meet any living Jews. When I finally met them, my ignorance not only embarrassed me but also compelled me to learn about Jewish life and reevaluate my own cultural upbringing.

The process of learning about Jewish-American culture was slow and often haphazard. A seminar on the foundations of Judaism made me entirely revise my thinking, hitherto grounded in a Protestant theological worldview. I went to Jewish-Christian dialogues in which Jews participated. I took part in a Yom Ha-Shoah service (Holocaust Remembrance Day) and for the first time met a Jew with a number tattooed on her arm. I attended an international gathering of Jewish Holocaust survivors. I visited a Jewish member of the Plowshare Movement (a nonviolent movement against the nuclear arms race) who was serving a three-year prison sentence for spattering blood on a nuclear warhead: he justified his action as part of an effort to prevent a second Holocaust. I occasionally went to Friday evening services at a small, progressive Jewish congregation in Philadelphia. In short, I was intrigued by everything

Jewish, as if I had to fill a large hole in my life. But I also felt tense, curious, and guilty when meeting Jewish people.

In 1985 I began to write about my thoughts and feelings on relations between Jews and Germans. At an evening of commemoration of the American Gathering of Jewish Holocaust Survivors in Philadelphia, I was deeply troubled by the discrepancy between the images in my head and the reality of Jewish survivors sitting next to me.

> Black and white images were my most prevailing memory of the Holocaust. The first Jews I met were documented on photographs: slave laborers, inmates, skeletons, corpses. And I remember images of arrests, roll-calls; piles of glasses, shoes, and clothes. My knowledge of Jews was limited to these documentations. On these photographs the Jewish people were dying time and again—eternal victims. They were transformed into a metaphor of dying. For a long time I did not even think of Jews as being alive. It took me 24 years to meet a living Jew—an American Jew—and the encounter was almost incomprehensible. How was I to react to a Jew who had not been killed during the Holocaust? What was I supposed to say, to do? I had to start from the beginning, a very painful and embarrassing beginning. (Krondorfer 1986:276)

My ignorance and embarrassment left me for a long time without a language in which to talk to my Jewish peers. I was unable to gauge their remarks and behavior. Did they speak to me, or not speak to me, because I was German? Did they speak to me differently than they would to one another, or to a Russian or an Italian? Should I bring up the issue of the Holocaust, or was this a terrain too painful and precarious to enter? Looking back, I think I was surprised that Jews would speak to me at all. At other times, I was equally surprised that they had opinions about Germany. It had not occurred to me that Jews my age would have explicit views on Germans and that I would be seen as one of "them," not just myself but also a representative of my country. The burden of an antagonistic history was still very much alive in my encounters with Jews.

Today it strikes me as curious how unself-conscious I was during my initial encounters with American Jews. In retrospect I realize that my suppressed feelings of guilt prevented me from fully admitting my convoluted emotions and from genuinely engaging in relationships with

Jews. "Isn't 'Björn' a Swedish name?" I have often been asked. Before answering, I'd always pause uneasily: "Yes, it's a Swedish name . . . but actually I am German." Once I revealed my national identity, what turn would our conversation take? At first, it almost did not matter what Jews said to me: regardless of whether they were friendly, indifferent, or resentful, I always felt somewhat intimidated. Sometimes I was angry without knowing why; sometimes I felt doubly guilty because I was angry; sometimes I vented my anger at inappropriate moments or disguised my feelings of guilt behind intellectual talk and submissive gestures. It took many years to comprehend the numerous tricks my emotions played on me. It was not easy to become aware of the cultural premises on which my American Jewish peers and I had been raised and to distinguish between appropriate self-assertion and destructive feelings of guilt—in short, to be both true to myself and sensitive to Jewish perspectives.

My most profound change began with a series of events that perhaps occur only to someone lost in a foreign culture. During my first year in Philadelphia I signed up for a class in African dance. I assumed that other white men would participate, but it turned out that I was the only white and the only male in a class of African-American women who treated me with some friendly teasing. At the end of one class, I struck up a conversation with a woman who rehearsed in the same studio, and she eventually asked whether I would be interested in joining a dance group centered around Jewish topics. I said yes—only to find myself a few weeks later the only male and the only German in an otherwise Jewish female dance company.

The company was short-lived, but we managed to present a few public performances before largely Jewish audiences. Needless to say, I was painfully self-conscious. After years of not even noticing the absence of Jews in Germany, I now performed with Jewish dancers for American Jewish audiences. As a company, we were all aware of my "otherness," but we never fully explored this issue. We cared for each other but knew that something was left unsaid. Our histories kept us apart regardless of how much amity we felt for each other.

Some of the members arranged a meeting to discuss the possibility of exploring our Jewish and German identities more deeply. Rather than talking, we wanted to employ the techniques of modern dance and experimental theater in an effort to understand the past and our rela-

tions today. Two German artists living in Philadelphia joined this experiment, and in the winter of 1985 a group of six dancers and performance
artists formed the Jewish-German Dance Theatre.

In this company, we began a process of exploration which, for some
of us, developed into a four-year commitment. Together we created
an environment in which we felt safe enough to reveal ourselves to one
another and uncover some of our hidden assumptions and fears. We
focused on personal histories and memories and employed our bodies
in the search for understanding the impact of the Holocaust on our
lives. As young American Jews and non-Jewish Germans, we realized
that we identified, respectively, victim and victimizer, sometimes trying to escape those roles, sometimes embracing them. We discovered
how deeply we were shaped by our cultural memories and different
ways of remembering the past. For Jews: the need to remember and to
express the pain over the tremendous loss in the Shoah; the need to
be allowed to be angry at Germans, to say "I hate you for being German." For Germans: the need to gain clarity about the feelings of guilt
that so strongly determine the relation to Jews; the need to be angry
without blaming Jews; the need to learn how to mourn the absence of
Jews in Germany. And for both Jews and Germans, the need to trust.
The ritual quality of the body-centered techniques we developed
allowed us to be angry with each other, to traverse social taboos, to
transgress the safe terminology of public discourse, to stumble over
pain hidden in our memories, to embody emotions rather than ratio-
nalize our historic legacies, and to find places of vulnerability and intimacy. We did not always succeed, but we achieved more than I had
ever anticipated.

The Jewish-German Dance Theatre created an evening-long production called "But What About the Holocaust?" which was performed in
several U.S. cities and before German audiences in October 1988 and
June 1989. On stage we revealed our struggles with the past, with ourselves and each other, and with our cultures and families. Occasionally,
we involved the audience directly, albeit cautiously (for the staging of a
production on the Holocaust by young American Jews and Germans in
itself generated enough emotional turmoil). Often, Jewish survivors
came to see our American performances. Many of them had avoided
contact with Germans ever since their liberation. And when we performed in small rural towns in Germany, we often encountered audi-

ences who had never before interacted with Jews or, if they were older, had not met a Jew since the 1930s.

In 1990, I was offered the opportunity to teach a course on the Holocaust at Lehigh University. By that time, I had worked through some of my emotional baggage regarding my role as a German, but I had no clear sense of the emotional ties of American students, particularly non-Jews, to the Holocaust, and I was surprised to hear that more than ninety had signed up for my class. As it turned out, many students were intrigued by the notion of a German teaching about the Holocaust. Some were indifferent to that fact; others, I suspected, hoped for the thrill of witnessing a moment in which I would unwittingly reveal my true "fascist" nature. A few of the Jewish students admitted halfway through the semester that they had been skeptical about my ability to teach the Holocaust and would have dropped the class had their suspicions proved true. But most intriguing to me were those students who expected an "objective" view of the Holocaust from a German instructor. I heard this from non-Jewish students who knew little about issues of the Holocaust as well as from Jewish students who were quite familiar with them. I sensed that their expectation of objectivity expressed both latent antisemitism (mistrust of Jewish teachers) and an intergenerational conflict within the Jewish community itself (resistance to the teaching of the Holocaust as an identity-forging Jewish event). But these students also expressed a desire to meet the "other": they wanted a German to authenticate the historical accuracy of the Shoah.

The American students at Lehigh, like many Germans the same age, lacked detailed historical information, and much time was spent providing a historical framework. That was the easy part of the course. I found it much more challenging to try to convey a sense of the political and moral intricacies and dilemmas that the Holocaust poses. The traditional lecture format seemed inadequate to this task. I therefore began to introduce some announced and unannounced role playing and thus turned the classroom into a space of experiential learning. For example, students often raised the question "Why didn't the Jews resist?" Despite my efforts to show evidence of Jewish resistance and to broaden the concept of resistance from a heroic armed struggle to a daily struggle for survival, the question kept coming up. The images of Jews being herded into cattle cars and gas chambers were too strong, and too remote from the world of the mostly upper-middle-class American students. I felt that only experiential learning would draw them out of their detachment, and I began to think of how to push the students to relate their question about resistance to their own experience.

I decided to use a written test as an opportunity to expose students to a situation of victimization (and possibly resistance). I asked the first student who showed up for class to guard the door and let the other students in one by one. As each student entered, I politely asked him or her to find a seat in either the left or the right half of the room. If someone asked why, I said I had rearranged the seating order because I was concerned about cheating. Nervous about the exam, they complied willingly, not knowing that my only criterion was the color of their hair. I distributed two sets of exams: those on the left with dark hair got easy questions and those with blond hair, on the right, got extremely difficult questions. Afterwards, we went through both sets of exams. As the students realized the difference between the tests, those on the right side got upset while those on the left wanted the exam to count for credit. I told them that my decision to grade the exam depended on their consensus. The two groups fought fiercely, but they never directed their anger and confusion against me. I eventually stopped the debate and asked them to look at each other. When they discovered that they were divided by the color of their hair, I revealed the setup. We then analyzed the mechanisms of victimization. "Imagine that not your grade but your life was at stake," I said. "In a system of total victimization, how would you know when to question authority, when to resist, when to turn left rather than right?" It was an eye-opening experience for the class. By using a creative ritual, I was able to soften the students' rigid moral and political assumptions about living and surviving from day to day in the ghettos and camps. They also learned about their own behavioral limitations when under pressure.

I came to believe that young Jews and Germans could truly understand each other only if they were provided with a protected environment, outside a traditional classroom, where they could interact with each other over a prolonged time around issues of the Holocaust. As a board member of an interfaith organization in Philadelphia, I was able to help implement such a project in the summers of 1989, 1991, and 1993.[3] Twenty college and university students participated in each program, half of them non-Jewish Germans, the other half Jewish and Christian Americans. The students studied, traveled, and lived together for a full month, first on the campus of Bryn Mawr College (with trips to New York and Washington), then in Berlin and at Auschwitz, in Poland. With the help of other facilitators,[4] I directed those programs in which the students learned about the history of the Holocaust, about their culturally diverse ways of remembering this traumatic event, and about their relation to each other in today's world.

This book is about these and other experiences in which post-Shoah Jews and Germans encounter each other. My personal story is woven into the fabric of my writing because I would not have been able to work with Jews and Germans of the third generation—or, for that matter, write this book—had I not gone through this painful but ultimately liberating process of discovering Jewish culture and the roots of my emotional turmoil. My German upbringing had left me ignorant about Jews and bewildered when I first met them. Embarrassment, confusion, guilt, anger, attraction, shame, anxiety—Germans and Jews are entangled in these feelings when they confront each other, and too often they do not know how to begin to sort them out.

The book is also an attempt to put the many incidents I witnessed or read about into a historical perspective and a cultural context. Much has been written about Jews and Germans after the Holocaust but little about the particular problems of the third generation, those born in the 1960s and 1970s, whose grandparents were adult moral agents during the Hitler regime. Whatever issues our grandparents and parents were unable to resolve in their lifetimes have been transmitted to post-Shoah generations—although the young often do not acknowledge the emotional, personal, and cultural ties that bind them to the Shoah and to each other as Jews and Germans. Many of the unresolved emotions and conflicts have gone underground, only to resurface quickly once Jews and Germans are put in the same room.

Lastly, the book is about developing a framework for improving post-Shoah Jewish/German relations in the future. Jewish/German relations are a culturally unfinished business. Change and improved understanding, I believe, can be fostered through creative models of communication and conflict solving. Insights from my training in religious studies and from my experience in ritual and performance studies have helped me to formulate such a framework.

Reflecting on my own unfinished journey, I believe that working toward reconciliation is a critical task, not only for Jews and Germans—

though they are the primary focus of this book—but also for other people divided by an antagonistic past and present. Since the Holocaust has attained a highly symbolic and paradigmatic character in the public's mind, the reconciliatory work between Jews and Germans might become paradigmatic as well. Should post-Shoah Jews and Germans be able to slowly recover from the wounds that Germans have afflicted on Jews (and also on themselves), then their road to recovery may become a model for other divided peoples. I hope that this book encourages others to follow a similar road.

Rituals of Reconciliation

To write as a German about reconciliation between Jews and Germans after Auschwitz is asking for trouble; as some critics have said, Jewish/German reconciliation after the Shoah is a fundamentally flawed and at best morally dubious project. The trouble already begins with the terms "Jew" and "German." What do I mean when I speak of Jews and Germans? Aren't some Jews also German? What exactly are "Jewish/German" relations? Is the relation between an assimilated American Jew whose family immigrated from Russia in the 1880s and a non-Christian German who was born into an affluent postwar democracy as fraught with pain, anger, and guilt as the relation between a child of Jewish survivors from Germany and a German child of Nazi functionaries? Do, for example, (former) East Germans relate to American Jews mostly as Jews or as Americans? Do American Jews differentiate between East and West, young and old Germans? Is it legitimate to speak about Jews and Germans in generic terms without differentiating between American and German Jews, between West and East Germans, between Jews and Christians, not to mention distinctions of class, gender, and age?

These questions touch on the issue of belonging which still threatens to tear apart the twentieth-century world. Do we define ourselves by nationality, ethnicity, culture, religion, class, or community? These questions affect the identity of "Jews" and "Germans." Because of a tradition of Christian Jew-hate and modern antisemitism, the categories of religion and race have worked to the detriment of Jewish life and survival in central Europe (cf. Krondorfer 1991a). Jews did not fare much better in communist states, which tried to eliminate national and religious identity by promulgating a classless society. Even in countries like America and

Israel, the description of Jewish identity remains a continuous puzzle. Is it religion, culture, or family history that determines Jewish belonging? Can a nonreligious person assimilated into the surrounding (largely Christian) community be a Jew? With respect to Germans, the issue is no less convoluted. Are Germans defined by a common language, by citizenship status, or by German ancestry? After Nazi ideology had introduced the pernicious concept of "German blood" as the decisive criterion, postwar Germany preferred not to think about definitions of Germanness, assuming that national boundaries would somehow regulate the issue. Only recently have these questions resurfaced. People from the former Soviet republics point to their German ancestry in order to claim German citizenship; Turks who have lived for many decades in Germany claim similar legal rights; Jews who arrived from the Soviet Union in the late 1980s have been denied these rights; Israelis emigrate to Germany; and neo-Nazis chant *Deutschland für Deutsche, Ausländer raus!* (Germany for Germans, foreigners out!). In short, at the dawn of the twenty-first century, there is still an explosive confusion about issues of belonging.

Questions of collective identity threaten to obscure any talk about Jewish/German relations. And yet, encounters between people who see themselves as belonging to either the Jewish or the German community are real, and we need to find an intelligible terminology with which to examine them. I have found it helpful, when writing about Jews and Germans, to think of distinctive "discursive practices" (chapter 1) and a characteristic "ethos" (chapter 2) for each community. By "discursive practice" I mean those public voices within each culture which have framed the issues relating to Jews, Germans, and the Holocaust. Not every German thinks, speaks, feels, and acts the same way; but in looking at a series of individual experiences and perspectives, patterns emerge which are different from Jewish discursive practices (though Jews do not speak as a unity either). The concept of discursive practices allows me to look at patterns characteristic of either Germans or Jews without claiming that all individuals follow these patterns. The concept of ethos helps out similarly, but it refers less to what is said publicly and more to what people deeply believe about their way of living and thinking.

Differences in the discourse and ethos of Jews and Germans show up not only in political speeches but also in the emotional reactions of individuals. Only by carefully listening to the particular experience of individuals can we discern distinct cultural ways of mapping these experiences. If similar rhetorical phrases or emotional and behavioral responses recur among different people in separate situations, patterns larger than individual idiosyncrasies are at work. At the same time, some individuals resist dominant discursive practices. People have always demonstrated that they are capable of breaking away from the public and static rhetoric of their communities. This freedom to "break away" is what allows reconciliation to occur.

Throughout this book, the term "Jewish/German" refers to Jews and Germans as sovereign communities, and not to German Jews—that is, Jews living in Germany.[5] The term "Jewish/German relations" is used here mainly to describe the relations of American Jews and non-Jewish Germans. Other groups, such as Christian Americans or Jews in Israel or Germany are mentioned occasionally, but the focus is on the encounters between Jewish-American and non-Jewish German people as two communities defined by different ethoses and discourses.

The stories I tell are all about individual Jews and Germans, mostly of the third generation. But who is the third generation? How do we distinguish it from the first and second generations?

The first generation can be described as people who lived through the years of the Holocaust. Their experiences—as victims, survivors, partisans, onlookers, bystanders, accomplices, or victimizers—shaped the discourse on the Holocaust in the first two decades after 1945. The second generation, in a narrow sense, refers to the children of Jewish survivors (this is its definition in the psychological literature), but we can broaden that definition to include the children of those Jews and Germans who have lived through the Nazi period. The voices of the second generation emerged in the late 1960s and continue to shape the current discourse.

The third generation, generally speaking, are the grandchildren of the first generation. They were born in the 1960s and 1970s. They have, with a few exceptions, not yet articulated a distinct discursive practice but have certainly been influenced by a communal ethos and public discourse. From birth on, Jews and Germans of the third generation are already embroiled in the discourse of preceding generations. Some of the bewilderment that young Jews and Germans feel when they encounter each other is precisely their (erroneous and naive) belief that they have not been touched by their culture's biases, ideologies, and distortions. In order to understand the third generation we must also understand the discourse of preceding generations.

The boundaries between first, second, and third generations are, of course, fluent and imprecise. It makes a difference whether first generation Jews and Germans were sixty, forty, or twenty years old when World War II ended, for their children and grandchildren came of age during different stages of the post-Shoah world. I consider myself, for example, as someone in between the second and third generations, too young to belong to the former (I was nine years old when second-generation Germans revolted against their parents and university teachers in 1968), but too old to be considered in the third generation. Despite these fluid boundaries, the categories of first, second, and third generation are useful. They help us mark the progressive distance from the Holocaust and to isolate recognizable differences between the generations.

But the problem of Jewish/German reconciliation goes beyond questions of belonging and semantic dilemmas. Critical voices in the Jewish community and some German intellectuals have frequently warned that reconciliation projects after Auschwitz are morally flawed, because the (Jewish) memory of the camps and the (German) desire to forget them are too strong to make reconciliation possible. Indeed, it could be said that Jews and Germans have irreconcilable perspectives on reconciliation. While most Germans tend to evade the past and stress forgiveness as the moral lesson of the Holocaust, many in the Jewish community are wary of reconciliation because it suggests forgetting the past and exonerating the criminals. Jews did not return to Spain for centuries after their expulsion in 1492. Why, then, should any Jew be concerned about reconciling with Germany only fifty years after the Shoah? The remarks of two German Jewish intellectuals come to mind in this regard. Gershom Scholem deemed the so-called Jewish/German symbiosis before 1933 a chimera and dismissed the possibility of post-Holocaust dialogue. Similarly, Theodor Adorno's famous dictum that no poetry can be written after Auschwitz implies that Jewish/German reconciliation projects are doomed to fail. Reconciliation, its critics claim, is a term that obscures a speaker's true motives: the desire to forget and be forgiven.

For a German to write about reconciliation is suspect precisely for that reason. *Only* a German would write about reconciliation, a skeptic might say; a Jewish author would approach the same subject under the heading of remembrance. Wouldn't it be better to limit my reflections on the Holocaust to my own country, rather than talking about post-Shoah Jewish/German reconciliation? Wouldn't I be bound to errors of judgment about Jewish experiences? And why this German obsession with Jews to begin with? I am reminded of Ludwig Börne's comment about his German compatriots in 1832: "I have experienced it a thousand times. . . . Some reproach me for being Jewish; others forgive me for being Jewish; and the third praises me for it. But all are thinking about it as if they are spellbound by this magic Jewish sphere." After Auschwitz, wouldn't it be wiser for Germans to stop obsessing about Jews?

I have argued elsewhere that antisemitism is still imbued in German culture and that individuals cannot easily disentangle themselves from it (Krondorfer 1991a). Like racism and sexism, antisemitism works on public and subliminal levels and is deeply rooted in a person's unconscious and a people's ethos. Growing up German also means that anti-Jewish images and passions have been inscribed into my being. In a study of children of Nazis, the psychologist Dan Bar-On concluded that "[German] children who tried to penetrate their parents' silence have first had to be aware that there were gaps or distortions in their parents' accounts; then they have had to identify the motives behind these versions of the past, confront them, and find a way to work through to the untold story" (1989:329).

Jewish communities are not spared similar conflicts. When I read Aaron Hass's comment that Jewish Holocaust survivors "have often been reluctant to relate their experiences, for fear of harming their children or of confronting aspects of their own past" (1990:166), I was strangely reminded of problems familiar to second- and third-generation Germans. Is it possible that the struggles of post-Shoah Jews and Germans, like those of enemy twins, resemble each other? Sabine Reichel (1989:147), who grew up in postwar Germany and met American Jews only after she moved to New York, asked similar questions: "Could it be that both postwar Germans and postwar Jews developed the same diffuse, stereotypical sense of the perpetrators and the victims? Didn't the two observe each other's legacy with the same lack of personal experiences and individual encounters?"

But is it legitimate to correlate the experiences of Jews and Germans after the Shoah? Would not such comparisons obscure the moral and

political distinctions between a nation of victimizers and a victimized
people? Would not such thinking arrive at a position of relativism in
which the suffering of victims is compared to the pain of victimizers?
Would it not distort the realities of two people and cultures that are
rooted in different traditions and developed quite distinct identities after
the Shoah—despite their ties to the same cataclysmic event?

I decided not to evade these and other uncomfortable questions but
to critically examine the responses, attitudes, and thoughts of both non-
Jewish Germans and American Jews. Time and again I discovered that
opinions and information concerning Holocaust-related issues cannot
be taken at face value. Unresolved emotions, cultural biases, personal
prejudices, and printed misinformation have led to a spiraling series of
distortions, gaps, silences, and misunderstandings. Any discourse on
Jewish/German relations has to work with and through these distortions,
for they affect a person's intellectual judgment as much as his or her way
of behaving, feeling, and perceiving. Suspicion about one's own
premises and a good deal of self-reflection are desirable principles in
any Jewish/German encounter, and I have tried to apply them to my
own thinking and writing.

To the already troublesome notion of Jewish/German reconciliation I
sometimes attach the ambiguous term "ritual," using "rituals of reconciliation" as a way of framing the problems of Jewish/German relations.
Traditionally, a ritual is understood as a prescribed ceremony, a strict
procedure, often religious in nature. But in the emerging field of ritual
studies, distinctions are made between specific rites (ceremonies that are
followed faithfully, like a bar mitzvah or baptism) and the larger idea of
ritual as a certain way of approaching the world (cf. Grimes 1990). To
me, interactions qualify as rituals if they are deliberate, embodied, performed, condensed, patterned, and somewhat symbolic and stylized.
Understood this way, rituals are no longer limited to highly regulated
religious or political ceremonies but include other forms of deliberate,
patterned, and condensed processes and interactions. Political commemorations of the Holocaust, for example, are often institutionalized
and standardized rites and as such represent the static, pre-critical, and
conservative expression of ritual. Recent research and literature, however, point out that rituals can also be process-oriented, subversive, and
flowing (cf. Grimes 1992). This book applies this insight to work toward
creative ritual expressions of reconciliation.

The phrase "rituals of reconciliation," then, invites conflicting interpretations. On the one hand, such rituals can manifest themselves as
deceptive, dishonest, and destructive public and private events. Post-
Shoah relations between Jews and Germans have been particularly sus-
ceptible to these negative aspects. As I show in chapters 1 and 2, the current discourse on Jewish/German relations and the ethos with which
young Jews and Germans grow up bolster communal and national identity by ignoring or misidentifying the other. The discourse and ethos
repeat patterns that distort and fictionalize the other, but they do not
improve cross-cultural understanding. To become aware of the specific
problems of the third generation we need to carefully examine the current status of Jewish/German relations.

But rituals of reconciliation can also become genuinely creative occasions for social and individual transformation. I hope to persuade the
reader that reconciliation does not have to remain an empty and deceptive vision but can be practiced in a manner that is sensitive to the needs
and perspectives of both Jews and Germans. As I envision it, reconciliation is a ritual practice or experience that strives toward transformation.
It liberates Jews and Germans from the stalemate of current discursive
practices and encourages them to seek new ways of relating to each other
without neglecting the history and memory of the Shoah. It requires a
willingness to take risks. Reconciliation is not a monument but a process,
not a museum but "a growing inventory of an active memory" (Maier
1988:121), not a theory but an experimental practice. Monuments, museums, and theories can be part of this process but never comprise the
whole. Genuine reconciliation, I propose in chapter 3, is a communal
and experimental practice in which third-generation Jews and Germans
remember the Holocaust, but also creatively engage in overcoming the
limitations and deceptions of the currently cultivated discourse.

Chapters 1–3 introduce the cultural context within which Jewish/Ger-
man relations have been shaped. This first part of the book argues that
the current discourse on reconciliation is negatively ritualized and alienates the young; it shows that both Germans and American Jews are
guided by deeply felt beliefs, or ethos, which often counter political
attempts to reconcile; and it lays the ground for envisioning reconciliation as a transformative practice that aims at helping third-generation
Jews and Germans to cope with the past. These three chapters make up
the first part of this book, "Memory and Identity."

The second and main part of the book, "Reconciliatory Practices," describes and examines processes in which some Germans and Jews of the third generation have actively shared journeys toward reconciliation. Chapter 4 explores family histories, for the dismantling of mistrust between Jews and Germans can only be founded on an honest accounting and knowledge of one's personal roots. Chapter 5 looks at interactions between the third and first generations and how young American Jews and Germans react to oral Holocaust testimonies. Chapter 6 moves away from personal memories to public memorialization, addressing the question of how the third generation responds to public sites commemorating the past, such as Holocaust museums.

In Chapter 7, the focus shifts to the creative work of Jewish-American and German artists of the Jewish-German Dance Theatre. Rehearsals and workshops show how body-conscious and dramatic exercises can resuscitate memories and increase trust between Jews and Germans. Chapter 8 looks at public reactions to reconciliatory efforts. Again, the work of the Jewish-German Dance Theatre serves as an example: how did German and American audiences interact with a group of young artists who publicly enacted their personal struggle with the legacy of the Holocaust? Chapter 9 ends the book by following a group of Jewish and German students to Auschwitz. When third-generation Jews and Germans visit together this landscape of evil, can they develop the courage necessary to trust and comfort each other?

The processes described in Chapters 4–9 are not restricted to cognitive understanding of the history of the Holocaust but engage the participants on personal, emotional, and physical levels. They are *rituals* because these encounters have been deliberately arranged as exemplary, communal, embodied, protected, and temporary processes. They are *rituals of reconciliation* because they consciously attempt to transcend the current stalemate of Jewish/German relations.

Hardly anything has been published specifically on encounters between Jews and Germans of the third generation, though individual accounts can be found in newspapers, magazines, films, conference proceedings, and, occasionally, books. I interpret the findings of this diverse literature as they apply to the cultural premises on which post-Shoah Jews and Germans operate.

The sources for my observations and assessment of Jewish/German relations are the summer programs on the Holocaust for American and

German students; the rehearsals, workshops, and performances of the Jewish-German Dance Theatre; and other personal encounters with Jews and Germans, including stories of my own family. Three volumes containing student journals and essays, pedagogical reflections, media coverage, and day-to-day outlines from the summer programs have been published (Krondorfer and Schmidt 1990; Krondorfer and Staffa 1992, 1994). In addition, I rely on my own journal and my memory, personal conversations, and subsequent correspondence with many of the participants. The rehearsals, occasional workshops, and numerous performances of the Jewish-German Dance Theatre in America and Germany have left an abundance of memories, rehearsal notes, videotapes and audiotapes, reviews, journal entries, and performance scripts. These sources, now collected in the archives of the Lincoln Center (New York) Library of the Performing Arts, are a vital part of this book. Readers can also consult four short publications on the company's work.[6] Besides the summer programs and the work of the dance theatre, I incorporate other personal material—from my family, teaching, and other experiences. Many of these stories reveal the day-to-day friction and affection between and among post-Shoah Jews and Germans.

The stories and reflections in this book will reveal that Jewish/German relations to this day remain uncertain and unresolved, deeply imbued with political, moral, and emotional ambiguity. As individuals and communities, we are uncertain about our sense of belonging. These uncertainties must be tolerated when we practice reconciliation. As the shadow of Auschwitz continues to darken the paths of Jews and Germans, we do not know yet whether a brighter and common journey lies ahead of us. But third-generation Jews and Germans have the opportunity to work toward reconciliation, for they are distant enough in time from the Holocaust to not be paralyzed by it yet close enough to be emotionally attached to its memory.

I Memory and Identity

The history of Jewish/German relations after the Holocaust is replete with examples of a ritualized public discourse in which apparently incompatible perspectives are negotiated.[1] The American Jewish community tends to argue that the Holocaust was so devastating and unique that it makes reconciliation, if not outright impossible, at least a highly suspicious undertaking. German society, on the other hand, tends to interpret the Holocaust as a historical aberration which neither defines Germans as inherently evil nor dooms Jewish/German relations.

If these differences merely concerned academic disagreements, we could put the issue to rest and wait for the outcome of the debate among historians, politicians, and theologians. But since these different perspectives are inscribed in the very being and ethos of the Jewish and the German peoples, it is crucial to understand how they have affected post-Shoah generations. For what is at stake here is not just the "correct" way of remembering the Shoah but the identities of Jews and Germans themselves. Since the memory of the Holocaust affects the construction of cultural and national identities, the discourse on the Holocaust is blended with community-forging ideologies—a mix that is passed on to post-Shoah generations. Third-generation Jews and Germans grow up with different perspectives on a past they seem to share; and in most cases they do not even recognize these differences until they accidentally meet.

The current rhetoric on Jewish/German relations and the Holocaust has had a negative impact on the third generation. It has become a repetitive and self-referential discourse that uses Holocaust memory to defend national and cultural identities but is largely irrelevant to the particular problems of the young. Yet, we must be aware of how this discourse has influenced the thinking of third-generation Jews and Germans and the Holocaust memorialization of their respective communities. Inevitably, members of the third generation express their relation to the Holocaust through an amalgam of truths and half-truths, historical knowledge and communal ideologies, family histories and cultural pride, prejudices and legitimate struggles for identity. Any "memorialization process," James Young (1990:174) writes in his study of Holocaust literature, has "an inescapable potential for 'historic re-vision.'" The way things are remembered becomes the way history is interpreted. In the best case, third-generation Jews and Germans encountering each other have a rare and remarkable opportunity to discover how the discursive practices of their respective communities differ and how they themselves participate in the memorialization process. In the worst case, they unself-consciously perpetuate a stale, ritualized discourse and fail to undo their biased views of each other.

Since every memorialization process is embedded in communal remembrance, it lends itself to ideological distortion. The potential for distortion grows as the temporal distance from the Shoah widens. If it is indeed true that German society as well as Jewish communities[2] have ritualized the discourse on the Holocaust, we must ask whether this temporal distance has had beneficial or detrimental effects on the third generation. Does temporal distance merely expedite the inscription of stereotypical roles and patterns, because new generations, cut off from direct experience of the Holocaust, are more vulnerable to ideological impositions? Or does it hold the key to creative transformation of the current impasse in Jewish/German relations?

Temporal distance from the Shoah is an ambiguous gift. On the one hand, it may impel third-generation Jews and Germans to conform to the ritualized public discourse, in which case relations between young Jews and Germans will continue to be caught in their communities' defensive struggles over national identity and cultural preservation. On the other hand, temporal distance may motivate them to experiment with transformative rituals and allow them to address sensitive issues that until recently have been too frightening to handle, such as their emotional investment in remembering the Holocaust or pleas for renewed Jewish/German relations.

Unfortunately, the crisis of current discursive practices leaves a vacuum among the young which can be filled with any number of political agendas. That worries me. For among those who criticize the current discourse on the Holocaust, there are many who are more concerned with cultural and national self-preservation than with cross-cultural understanding. What is needed, I suggest, is a creative transformation that does not simplify the issues at stake. We must actively initiate new reconciliatory practices to help third-generation Jews and Germans understand the intricate links between the formation of their identities and the function of memory. Part of the work of improving Jewish/German relations is to examine the assumptions on which one's own culture is operating, and I will turn to this task in the first three chapters of this book.

1 Discourse

Victim and Victimizer

I think that there is nothing wrong with visiting that cemetery [in Bitburg] where those young men [German soldiers] are victims of Nazism also. . . . They were victims, just as surely as the victims in the concentration camps.
—U.S. president Ronald Reagan, White House, 18 April 1985

To the survivors of the Holocaust: . . . Many of you are worried that reconciliation means forgetting. Well, I promise you, we will never forget.
—President Reagan at Bitburg, 5 May 1985

A few minutes ago, the President of the United States of America and I paid homage at the military cemetery to the dead buried there and thus to all victims of war and tyranny.
. . . [T]he visit to the graves in Bitburg is . . . a widely visible and widely felt gesture of reconciliation between our peoples.
—German chancellor Helmut Kohl at Bitburg, 5 May 1985

The highly publicized events at Bitburg were one of those explosions that rock the boat of Jewish/German relations every few years. In 1985, German chancellor Helmut Kohl and U.S. president Ronald Reagan made international headlines when they visited the German military cemetery in Bitburg, which included the graves of some members of the Schutzstaffel, or SS. At the cemetery, Chancellor Kohl praised the "gesture of reconciliation" between Germans and Americans and declared all the dead the "victims" of the war, a German formulation that reflects a Holocaust victimology in which perpetrators are not distinguished from various victim groups. To counter the mounting international indignation, Kohl went to the concentration camp at Bergen-Belsen two weeks before Bitburg.

23

There, on 21 April 1985, he called upon the "memory" of the "innocent" and praised the reconciliation between Germans and Jews: "We are gathered here in memory of the many innocent people who were tortured, humiliated and driven to their deaths at Bergen-Belsen, as in other camps. . . . We are grateful that reconciliation was possible with the Jewish people and the State of Israel, that friendship is again growing particularly among young people." President Reagan, too, changed his rhetoric of reconciliation in order to dispel the fears of American Jews. By the time he had arrived in Bitburg, he no longer justified his visit by saying that German soldiers were "victims, just as surely as the victims in the concentration camps," but linked reconciliation with the promise "never to forget," a phrase borrowed from the Jewish-American discourse on the Holocaust. But the damage had been done and many Jews remained outraged by this official gesture of German/American reconciliation, which threatened to blur the distinction between Jewish victims and German victimizers. Elie Wiesel, in an address at the White House on 19 April 1985, carefully worded his condemnation of Reagan's plan to visit Bitburg and praised the reconciliatory efforts between the Jewish and gentile communities in America: "Mr. President, speaking of reconciliation, I was very pleased that we met before, so a stage of reconciliation has been set in motion between us. . . . We were always on the side of justice, always on the side of memory, against the SS and against what they represent" (quotations from Hartman 1986).

These speeches point up the rhetorical and ritualized aspects of a public discourse that indiscriminately employs the language of reconciliation and remembrance. They exemplify a moment in the history of post-Shoah Jewish/German relations in which different players have used the same terminology for different purposes. An almost liturgical chant of "remembrance" and "reconciliation," "victim" and "victimizer," helps preserve and define collective identities with respect to the past. This discourse, which has hardly changed in the decades since the war,[1] has attained a ritualistic quality that is static and conservative rather than creative and transformative. As a result, the third generation has shown signs of boredom and disinterest in Holocaust-related issues; the rhetorical redundancy does not motivate them but alienates them. "Commemorations often fail to engage emotionally and intellectually the younger generations," observed Judith Miller, an editor at the *New York Times*. "[They] may, indeed, be wasted on the young" (1990:55).

Third-generation Jews and Germans grow up in communities engaged in claims and counterclaims over the "correct" interpretation and memorialization of the Holocaust. But mostly, "the Jew" and "the German" are for the third generation fictive images, without flesh and blood, shuttled in a game of mutual accusations, denials, apologies, and goodwill gestures. When, for example, German political opinion prides itself on the democratic changes in postwar Germany, Jewish communities are likely to respond by pointing to antisemitic sentiments in that country. When, on the other hand, Jewish communities interpret Germany's declarations of guilt and proclamations of reconciliation as attempts to exonerate the nation, Germans are quick to note their educational system, which, they claim, meets the special obligation of teaching the lessons of the past. Some Germans charge Jews with hypersensitivity, while some Jews take the complaint of young Germans that they "have heard enough about the Holocaust" as evidence of resurgent Jew-hate. In short, what the Jewish community claims is an appropriate description of Jewish/German relations many Germans perceive as an accusation; and what German society offers as a proper depiction the Jewish community interprets as apologetic attitudes.

Miscommunications abound. Neither speakers nor listeners seem to know whom and what to trust. Can we trust the other's representation and motivation? Do we use similar words but speak a different language? When we mention the lessons of the Holocaust, are we thinking about the same lessons? When we call for dialogue and reconciliation, what is our agenda?

Even benign manifestations of this rhetoric suffer from ritualization, a form of automatic response that is no longer trusted or has been corrupted. A close look at the intentions and agendas of many commemorative events, Holocaust conferences, dialogue groups, and educational programs reveals that the apparently congenial nature of these events often disguises ideological friction. Moral claims can be used to ignore and conceal conflicts and rivalries with which Holocaust institutions are afflicted. Often, Holocaust organizers, educators, and scholars appeal to specific victimologies encoded in key words such as "remembrance" (which rallies the Jewish community) and "guilt" (which mobilizes and angers German society). No doubt, the moral quality of this language still has the power to motivate people to action, spurring them to create educational programs, sponsor cultural events, support political agendas, or decry antisemitic acts. Nevertheless, the discourse long ago shifted from the moral to the political arena and is often a barely concealed war of words. Terms such as "victim" and "victimizer," "reconciliation," "remembrance," and "guilt" are no longer intended to offer an accurate description of the current status of Jewish/German relations. Rather, they are used to defend one's sociopolitical identity and to redefine one's place in the power structure.

The events in Bitburg show how national and cultural identities are negotiated within changing power structures. Bitburg not only represented the convergence of conflicting interests between the Jewish, German, and American communities but also signaled an attempt to redefine the public discourse on the Holocaust. The visit by Chancellor Kohl and President Reagan to the graves of German soldiers provided the context within which the meanings of the words "reconciliation," "remembrance," and "victims" were enlarged to apply to Jews as well as Germans including SS soldiers. When Reagan, in his 18 April speech, justified his visit to the cemetery, he caused anguish in the Jewish community by saying that "those young men [German soldiers] . . . were victims, just as surely as the victims in the concentration camps."[2] A political gesture of reconciliation between the German and American nations was celebrated at the cost of antagonizing the Jewish community by threatening to dissolve the distinction between (Jewish) victim and (Nazi) victimizer.

To be sure, German Veterans Day ceremonies had been held in Bitburg before, in the presence of U.S. air-base commanders, and conservative segments of German society have in various ways commemorated German war victims since 1945. What made Bitburg in 1985 different from previous events was that German politicians used the occasion to move their Holocaust discourse from a parochial level to international recognition. Germany wanted the international community to release it from the role of victimizer (cf. Rabinbach 1986:6). At the time, the official speechwriters still deemed it necessary to employ the official jargon, albeit with the intent to bloat and invert the imagery.[3] "Overcoming the past means changing the symbols of the present, and this is just what the rites at Bitburg were intended to do," writes the anthropologist David Kertzer in his book on the ritual construction of political reality (1988:95). Sanctioned by Reagan's presence, the phrase "remembering the victims" now applied to Jewish victims of the Holocaust as well as German soldiers who died in the second world war.

In the United States, a coalition of Jewish, Christian, and veterans groups spoke out against Reagan's visit to Bitburg (cf. Bole 1986). In Germany, the opposition included church, union, Jewish, and leftist groups (cf. Miller 1990:45–51). Trying to ward off Kohl and Reagan's conservative attempt to redefine the linkage of memory and identity, the opposition forces were holding on to the original version of the victim/victimizer image, distinguishing Jewish victims from Nazi perpetrators. When Elie Wiesel spoke at a ceremony at the White House shortly before Reagan left for Germany, he emphasized this distinction: "That place [Bitburg], Mr. President, is not your place. Your place is with the victims of the SS."[4] With the principals embroiled in a fight over language, Bitburg brought to the fore the underlying principle of a rhetorical danse macabre that has been rehearsed and performed since 1945: the stronger the German rejection of the role of victimizer, the stronger the Jewish assertion of their victimization. The main function of this entrenchment, I believe, has been to impede any genuine encounter between Jews and Germans.

For those who engage in this kind of political rhetoric and victimology, there are no doubt benefits. It allows them to enter into a ritualized dialogue without risking the principles and rationale by which they produce their identities. Indeed, the continuous battle over the assertion or dismissal of the victim/victimizer dichotomy has helped both Jews and Germans redefine and rearrange their national, political, and cultural post-Shoah identities. To relinquish this rhetoric would mean to give up part of their still fragile identities, something that neither side is willing to do. Instead, they remain in the grip of the past and continue to negotiate and defend the meaning the Shoah holds for their efforts at self-definition.

To form one's collective identity in the light of the past is, of course, an adequate way of strengthening the separate identities of Jews and Germans and the basis for building a healthier relationship between them. However, the current political rhetoric—whose benign forms seek to suppress underlying conflicts and whose insidious manifestations exploit language for various political agendas—does not improve communication. There has been defensive rhetoric but no willingness to risk emotional honesty, political gestures but no intimacy, talk but no trust.

This seems to suggest that we should abandon all talk about victims and victimizers, for it does more harm than good to Jewish/German relations. But that is not my intention. The distinction between victim and victimizer must be upheld for the sake of historic accuracy: it adequately describes the Holocaust and Germany's antisemitic traditions. Young Jews and Germans need to familiarize themselves with this history if they want to understand their present relationships. The scale of cruelties inflicted upon Jews has been so immense, and the impact of visual evidence of the genocide so strong, that the victim/victimizer dichotomy is not going to fade away. It has determined the discourse in the past and will continue to shape it in the future.

However, the repeated exposure of Jews and Germans to the visual evidence of the Holocaust has also been counterproductive to genuine reconciliation. The abundance of images that have seeped into popular culture (cf. Rosenfeld 1986) has not only numbed the third generation but also provoked emotional resistance against the victim/victimizer dichotomy—including similar antithetical pairs such as Jew/German, innocent/guilty, good/evil. What is pernicious about such a polarized victimology is its potential for subconscious and ideological misappropriation. It has the power to prescribe and inscribe the roles young Jews and Germans ought to play. The recent recurrence of neo-Nazi attitudes among some of Germany's youth is the most visible and distressing sign of such misappropriation. These young people resolve the tensions contained in the victim/victimizer dichotomy by defiantly and rebelliously embracing the role of victimizer. For some young Jews, on the other hand, the attraction of the radical and aggressive Jewish Defense League may originate in a similar, yet inverse, motivation: they rebel against the inscribed role of victim.

For most third-generation Jews and Germans, however, the discourse on victim/victimizer has less drastic effects. Most young Jews and Germans employ images of victim and victimizer thoughtlessly: they use them to draw historic distinctions or moral lessons, to defend their position or to rebel against the past, to describe themselves or to inscribe the role of the other. "The next generation will be free of responsibility and free to mythologize and theologize without check of reality," the Jewish writer Anne Roiphe notes with some concern in her reflections on the Holocaust (1988:25). This casual attitude might be frustrating to some, but I look at it as an opportunity to help the young to work through their ideological and emotional confusion. Free to mythologize, the third generation is vulnerable to ideological distortions. But they can be helped to become aware of those distortions with respect to the history, memory, and memorialization of the Holocaust if improving Jewish/German relationships is our goal.

"You Could Have Been One of Hitler's Boys"

Two incidents in Philadelphia made me aware of how much I had been struggling with the victim/victimizer dichotomy. Toward the end of our first year in America, my wife and I were invited to a party in the suburbs. The other guests were white, Anglo-Saxon, mostly liberal Republicans a good twenty-five years older than we were. I was talking to a middle-aged woman when she unexpectedly remarked, "You are such a good-looking young man, with your blond hair. You could have been one of Hitler's boys." What she intended as a compliment hit a raw nerve. Never before had it happened, and never since, that I got a compliment because of my "Aryan" looks. I was embarrassed because someone had linked my physical appearance to a past with which, I thought, I had nothing to do.

Six months later, it was my turn to put my foot in my mouth. I participated in a workshop in the downtown studio of a painter. He showed me some of his work and we got into a conversation about our respective identities as Jew and German. For a reason I do not remember, we started talking about politics in Nicaragua. Assuming that he, as a Jew, would support a liberal agenda, I mentioned my recent readings in liberation theology. To my surprise, he defended Reagan's policy of financing the right-wing insurgents, the Contras. "How can you, a Jew, support such policies? Especially after the Holocaust, I thought you would be on the side of the victims," I blurted out. He replied angrily, "Especially as a Jew after the Holocaust, I am on the side of the strong." The conversation ended abruptly. As much as I had been caught off guard when I was complimented for my Aryan looks, I likewise did not expect that some American Jews had deliberately renounced the status of victimhood and sided with American interventionist policies.

The confusion I felt made me aware that something about my German identity was unresolved and that people read each other through the eyes of (symbolic) victim and victimizer. Similar situations have been played out between Jews and Germans hundreds of times; I have witnessed many of them in my work with the third generation. Suzanne, for example, an American Jewish participant in the 1989 summer program on the Holocaust, expressed an anxiety not atypical for young, educated, American-born Jews. On the third day of the program, after tensions between the American and German students had already surfaced, she wrote in her journal: "I simply cannot know if I will be able to reveal myself before this [German] third generation—there are still many biases and prejudices abounding on all sides. I am also more deeply dedicated not to compromise my history, my people, my self." Suzanne's statement clearly expresses a sense of vulnerability. Confronted with young Germans, she emphatically affirmed her Jewishness, thus resisting an imagined process of victimization.

Iris, a West German participant in the 1991 program, similarly struggled with her identity:

> In this program, the perspectives of victims and victimizers collide again in my head and soul. . . . Our different backgrounds and perspectives quickly became apparent. As a West German, non-Jewish woman, I am part of the tradition of victimizers: My grandparents are from Germany; their thoughts, feelings, actions, and non-involvements belong to the society of victimizers and bystanders—my grandparents!
>
> I was familiar with the story of suffering of my grandparents— they were perhaps straws in the flow of time. But in light of the horrors of German crimes, the unimaginable sufferings of the victims, and the stories of survivors, the German stories of affliction sound absurd, perverse, and riddled with self-pity. Is that the madness of ordinary life? (Krondorfer and Staffa 1992:39f)

In this passage, Iris questioned her uncertain national identity and even dared to identify briefly with the "tradition of victimizers." But she quickly removed herself from the scene of the crime and pointed to her grandparents as the true perpetrators. She then proceeded to reflect on how to reconcile the suffering of her grandparents with the suffering of Jewish victims.

Such statements as these demonstrate that victim/victimizer imagery is operative in the minds of the third generation, though it is always used ambiguously. Young Jews and Germans refer to victims and victimizers to defend themselves, draw boundaries, make moral judgments, or describe historical reality. Whereas Suzanne's first reaction upon encountering young Germans was to defend and protect her cultural identity, Iris adopted a self-critical but also self-absorbed approach in which the "Jewish victim" figured merely as a backdrop.

Why are their perspectives and appropriations of the victim/victimizer dichotomy different? What messages did they absorb from their cultures? What assumptions of their cultural heritage do their perspectives affirm or reject? What communal and societal struggles are reflected in their statements? The answers lie in the discursive environments in which Iris and Suzanne, and the third generation in general, grew up. The German discourse, I argue, has failed to mourn the victims and has rebelled against identification with the victimizers. The Jewish discourse, on the other hand, is driven by the need to make the experience of utter victimization meaningful; as a result, it has made the role of the victim central to efforts at community building.

A German Discursive Practice: Rebellion against the Victimizer

Germany was an antisemitic culture before Hitler came to power and remained antisemitic even after the war (cf. Krondorfer 1991a). Much of the German population consented to or actively supported the persecution and murder of Jews, while the rest, with a few exceptions, remained indifferent toward their plight. That the victim/victimizer discourse has retained such prominence in Germany to this day is a direct result of the Nazis' unprecedented brutality and use of modern technology with which they tried to annihilate the Jewish people and Jewish culture.

Confronted with ample evidence of the systematic and institutionalized killing of Jews, Germans after the war could not escape the persuasiveness of the victim/victimizer dichotomy, notwithstanding the adoption of various strategies of denial and avoidance. By their mode of discourse Germans alternately

—relativized victim and victimizer ("Not only Jews were victims but also gypsies and communists"; "Not only Germans were victimizers but also Ukrainians and the Allies")
—trivialized Jewish victims ("Everybody is a victim of the Nazi regime")

—universalized the meaning of the Shoah ("All humans are capable of doing evil"; "Everybody is a survivor of some sort")
—compared the Holocaust to other mass killings (the bombing of Hiroshima, the Vietnam War, a potential nuclear "holocaust");
—denied any personal involvement ("The Nazis did it but nobody in my family was involved");
—skirted the issue altogether ("Nobody wants to talk about it"); or
—denied the reality of what had happened ("There are no victims"; "We Germans were not involved").

These and similar strategies were meant to lessen the impact of the Holocaust on the postwar German psyche.[5] But in fact they show that even when repressed, distorted, and inverted, the victim/victimizer dichotomy informed the society's attitudes toward Jews, the Holocaust, and Jewish/German relations.

After the war, when Germany plunged into an overzealous effort toward restoration and normalization, the various strategies of avoidance came in handy. Germans presented themselves as "ordinary" people with "ordinary" worries who did not want to be reminded of the extraordinary brutality and indifference they had acted out a few years earlier. Under the guise of ordinariness, high-level Nazi functionaries and administrators were eventually reintegrated into the democratic institutions of a thriving capitalist economy (cf. Giordano 1990). "Instead of a political and spiritual processing of the past and the search for new ideas, ideals, and concepts, the German economy developed explosively," the psychoanalyst Margarete Mitscherlich said of the situation (1984:19). In their hurry to rebuild, Germans forgot to address their own moral and human failures and to mourn their victims (cf. Mitscherlich 1975).

The German inability to mourn may have been the main source of the continuous presence of anti-Jewish sentiments in postwar Germany. A process of mourning is essential for gaining a realistic understanding of one's family history and a nation's past and for establishing a reasonably healthy identity. It may also help to build up caring relationships with the descendants of the victims of the Holocaust. This, however, did not happen. Instead, Germans kept family histories in the dark, applied a variety of defensive and rebellious strategies with which they hoped to escape the identification with the Nazi perpetrator, dismissed the relevance of learning about Jews and Judaism, and engaged in haphazard and guilt-ridden relations to the Jewish community.

As a result of this widespread societal attitude, Holocaust education in Germany was riddled with flaws. Until the mid-1960s, the "Final Solution" was hardly ever mentioned in Germany's schools; not until after the student rebellion of the late 1960s did awareness of German fascism and the destruction of European Jews grow. This awareness was slowly transferred to school curricula, media coverage, church activities, and adult-education programs. But the teaching of the Holocaust remained awkward. The Shoah was either tucked away in the general history of World War II, mentioned as an especially gruesome aberration of the Nazi regime, or called a by-product of Hitler's dictatorship. During my high school years, in the mid-1970s, I learned about the Holocaust mainly through documentary films, photographs, and brief passages in a history textbook. The issue was also briefly touched upon in my confirmation class at a Protestant congregation. Perhaps most memorable was a visit to Stutthof, a concentration camp in Poland, with my parents (though I do not remember them explaining much). What I and many students after me learned about the Holocaust was some basic data and facts. But nobody taught us how to relate to the Shoah emotionally.

Furthermore, we learned little about antisemitism and almost nothing about Judaism and contemporary Jewish life. Whatever knowledge we gained about Jews and Judaism came from our religion classes, which, in contrast to the practice in the United States, are offered in the public-school system. Jews were presented through the eyes of Christianity: they were mainly the "hypocritical" and "legalistic" Pharisees, the ancient antagonists of Jesus in the New Testament. Only later did I discover that the little we learned about Judaism had no relevance to how Jews understand their religion and themselves.

The situation improved in the 1980s. After the American television series *Holocaust* was shown on West German television in 1979, the term itself had finally arrived. Previously, the German discourse had referred to the killing of Jews as the "Final Solution" or as the Nazi policy of annihilating the Jews. The television series enabled "millions of postwar Germans to shed tears, for the first time, for the people next door," remarked Susan Neiman (1992:129f), a young American Jew who lived in Berlin for several years. "Maybe tearjerkers are needed in a land where rage is so easy, mourning so hard."[6] Now, textbooks began to present more comprehensive material about National Socialism and the Holocaust (cf. Renn 1987), and some teachers encouraged their students to research the Nazi period. A few of these projects went far beyond regular classroom assignments and resulted in the restoration of old synagogues or in efforts by local communities to invite Jewish survivors back to their old hometowns. As impressive as some of these achievements were, they remained atypical of the general picture. German students to this day say that they "have heard enough about the Holocaust"—a statement that does not reflect their actual knowledge of the Shoah but reveals their emotional resistance to the subject.

Most German students "know about" the Holocaust but do not recognize the names of specific ghettoes, camps, laws, or the people who had been involved in the killing or organized the Jewish resistance. They are also quite ignorant of the complexity of survival or details about the living conditions in camps. Inundated with images of the Holocaust, third-generation Germans do not claim the past as their own but reject it as "past history" (vergangene Geschichte). In the absence of Jews, young Germans perceive themselves as victims of their own history or of those forces that continuously remind them of the Holocaust. They lack a constructive way of acknowledging the inheritance of belonging to a culture which produced bystanders, accomplices, and victimizers—and only a small number of active members of the resistance. They restrict the identification with the perpetrator to the generations of their parents and grandparents and for themselves adopt the opposite role, identifying, for example, with Palestinians as "victims" of Israeli policy and of the "imperialist" Jewish-American lobby. They universalize the role of victimizer ("other nations have committed crimes as well"); worse, a few imitate the victimizers by joining the ranks of neo-Nazis and skinheads.

After completing school, third-generation Germans are entirely unprepared for situations in which they meet Jews. Because their teachers were themselves ambiguous about their emotional and personal investment in the history and memory of the Holocaust, the third generation was instructed in mostly intellectual, political, analytical, and sometimes moral terms. Teachers did not help them develop mechanisms for coping with either the emotional impact of the material or encounters with Jews. Philosopher Theodor Adorno once remarked about German Holocaust education that it is first "necessary to educate the educators," so that "the attempts at public enlightenment to explore the past" do not "awaken a stubborn resistance and bring about the exact opposite of what is intended" (1986:126). This, I believe, has happened in Germany. Not only is the Holocaust taught as a by-product of National Socialism; not only are Jews an unknown entity; not only are the depth and scope of antisemitism misunderstood; but there is also precious little awareness of one's family history and one's emotional entanglement in the Shoah. To young Germans, the Holocaust has become a strangely abstract, yet ever terrifying reality, or "unreality." Nobody taught them how to cope with the possibility of their family's involvement in the genocide. And nobody taught them how to grieve the loss of the former Jewish population of Germany and Europe, or to gain a realistic view of Jewish life today, that is, a view without a latently antisemitic slant.

The strategies for avoiding the identification with victimizers correspond to a prospering of victim imagery in German discourse. Older generations often say that they were victims of outer circumstances, of Hitler, the advancing Soviet army, the Allied bombing raids, or Jewish conspiracies. Younger generations claim to be victims of their country's past, their grandparents and parents, capitalism, or contemporary politics.

As regards the image of Jews as victims, the German discourse also displays a high degree of ambiguity. "Every time I see you I think of Dachau," Susan Neiman was told by a German friend; and after years of living in Berlin, Neiman concluded that for "Germans born after 1930 . . . 'Jew' became a concept with a role in their world; as enemy of the people, as accuser and victim, as anything else but a fellow like me" (1992:138, 303). When discussing Jewish/German relations and Holocaust-related issues, Germans—irrespective of their political outlook—expend much emotional energy in proving or disproving the innocence and goodness of Jews as victims. This, I suspect, serves the purpose of boosting the Germans' blemished self-image by means of a fictionalized image of Jews. In fact, German postwar strategies of avoidance can be interpreted in some measure as a defense against the (often imagined) accusations that Germans are evil and Jews are good.

Two basic stratagems follow from this defensive attitude: one aims at disproving the innocence of Jews, the other at proving their goodness (cf. Rabinbach 1986). The first stratagem is often unacknowledged and hidden behind political polemics. The compulsion of Germans to discuss and criticize Israeli politics is a case in point. Regardless of whether they have actually met Jews or know much about the Middle East, they make authoritative statements and judgments about Israel. That Zionism equals racism and that the Israeli policy toward the Palestinians mirrors the Nazi persecution of Jews are widespread assumptions. Israelis are Jews who have lost their innocence. "An anti-Zionist self-conception is no protection against anti-Semitic stupidity," the German sociologist Detlev Claussen writes about the German New Left's identification with the enemies of Israel. His critique, I believe, applies to Germans of all ages across the political spectrum (1986:57; cf. Schneider and Simon 1984).

The second stratagem, the attempt to prove the goodness of Jews, is expressed in various ways: the Jewish "co-citizen" (*Mitbürger*) of past and present is idealized ("Jews are smart, like Einstein, Freud, and Marx"); the German/Jewish symbiosis is praised ("German Jewry was the Jewish high-culture of Western Europe"); Jewish culture is nostalgically embraced (as in Germany's current adoration of Yiddish culture). Those who make these philosemitic statements have been reproached for their idealistic pillaging of Judaism. Philosemites, so the charge goes, adopt from Judaism whatever they perceive as good, project it onto their praised object, and fail to understand the intricacies of reality. "References . . . to the great achievements of Jews in the past, however true they may be, hardly do much good and smack of propaganda" (Adorno 1986:127). The disappointment that must ensue when the idealized image of Jews ceases to correspond to the reality of contemporary Jewish life can lead to resentment and arouse hostility. This is, I suspect, the reason philosemitism has been called the inverse of antisemitism.

The accusation of being an antisemite in a disguise of philosemitism can lead to double reversals and therefore requires double-thinking. Certainly, a kind of German and Christian philosemitism exists that can be called suppressed antisemitism. By the same token, there are antisemites who suspect behind all non-Jewish support of Jewish culture an antisemitism disguised as philosemitism. Since antisemites cannot conceive of any genuine empathy with Jews, they use the "philosemitism-equals-inverse-antisemitism" argument to neutralize every pro-Jewish statement. Those familiar with the politics of the German discourse on antisemitism know that this debate can lead to an infinite chain of charges and countercharges (cf. Frank Stern 1991; Claussen 1986; Seligmann 1991:109ff).

The German discursive practice on victim and victimizer is deeply ambiguous. Some have erroneously described themselves as victims or have otherwise twisted the notion of victimhood. Other have adopted a rebellious attitude toward any identification with the victimizers; but this rebellion still employs the victim/victimizer imagery in search of a post-Shoah German identity. In these largely unself-conscious processes, the Holocaust loses its historical specificity and becomes a metaphor for other actual, potential, or purported atrocities: the nuclear "holocaust," the Cambodian "holocaust," the AIDS "holocaust," the abortion "holocaust." "If historians diffuse the target," the Harvard historian Charles Maier wrote, "the Final Solution will become a specimen of social-Darwinist eugenics gone wild, capitalist crisis, twentieth-century inhumanity, a sea of complicity in which everyone founders—everything but a crime committed by some Germans against many Jews" (1988:166). The paradigmatic and metaphoric use of the term "Holocaust" detracts from one's own investment in a particular history and culture.

Compared to this general rebellion against any identification with the victimizer, Iris, the German student quoted above, expressed a refreshing awareness of the pitfalls of German discourse. She wrote that "as a West-German, non-Jewish woman I am part of the tradition of victimizers." At least briefly, Iris dared to identify with the perpetrators. However, her challenge of German victimology was cautious, since she continued the sentence with a reference to her grandparents: "My grandparents are from Germany . . . [and] belong to the society of victimizers and bystanders." Iris's swift move from talking about herself to talking about her grandparents conveys the threat that the role of victimizer poses for young Germans.

After four weeks of living together with young American Jews, Iris wrote that her "identity begins where I remain vulnerable. . . . I envision a society in which different cultural and ethnic groups can live with each other on an equal basis." That Germans of the third generation make themselves vulnerable when encountering their Jewish peers is an indispensable step along the path of reconciliation.

A Jewish Discursive Practice: The Victim as Agent of Social Cohesion

Critics of the current debate over the place of the Holocaust in contemporary society—I am thinking here of both sympathetic and unsympathetic voices, but not of revisionist attempts to downplay or deny the Holocaust—point to a certain "Holocaust fixation" in Germany, Israel, and America (Wolffsohn 1988:62). They argue that this leads to a self-referential "memory industry" (Ophir 1987:61) or "Holocaust industry" (Miller 1990:231) made up of museums, archives, publications, commemorations, conferences, educational institutions, exhibits, cultural events, films, and the like. This "industry," they claim, is engaged in a ritualized, repetitive discourse, and its institutions compete for the same audiences and financial resources. "The Holocaust," Henryk Broder remarked, "has turned into a social ritual, an occasion for parading one's evening gowns and for delivering speeches. A number of dignitaries and functionaries have found a playground. . . on which to retravel the road to Auschwitz without danger" (quoted in Seligmann 1991:107).

Whereas the German discourse on Jews and the Holocaust is caught up in its own biases, distortions, limitations, and strategies of avoidance, Israeli society, by contrast, insists on specificity and identifies the Holocaust as a unique period in the history of Jewish suffering and exile. But critics of the Israeli construction of a "memory industry" charge that the Shoah has turned into a secular religion which functions as historical and ideological glue for keeping a fragmented society together. The Holocaust has undergone a "process of 'sanctification,'" the Israeli philosopher Adi Ophir has warned; as the Holocaust is mythologized and demonized, it "blurs the humanness of the Holocaust, . . . directs us almost exclusively to the past, to the immortalization of that which is beyond change, [and] encourages memory as an excuse for one more nation-unifying ritual and not as a tool for historical understanding" (1987:63).

Among Jewish Americans, the Holocaust similarly provides social cohesion. Unlike in Israel, the Jewish community in America does not live in the physical presence of an antagonistic force (Arabs, Palestinians) but faces identity-eroding social forces, such as assimilation, intermarriage, and religious pluralism. To counter the trend toward assimilation and disaffiliation, the Jewish discourse on the Holocaust often serves as a reminder of the importance of remaining Jewish. "Don't give Hitler a posthumous victory" is a phrase frequently spoken, especially to those who are assimilating and considering intermarriage. In 1967, the philosopher Emil Fackenheim even declared it the 614th commandment of Judaism: "The authentic Jew of today is forbidden to hand Hitler yet another, posthumous victory" (1989:294). New generations of American Jews are growing up with this warning, for it is they who are particularly inclined to embrace an American way of life which, on the one hand, accords minorities a certain charm but also perceives them as obsolete, folkish, and sometimes menacing. To many, perhaps most, American Jews of the third generation, their centuries-old European roots are like a distant relative to whom one must pay respect but who remains distant and unfamiliar. They grew up, like their non-Jewish peers, with images of the Holocaust produced by American popular culture, which thrives on situations that seem morally unambiguous.

Most children and grandchildren of survivors still feel deeply connected to the Holocaust. However, third-generation Jewish Americans as a whole seem to feel more and more detached from the Holocaust as temporal distance grows. The American positivist outlook and the forces of assimilation work counter to the traumatic and apocalyptic worldview that the Shoah offers. At the same time, Jews are concerned about the growing popularity of revisionist voices that deny the Holocaust. By the 1970s, many survivors felt compelled to tell their stories publicly. The social tensions of temporal distance from the Shoah, assimilation, and revisionism revived Jewish interest in Holocaust education programs. The Shoah became part of the curricula of many Hebrew schools, being taught not only as an important event in history but also as an event crucial to Jewish identity.[7]

In the 1970s, Holocaust education spread quickly, extending beyond the Jewish community and reaching non-Jewish Americans. Educational institutions, often in cooperation with Jewish and interfaith organizations, developed curricula that looked at the Holocaust as both a Jewish trauma and a paradigm for the crisis of modern civilization that could teach lessons about racism, antisemitism, hate, and bigotry. When "the experience of the Holocaust . . . [entered] the mainstream of American political life, it [was] inevitably Americanized," Michael Berenbaum wrote, and was "reshaped to participate in the fundamental tale of pluralism, tolerance, democracy, and human rights that America tells about herself" (1981/2:9; cf. 1990:3–16). In 1969, for example, only two courses on the Holocaust were offered at American universities. This number increased to two hundred by 1979, and "in the 1980s, the number has increased tenfold to two thousand courses" (Berenbaum 1990:61). According to the findings of a 1991 survey released by the Anti-Defamation League and the United States Holocaust Memorial Council, 73 percent of the American population regards the Holocaust as a significant historical event, and 85 percent believes that it is important to continue Holocaust education so that such an event will not happen again.[8] The Holocaust, it seems, has secured a place in American education.

But American Holocaust education is not without problems. "Whose history is to be taught: the perpetrator's, the victim's, or the bystander's?" Berenbaum asks (1990:61). The soaring interest in the Holocaust among Jewish-American communities might be "an epidemic of necessity," Robert Alter writes, but the danger of making the Holocaust a center of Judaism itself is that "serious distortions of . . . Jewish life [may] occur when the Holocaust is commercialized, politicized, theologized, and academicized" (1981:49). If the Shoah became the central content of Jewish life, Alter warns, it would bury and distort the religious and cultural values of Judaism. Young Jews might remain loyal to Judaism for fear of a potential new destruction but would not identify with the Jewish tradition for positive reasons.

What is the impact on the psyche of young people if they are taught of such intense suffering and victimization? In his assessment of the contemporary experience of American Jews, Leonard Fein wonders whether the old Jewish "passion of religious messianism" as well as the "utopian passion . . . of secular messianism" have been replaced by an "apocalyptic passion" (1988:65). Focusing on the Holocaust as apocalyptic passion makes its history vulnerable to ideological misappropriation. To emphasize this point, Fein cites a fund-raising letter from the National Council of Synagogue Youth:

> In the 1940s Jews faced annihilation. In the 1980s we face it again! This time, however, we face a much more insidious enemy. This time you and I face the scourge of assimilation. Dare I call it a second holocaust in the making? . . .
>   There are no longer Nazis to fight. There is no single force to battle—except—ourselves. (1988:146)

This appeal illustrates the peculiar turns the Jewish discourse on the Holocaust can take: the image of the victim is called upon to hold the community together. It is the tie that binds.

The context within which the memory of the Shoah is evoked determines the ideological content. Such key phrases as "remembrance," "innocent victims," and "never again" mean one thing in the context of Yom Ha-Shoah commemorations among survivors, where they sum up and summon individual pain, but something else in the context of a fund-raising letter. At other times, it is the wording itself, or perhaps the repetition of certain words, that betrays a stale discourse. Phrases such as "innocent victims" and "fascist monsters" (cf. Alter 1981:51), which have the power to inscribe the roles of Jews and Germans, are a case in point. Speakers and writers have tried to convey a terror which, as Elie Wiesel stated, is beyond the grasp of language, tucked away in silence. But once removed from a historical context, hyperbolic expressions assume a life of their own, inhibiting attempts to break out of the current stasis of Jewish/German relations. Adjectives like "good" and "evil," "guilty" and "innocent," were often attached to people; the "good Jew" and the "evil German" came to possess an ontological, biological, or otherwise unchanging status.[9]

As early as 1946, when observing the war-crimes trials at Nuremberg, Hannah Arendt wrote to Karl Jaspers about the dangers of such representation. "The innocence of the victims," she said, "is as non-human as the guilt [of the victimizers]. No human being can be so innocent as [the victims] were in front of the gas chambers. . . . Neither in human nor in political terms can we cope with a guilt which is beyond all criminal guilt and an innocence which is beyond kindness and virtue." Guilt, Arendt claimed, could not adequately describe Nazi atrocities; "the Nazis are so cheerful in Nuremberg" because they know "there is no adequate punishment for their crimes" (quoted in Diner 1986:245). Nor could the victimizers be described simply as evil monsters, a point Arendt made in 1961 when reporting on the trial of Adolf Eichmann in Jerusalem (Arendt 1963). On the other hand, the notion of innocence, she felt, was similarly inadequate to describe the plight of Jews. Jewish victims were bound together in their innocence as regards the genocide, but they were not innocent as regards their human nature. "We Jews are burdened with millions of innocent [victims]," Arendt wrote in the letter to Jaspers, "which explains why all Jews today think they personify innocence itself."[10]

We do not have to accept Arendt's sweeping claim that "all Jews today" think of themselves as innocents in order to appreciate her reflections on the ambiguous meaning of guilt and innocence. Her thoughts, often mistakenly viewed as cynical, to me convey the despair over the general "contradiction between the impossibility but also necessity of writing" about the Holocaust (Rosenfeld 1980:8). Indeed, the casual use of "innocence" has led to awkward conclusions. On one level, "innocence" may also imply "guilt," as if the Holocaust could have been justified had Jews been proven guilty of certain crimes. But only a perverted "Nazi ethic" (Haas 1988) tried to charge Jews with fabricated crimes, such as the Jewish world conspiracy, thereby trying to blame the victim. Jews were, of course, innocent of these charges and, to my knowledge, the term "innocent victim" has not been used as a judicial concept to disprove the Nazi accusations. Jews did not have to be legally innocent in order to become victims.

The phrase "innocent victim" also implies that Jews were passive and inactive. But such an idea, which is also expressed in the phrase "Jews went like sheep to the slaughter," constitutes a political judgment and does not reflect reality. It assumes that Jews did not resist and ignores the tremendous difficulty of organizing resistance in a context of total victimization. In his reflections on survivor testimonies, Lawrence Langer responds to the frequently asked question of why Jews did not resist: "The first answer is that they did; the second is that sometimes it made no difference; and the third is that, under those circumstances, more often than not they couldn't" (1991:20f; cf. Rosenthal 1988).

The term "innocent victim" is not only legally and politically inept but also inappropriate as a moral category. It cannot convey the moral quality of being unblemished or good, as Arendt has correctly observed. Every victim was "good" when compared to the overwhelming evil of the Final Solution. But even as victims, Jews were still active and moral agents who had to make decisions. (The continuing debate about the integrity of the *Judenräte* is but one example.)[11] In short, neither legal, political, nor moral definitions of innocence can accurately describe the situation of Jews during the Shoah. The victims of the Final Solution did not have to be law-abiding, passive, or good people in order to be annihilated; they just had to be human beings who happened to be Jewish.

One might expect that Jewish survivors would be most strongly invested in perpetuating the discourse of innocent victims and evil victimizers; and clearly a strong sense of innocence prevails in their literary testimony.[12] Child survivors in particular experienced the German onslaught as a complete rupture of their "innocent" childhood (cf. Fisher 1991). This innocence is perhaps best described as bewilderment and disbelief in response to the cruelty they faced. Their world and their belief in basic human values collapsed, subverted by the Nazis. To understand innocence in this way dissociates the experience of total victimization from the distorting assumption of "innocent victims" as necessarily law-abiding, passive, and good people.

The reactions of survivors to Germans as (past and potential) victimizers differ greatly. Many survivors will not speak to Germans, vow never again to set foot on German soil, and boycott German products. But there are as many who either actively seek contact with younger Germans or do not shy away from accidental contacts. Many are very conscientious about differentiating between the evil they experienced and ideological generalizations. They have suffered at the hands of German soldiers, SS units, their neighbors, and bystanders, but in their oral testimonies they also tell of (admittedly rare) instances of receiving unexpected help from Germans. Their pain is deep, and yet they often are willing to embrace Germans of the third generation, the grandchildren of their victimizers.[13]

We know that some of the bitterness and anger that survivors were unable to express (because they were too deeply injured) has been voiced by their children. It is not unusual for children of survivors to show their anger toward Germans and to be reluctant to meet the postwar German generation. In Philadelphia, for example, young German volunteers of Action Reconciliation (a German organization working for peace and social justice in countries that suffered under the Nazis) tried to arrange a meeting with the Association of Children of Holocaust Survivors in the early 1980s but were rejected. The children of survivors feared that such a meeting would cause too much agony and confusion. At the same time, however, some of their parents had already met with third-generation Germans on an individual basis. Not until the late 1980s did second- and third-generation Jews and Germans begin to meet, irregularly, at workshops with Action Reconciliation, in which they cautiously addressed issues of Jewish/German relations. Finally, in the summer of 1991, the Association of Children of Holocaust Survivors in

Philadelphia officially sponsored a social gathering between Germans and Jews of the third generation, a breakthrough that would have been inconceivable a decade earlier. "Ten years ago," a child of survivors recently told me, "I would not have stayed in the same room with you."

If Jewish survivors and their children differ in their responses to Germany and Jewish/German relations, how do young American Jews without personal ties to the Holocaust react to these issues? How do they approach Germans?

Given the spatial and temporal distance from the Shoah, we might expect them to be less entangled in the image of "evil Germans." However, this is often not the case. I know of many encounters, including personal ones, in which young American Jews had a hard time distinguishing between Nazi Germany and contemporary Germany. Germans and Nazis were interchangeable characters on a conceptual or emotional level, and sometimes on both levels simultaneously. "I never met a German before," an American Jewish student said during one of the summer programs, "but the image I've gotten is from [the television series] *Hogan's Heroes*—loud, drunken, clumsy, stupid." Young American-born Jews can be invested, sometimes vehemently, in perpetuating a negative image of Germans, including those born after the Shoah. "Their questions about Nazis and Germans," Sabine Reichel, a second-generation German, reports, "which at times seemed trite and simplistic and which I felt distracted from the real issues, were drawn from an insulated capsule filled with vague suppositions and self-formulated conclusions that were not easy to penetrate" (1989:147). This emotional investment of young American Jews, especially in the absence of real encounters with Germans, shows that they have developed a stereotype of Germans that has a life and function of its own outside any historical framework.

There are, of course, legitimate reasons for not liking Germans. After all, Germans did annihilate Jewish lives and European Jewish culture. But this does not mean that we should blind ourselves to other social forces that contribute to the stereotyped image of Germans among young American Jews. War movies and television shows promote this stereotype, and American isolationist tendencies cultivate a certain insensitivity to countries across the Atlantic. In addition, the particular struggles of the American Jewish community against (real or imagined) hostile forces—such as internal erosion (assimilation) and external harassment (living as a minority culture within a Christian world)—feed and are fed by the victim/victimizer dichotomy. Between the need to remember and the fear that "the Holocaust now threatens to become the starting point for Jewish life" (Fein 1988:69), American Jews must ponder their options. Specifically with respect to the future of American Holocaust education, the discourse on victim and victimizer can be (mis)used to prescribe the roles Jews and Germans ought to play, thus preserving the status quo. But when this discourse is used to differentiate and specify, it can open doors to the painful but ultimately transformative work of reconciliation.

When Suzanne, upon meeting young Germans, said that she "was more deeply dedicated not to compromise my history, my people, my self," her sentiment echoed a discursive practice that insists that reevaluating one's relationship with Germans threatens Jewish identity. But at the end of four weeks of living and studying together with her German peers, Suzanne conceded that she had "met some marvelous, open, warm, dedicated" Germans and could "envision a future for our personal and political relationships." On the last day of the program, she wrote in her journal: "I have found a voice, but the proper audience has not really presented itself. It is time for me to go find that audience, to construct it, and educate" (Krondorfer and Schmidt 1990:30).

I have argued that the discursive practices of Germans and American Jews are invested in formulating and maintaining a discourse that describes Jewish/German relations in terms of victim and victimizer, innocent and guilty, good and evil. The German discourse holds on to these dichotomies in order to establish German identity vis-à-vis a fictionalized image of Jews. The American Jewish discourse, on the other hand, has seized on the image of victim in the face of a hostile world because, as a minority community, such identification can strengthen its sense of belonging. Yet the prominence of certain antonyms (innocent/evil, us/them) suggests that the Jewish discourse, too, simplifies and mythologizes complex situations. In the public discourse of both Jews and Germans, the victim/victimizer dichotomy has moved from descriptive assessment to inscriptive ideology. It inscribes—or perhaps prescribes—the roles Jews and Germans must play in a highly ritualized discourse, in which ideas like guilt, forgiveness, remembrance, victim, and perpetrator are freely and casually applied, although with ever-dwindling meaning. Ideological inscriptions not only are ahistoric but also foil moves toward social and individual change. This resistance to change is, I believe, an unwillingness to probe the potential value of renewed relationships between Jews and Germans.

Despite the need to differentiate between descriptive assessment and inscriptive ideology, the victim/victimizer discourse is irrevocably ambiguous, moving indiscriminately from one term to the other. It can describe historical and political reality, but may simultaneously impose communal and national ideologies on new generations. An analytic mind may deplore such opacity; but as far as practical efforts of reconciliation are concerned, it is material to work with. When third-generation Jews and Germans share how they and their communities memorialize, or "re-vision," the Shoah and how they "envision" their present and future lives in a post-Shoah world, the victim/victimizer discourse emerges in all its shades and colors, as we have seen already in the statements of Iris and Suzanne. It makes little sense, at workshops and other programs, to tell them that their observations are wrong, as a judgmental attitude would only cause them to suppress the emotional and ideological confusions instead of revealing them. A facilitator can, however, sensitively point out why certain interpretations of the victim/victimizer discourse are incomplete and how they are governed by deep cultural beliefs and attitudes.

I suggest a dual approach to the victim/victimizer discourse. The third generation must learn to affirm the legitimacy of describing Jewish/German relations in terms of victim and victimizer; anything else would falsify the history of the Shoah, Germany's antisemitic traditions, its rebellious strategies of avoidance after 1945, and the continuous strain on Jewish/German relations. But the reverse is true as well: to hold on to an inscriptive and prescriptive reading of victim and victimizer would stall earnest attempts to transform the current dominant discourse, in which Jews and Germans have been caught for too long.

2 Ethos

Remembrance and Guilt

As we examine the effects of the Holocaust we come directly into the angers felt by all sides.

—Anne Roiphe

Probably a *knowledge* of history in and of itself makes up a comparatively small part of one's sense of identity. More relevant is one's *relationship* to history.

—Barbara Heimannsberg

Ethos and Discourse

The Jewish-American and German discursive practices, each for its own reasons, have relied on the victim/victimizer dichotomy to construct collective identities. For European Jewry the Holocaust meant destruction and annihilation, but for American Jews today Holocaust memory serves as a unifying force. The opposite is true for Germany: whereas genocidal antisemitism galvanized Nazi Germany in the past, Holocaust memory today usurps Germany's search for a new national identity. Because of these different perspectives, third-generation Jews and Germans have received mixed messages about the Holocaust, reinforcing social frictions between them.

Post-Shoah Jews and Germans have been taught historical facts and moral lessons but they have also learned to accept their culture's silences, omissions, and taboos. Germans may have learned never again to victimize Jews, but they do not know any; American Jews may have learned not to be victimized ever again and to see "the German" as paradigmatic enemy, but they do not know the society in which young Germans grow up today. It is one of the ironies of the current state of Jewish/German relations that the Holocaust and its moral lessons are taught by educational institutions on both sides of the Atlantic while, at the same time, neither community has taught its children how to relate to the other group. For American Jews and non-Jewish Germans of the third generation, the "other" is not a real person but an imaginary figure. Thus, the key players in the history of the Holocaust have become fictive structures of the mind.

Encounters between Jews and Germans are encumbered by numerous misunderstandings. Neither side is aware of the degree to which the other identifies it with these fictionalizations, biases, images, and attitudes. These identifications reach deeper than discursive practices. They are part of a people's ethos, which, according to anthropologist Clifford Geertz, is "the tone, character, and quality of their life, its moral and aesthetic style and mood; it is the underlying attitude toward themselves and their world that life reflects" (1973:127). Whereas discursive practices are the ways in which people present themselves, the ethos of a people is rooted in the belief that their assumptions, choices, and behaviors are correct and valid. The Holocaust has certainly left its mark on the deeply felt views of Jews and Germans on morality, history, and human interaction. This ethos not only has informed the behaviors and attitudes of first-generation Jews and Germans but has also been transmitted to subsequent generations through mundane practices, often on preverbal and subliminal levels. To be sure, a people's ethos is also reflected in its discursive practices, and vice versa. However, the two concepts are not identical: if discursive practices are what is said, an ethos is what is deeply felt.

As regards the Shoah, American Jews are guided by an ethos of remembrance, Germans by an ethos of guilt. The difference can be illustrated by looking at the role memory plays in each community. American Jews cherish the memory of those who died in the Shoah, and they interpret remembrance as a means of Jewish survival. Remembrance is the marrow of Jewish identity. For Germans, informed by an ethos of guilt, Holocaust memory is more like a tumor that threatens their identity and belief in their own humanity. Remembrance seems to have no function other than to elicit unresolved emotions.

Because the Jewish and German peoples are each governed by their particular ethos, memory and remembrance cannot mean the same thing to both. This explains, perhaps, why Jews are never fully comfortable when Germans speak of the importance of remembering the victims. What does it mean to a German to remember the victims? What does it mean to Jews if Germans remember them? Recurrent pledges by representatives of German religious and political institutions to "never forget" cannot eradicate Jewish discontent and mistrust. When Jews remind Germans of their duty to keep the memory of the Holocaust alive, and Germans either refrain from doing so or do it because they perceive it as morally correct or politically opportune, both Jews and Germans are acting out a kind of addictive behavior. They engage in a cycle of repetitive rhetoric but remain persistently dissatisfied: the symptoms are treated but the cause is not addressed.

What are the options? Clearly I am not advocating that Jews and Germans forget the past. Rather, I am calling for more honesty in Jewish/German encounters. One of the sources of miscommunication and dishonesty is the discrepancy between how people present themselves (discourse) and what they deeply believe in (ethos). Rectifying this discrepancy is a step toward a more honest relationship. How can Germans remember the victims if they have not yet begun to grieve for them? Do they not need first to develop a language that is sensitive to Jewish perspectives and does not hide behind safe rhetoric? How can Jews listen to Germans if the issue of trust is not resolved? Is it possible to conceive of reconciliatory practices that go beyond the German desire to be forgiven and the Jewish fear that Jewish injuries will be forgotten?

For older generations it is perhaps too late to reduce the accumulated distrust. Pain and shame are still too vivid to permit people who have lived through the Nazi era to improve their listening skills, start the grieving process, and learn how to become more vulnerable. The third generation, however, can dare to reconcile because they are distant enough in time but still emotionally attached to Holocaust memory.

But even for third-generation Jews and Germans reconciliation is no easy task. "Most Germans born after the war want to escape from this inevitable tie [to the Holocaust]," the historian Michael Wolffsohn writes, "while Jews cannot escape it without endangering their Jewishness" (1988:54). When post-Shoah Jews and Germans meet, they arrive with different expectations. Rebellion, anger, dismissal, indifference, insecurity, concern, distress, anxiety—these are part of the emotional repertoire with which they react to the transmitted memory of the Holocaust. Their responses mirror the mixed messages and beliefs they have received from their respective communities. Third-generation Jews and

Germans intuitively recognize the discrepancy between the official discourse on the Shoah that their communities practice at solemn occasions and the nonverbal and ambiguous messages they received at home and through their social networks. "For the fact is that material which is not spoken, which is only transmitted nonverbally, cannot be directly recalled, and yet definitely has an influence on . . . psychic consciousness as well as [the] unconscious," the psychoanalyst Sammy Speier writes about the transmission of the Holocaust trauma (1993:69). Gestures, moral attitudes, daily routines, casual comments, family albums, and family narratives have all nourished the third generation's belief in the integrity of their culture's assumptions about the past. To examine these deeply felt beliefs critically is thus inevitably to probe one's identity.

The Jewish Ethos: From Destruction to Redemption

The theme at Holocaust remembrance ceremonies at the Israeli kibbutz Lohamei Hageta'ot, founded by former partisan members and survivors of camps and ghettos, is always the same: "From Destruction to Remembrance" (Young 1990:185). This theme empowers the community during Yom Ha-Shoah commemorations and other occasions, such as anniversaries of the Warsaw ghetto uprising, gatherings of survivors in Washington, Jerusalem, and Philadelphia, anniversaries of Kristallnacht, or the opening of the Holocaust Memorial Museum in Washington, D.C. It also turns up in publications, Jewish art, and Hebrew school instructions. Remembrance, always important to Jewish tradition, became imperative after the Shoah. At Yad Vashem, the Holocaust museum in Jerusalem, a saying from the Baal Shem Tov, the eighteenth-century founder of Hasidism, is inscribed in the memorial hall: "In remembrance lies the secret of deliverance." The inscription illustrates how post-Shoah communities have woven sources of spiritual wisdom into the memory of the horrors of the Holocaust, incorporating the modern genocide into previous experiences of exile, suffering, and messianic promises. "From ashes to rebirth." "The obligation to remember." "From destruction to deliverance." These and similar phrases testify to the Jews' ability to survive and celebrate their post-Shoah lives.

What many young Germans do not realize is that the ethos of remembrance is directed toward the future. To Jewish people it is not simply a looking back at the past or being stuck in the past, as many Germans fear. To many third-generation Germans, Jews are either biblical figures (as taught in Christian education) or victims of the Holocaust. "If first impressions are crucial," Sabine Reichel writes, "my relationships with Jews got off to a heart-wrenching, alienating start. Jews were introduced to me dead: as enormous piles of skin and bones, twisted limbs and distorted faces, waiting to be tossed into carts bound for the crematory. . . . I met them through old newsreels in the sixties—wordless, grainy celluloid figures caught in a deadly pantomime" (1989:133). Jews represent the past in the psyche of Germans and in the Christian psyche in general. But the ethos of remembrance always points toward survival and redemption, to the celebration of Jewish life after the Shoah.

Jews may interpret redemption as the rebirth of Israel or support of the Jewish diaspora; as acknowledgment of Jewish resistance during the Shoah or survivors' joy in having raised children and grandchildren; as a messianic promise or the political backing of Israel; as the celebration of religious diversity or the search for a renewed spirituality. Though the interpretations are manifold, the ethos of remembrance always carries a promise, a dynamic move from victimization to survival and life.

Today, discussions among American Jews about the relevance of the ethos of remembrance focus on the centrality of the Holocaust. How prominent a role should it play in community life and the upbringing of children? The view that the Holocaust and the founding of the state of Israel are two events vital to modern Jews is rarely disputed. But some fear that the memory of the Holocaust has thoroughly secularized the concept of remembrance and has defined Jewishness in merely negative terms. Others warn that excessive remembering can be harmful, and still others argue that Jewish anger is a necessary component of remembrance. "That Jews are angry is a fact . . . and will shape our actions, our moral choices, our designs for living in the years to come," Anne Roiphe has written (1988:26). The psychoanalyst Martin Bergman has noted that "too much stress on remembrance is an oppressive way to live" (quoted in Roiphe 1988:216). And a prominent American Jewish scholar has pungently remarked: "What is the first lesson a Jew learns? That people want to kill Jews" (Fein 1988:59).[1]

Michael Berenbaum, the project director of the United States Holocaust Memorial Museum, suggests that "the current discussion centers on two major questions: (1) Does the Holocaust occupy an excessively prominent position in contemporary Jewish consciousness, threatening to obscure the promise of Sinai, the triumph of Israel, and the totality of previous Jewish history? (2) Does the Holocaust have normative implications for Jewish history and theology?" (1990:27). If the Holocaust occupies an "excessively prominent position," Judaism loses its religious roots and its messianic promise. The third generation will grow up lacking a positive identification. So argues, for example, the Jewish philosopher Michael Wyschograd (1971; cf. Katz 1983). On the other hand, the Holocaust changed the world so radically, according to Richard Rubinstein (1966), that we cannot turn away from its normative implications. In a post-Shoah world, all moral and political talk, even God-talk, has to be different.

The debate is far from resolved. It is important, however, to be aware of how deeply third-generation Jews are affected by the diverse interpretations of the ethos of remembrance. Faced with the question of how to teach the legacy of the Holocaust to the third generation, the psychologist Steven Luel, himself a son of survivors, has written:

> We of the second generation are rearing or are about to rear the third post-Holocaust generation. How do we wish to present the Holocaust to them? To what extent do we wish them to share our anxieties, rages, and hurts? On the one hand, we want to remind them through remembrance and transmission of the horrific truth. On the other hand, the second generation will be best equipped to rear the third if, in preparation, they extract themselves from a self-injurious attachment to the Holocaust. . . .
>
> This will mean, first, that the Holocaust must become less of a painful emotional problem for us and remain predominantly in historical, philosophical, and intellectual contexts for our children. . . . We must find a *via media* between the obligation to remember, with its unavoidable sadness, and the obligation to lessen the obsessive rumination, . . . the distrust of the "other," the anger, the apprehensive expectation and its accompanying hypervigilance. (1984:172f; cf. Hass 1990:154ff)

As Luel observed, second-generation Jews have to work through their own emotional "attachment to the Holocaust" before they are able to help their children relinquish anger and distrust, for the children pick up whatever hidden messages they receive from the deep beliefs of their family and social networks. I am skeptical, though, about Luel's sugges-

tion that the Holocaust be taught "predominantly in historical, philosophical, and intellectual contexts." Although such cognitive learning
helps to prevent facile ideological impositions, it will be tainted by various unconscious agendas if the emotions of students, parents, teachers,
and the community at large remain ignored and suppressed. The "work
of remembering," the psychotherapist Barbara Heimannsberg writes,
must be "an integrative process in which senses, thoughts, and feelings
work together" (1993:169). The affective impact of the memory of the
Holocaust on the third generation cannot be underestimated.

"The All-American Boy with the Black Box"

The story of Steven, a twenty-year old participant in one of the summer
programs on the Holocaust, illustrates the affective impact of Holocaust
memory on young American Jews. Steven clearly belonged to the third
generation in age and temporal distance from the Shoah; but, technically, he was also of the second generation, because his father had survived the Holocaust at a young age.

At the beginning of the summer program Steven did not acknowledge his intimate attachment to the Shoah as a child of survivors. Only in
the course of the summer did he realize how large a part of his identity
had been governed by the ethos of remembrance. In a letter a year after
the program, he wrote:

> Prior to the exchange program, I knew that technically I could be
> classified as a child of a survivor but for a variety of reasons I never
> identified as one. . . . Only one of my parents, my father, was a sur-
> vivor. . . . Despite the fact that my father was uprooted and lost all of
> his family, save one brother, my father rarely talked about the Holo-
> caust. . . . In addition, due to the fact that I was generally younger in
> age than most of the "second generation," it was difficult for me to
> identify with this group of my peers.

I met Steven for the first time during the application interview.
Steven appeared to be an educated young man who knew what to think
and say about the Holocaust. At one point during the interview he inti-
mated that his father was a survivor. When asked how his family history
might influence his role in the program, he suddenly became very shy
and groped for words. He did not think, he said in a faltering voice,

that he would be overemotional. He had not really talked about these matters with his father but did not consider this to be relevant because he did not think of himself as a child of a survivor. As Steven left the room, he seemed distressed. "When I was interviewed by the committee," he remembered a year later, "my fears proved to be justified. The panelists focused on my relationship with my father and how this would affect me during the program. This made me feel extremely uncomfortable."

When Steven arrived at Bryn Mawr College a few months later to participate in the four-week program, he was again the quick-witted and enjoyable character I remembered from the first half of the interview. He did not say much but had a rare gift of using humor to put his finger on issues others did not dare to mention. He did not share many of his feelings or identify himself as a child of a survivor. During a session on the second generation, to which we had invited a rabbi and a psychologist who were children of survivors also (but twenty years older than Steven), Steven mentioned that he was skeptical of the psychological research on the second generation and rejected the narrow framework of psychoanalytic case studies.

Two weeks into the program his attitude changed. The morning before we were due to leave for Germany, Steven finally acknowledged his family background. He had called his sister the evening before and must have had a very intimate conversation because he now told the group about his growing up in a survivor family. Steven also mentioned his sister's long years of suffering from anorexia. "I wasn't worthy to prosper," Steven quoted his sister's self-analysis of her disorder. "Becoming anorectic and getting my body under control was a self-imposed concentration camp." His sister's body image and the Holocaust metaphor she used must have affected Steven deeply, for he now began to reconcile himself to his family history. Realizing that his sister was viscerally reliving the memory of the Holocaust and almost literally embodied the ethos of remembrance, he recognized his own emotional entanglement:

> The "breaking point" came when I phoned home before the group left for Germany. By intent or coincidence, I can't recall, I spoke to my sister at length. For the first time in my life, I spoke to her as one child of a survivor to another. . . . If this was the cathartic experience for which I was searching, I did not feel particularly great about it

afterward. Some confounded web, which I thought I had escaped, had indeed entangled me as well. I was the All-American Boy who suddenly found out that he too is carrying around that "Black Box." My findings not only depressed me but also angered me and in turn motivated me to continue forth in the program and thereafter.

At the conclusion of the program Steven wrote an essay about the impact of the Shoah on children of survivors. As a source of inspiration he had consulted Helen Epstein's book *Children of the Holocaust* (1979). "But most of all," Steven wrote, "I think that I will draw upon myself and my family, since I have come to identify myself more profoundly as a child of survivors" (Krondorfer and Staffa 1992:31). In this essay Steven still kept his distance, reporting more on Epstein's findings than on his own family. Not until a year later was he capable of writing the letter quoted above: "After the program, I felt much more comfortable with my newly found identity," Steven concluded. "If it were not for the program, the process of self-discovery would have taken much longer or perhaps not have occurred at all. I am not only more in touch with myself now but I feel that I also understand my father a lot better. I view him with more compassion."

Steven's development demonstrates the importance of helping young generations to appreciate and come to terms with the emotive aspects of memory. Listening to other children of survivors and being confronted with Germans prepared Steven to get in touch with his own identity. Eventually he found the courage to face his particular family history. In the purely "historical, philosophical, and intellectual context" (that psychologist Luel envisioned as the appropriate learning environment for the third generation) Steven would not have grown into his own being. Prior to the program, he had been perfectly capable of handling discourse on the Holocaust but unable to acknowledge the ethos of remembrance that informed his identity (and may have been a cause of his sister's dysfunctional behavior). "For once, I hoped to approach the Holocaust not from only an intellectual level but on an emotional level as well," Steven wrote about his motivation in joining the program. "Why had I never passionately reacted to the Holocaust? Was I scared?" After the summer program, Steven was not only comfortable enough to give public talks as a child of a survivor but also able to realize his need to improve his relationship with his father.

The German Ethos: Guilt and Forgiveness

Whereas the Jewish ethos moves from remembrance to redemption, the German ethos is caught in a self-referential system of guilt and forgiveness. West German society strove to atone for its crimes through reparation payments, financial assistance for the small Jewish community in Germany, diplomatic relations and economic support for the state of Israel, intellectual debates, and educational programs (or, in East Germany, through welcoming Jews as long as they were also communists). Whether these efforts were successful does not concern us here.[2] What is intriguing is that Germany has not articulated an equivalent to the Jewish theme of moving from destruction to redemption. No phrase exists to symbolize Germany's moral and political intention to integrate the memory of the Shoah. Ideologically, postwar West Germany has interpreted the Nazi period as an aberration and tried to reconnect with its democratic pre-1933 traditions. In retrospect, it seems that the older generations spent their energies after 1945 in proving to themselves, their children, and the world that they are ordinary people who were involuntarily subjected to the Nazi regime. But a vision of how to constructively integrate the past into the present and future is missing.

What is not openly articulated nevertheless lives on in disguised form. When talking to Germans of all ages about the meaning of the Holocaust two issues emerge with predictable regularity: guilt and forgiveness. A peculiar dynamic between unacknowledged guilt and desired forgiveness is hidden in the German discourse. Unlike the Jewish ethos of remembrance, which is rooted in historical experience and points to the future, guilt and forgiveness are locked in a circular system, lacking both vision and empowerment.

Guilt and forgiveness often reveal themselves in contradictory viewpoints and behaviors. Some Germans reject the concept of guilt intellectually but still yearn for forgiveness. Others articulate the notion that no human has the power to forgive them for the Nazi crimes but still feel guilty when they meet Jews. Others again claim indifference to issues of guilt and forgiveness but join in bashing Israel or react with anger when reminded of the past because they interpret remembrance as a "Jewish" unwillingness to forgive and forget. They rebel against their feelings of guilt and the Christian concept of forgiveness but harbor antisemitic feelings. They take pride in their government's reparation payments but grossly exaggerate the amount or otherwise show their resentment.

To give but two examples: when Simon Wiesenthal asked whether he should have forgiven the young German soldier who, on his deathbed, confessed to Wiesenthal, a Jew and at the time a prisoner, that he had participated in mass killings of Jews, the well-known German writer Luise Rinser "shudder[ed] at the thought that you let that *repentant* young man go to his death without a word of forgiveness."[3] Cardinal Joseph Höffner, in a sermon in Cologne Cathedral three days after Kohl's and Reagan's visit to the Bitburg cemetery, declared, "We should not, again and again, exhume past guilt and mutually committed injustices, in constant self-torment. We should not constantly weigh guilt against guilt and use it as a weapon, one against the other. All guilt is abolished in the mercy of Jesus Christ, who taught us the prayer: 'Forgive us our sins, as we forgive those who sin against us.'"[4]

These statements are not untypical. They anger me because they voice the expectation that the victims have a duty to forgive the victimizers. Worse, such statements are an attempt at self-exoneration ("all guilt is abolished") and seem to imply that Jews were guilty too ("we should not weigh guilt against guilt"). But despite the articulated stubbornness, I sense a frustration that seems to be caused by the futility of insisting on forgiveness. Did Rinser, Höffner, or others with similar thoughts ever ask themselves what it would actually mean if a Jew forgave them? Would it ease their feelings of guilt? Would it amount to giving Germans permission to forget the past? Do Germans need forgiveness in order to regain equal moral status with Jews? Do Germans need external approval for having mastered the past? *"Vergebung ist das Gebot der Stunde,"* "Forgiveness is the need of the moment," a German farmer in his sixties declared after he saw videotaped interviews of Jewish survivors who had lived in his village before 1938.[5] Guilt and forgiveness are ultimately caught in a defensive, circular system with nowhere to go. Forgiveness presumes guilt, however ambiguously experienced, and guilt thirsts for forgiveness, however ambiguously desired. But forgiveness does not smother the memory of the Shoah nor will it resolve unresolved feelings. Not the withholding of forgiveness, but repressed memory is the source of unresolved feelings. "In Germany, it seems, time doesn't heal wounds; it kills the sensation of pain," Peter Schneider wrote in his novel *The Wall Jumper* (1983:30). It is the German ethos of guilt, not the Jewish ethos of remembrance, that is truly fixed in the past.

There are attempts to break out of the rhetoric of forgiveness and guilt. In his famous speech to the Parliament on 8 May 1985, West German president Richard von Weizsäcker set an example. "Remembering," he said, "means recalling an occurrence honestly and undistortedly. . . . There can be no reconciliation without remembrance." About the postwar generations, he said that "they cannot profess a guilt of their own for crimes they did not commit. No discerning person can expect them to wear a penitential robe simply because they are Germans. But their forefathers have left them a grave legacy. All of us, whether guilty or not, whether old or young, must accept the past. We are all affected by its consequences and liable for it" (quoted in Hartman 1986:263, 265). I wish to believe that Von Weizsäcker's speech was not guided solely by political motives but constituted a serious attempt to find a new and nuanced language.[6] "One must now regretfully wonder whether Weizsäcker's speech should be seen as the authoritative and representative voice of Germany," Fritz Stern remarked, "or whether in retrospect it will come to be regarded as a coda to a period of soul-searching, as a perhaps unconscious premonition of a new wave of embittered, self-pitying indifference that may now be emerging in Germany" (1987:19). Be that as it may, the president's speech represented at the time an enlightened aspect of the ethos of guilt. It affirmed that future generations would have a responsibility toward this legacy. Guilt, remembrance, reconciliation—these were Von Weizsäcker's key words. The memory of the Holocaust infuses guilt, on whatever subtle level, and young Germans will react to it. When American Jews meet their German counterparts they have to reckon with the fact that the issue of guilt informs the attitudes and behaviors of young Germans on an intellectual as well as an emotional level.

"Were We Supposed to Feel Guilty Again?"

In Peter Sichrovsky's *Born Guilty* (1988), a collection of interviews with young Germans about their views on Jews and the Holocaust, Stefanie, a nineteen-year-old student, said, "Don't misunderstand me. I'm not a racist. I've got nothing against Jews. They don't mean anything to me. I don't even know any. But to keep on accusing me that I with my nineteen years share in the guilt of all the crimes against the Jews [*daß ich mitschuldig an der ganzen Sauerei gegen die Juden bin*], that's ridiculous.

What does it mean we took everything away from them back then? What have we got today? . . . You know, sometimes I wouldn't mind being one of those poor little Jews" (1988:33). Stefanie's opinion is an extreme example, and we learn more about her hostility toward Jews in the remainder of the interview. Stefanie defends her grandfather, who was sentenced to death as a war criminal, and belittles her aunt, who has shown empathy for Jews and foreign workers after the war. What I find remarkable in the interview is Stefanie's unawareness of her own contradictory attitudes. She claims that she is indifferent toward Jews and not a racist, but one senses how angry, hostile, and defensive she is.

A person like Stefanie will probably never join a program in which Jews and Germans encounter each other (though she might be the one with the gravest need), and Germans who volunteer to get to know their Jewish peers are unlikely to express such hostile views. But Stefanie is not alone in her confusion. Young Germans from all walks of life are suffused with guilt and anger. These feelings might be subtle and unacknowledged, but they come to the fore when issues of antisemitism and the Shoah are addressed or when Germans actually encounter Jews. "I am not guilty but responsible," enlightened voices say, thus differentiating between the actual guilt of the Nazis and their own responsibility today. "Why should I feel guilty?" others ask, stubbornly insisting on their indifference toward the Shoah—although we can assume that their claim is but an attempt to suppress ambiguous and unresolved feelings.

During the 1988 tour of Germany, the members of the Jewish-German Dance Theatre were confronted with the issue of guilt in almost all post-performance discussions, especially among young people. Here are some of the comments we heard from people between eighteen and thirty-five years of age.

I was born in 1970 and I have nothing to do with it. Why should I feel guilty?

I heard enough about the Holocaust. It's time to move on.

Why should we be concerned about Jews today? That's in the past. If we want to fight against racism, we need to care about our Turkish neighbors.

I feel ashamed but I don't know any Jews.

Rather than talking about the past, we can learn from the Holocaust to be responsible for today's injustices.

What about Israel and the Palestinians? Are Jews not guilty of racism as well?

Do you want to make us feel guilty with your performance? Why dwell on the past?

In the 90-minute performance "But What About the Holocaust?" the word "guilt" was used only twice; and in our post-performance discussions we did not volunteer the word. A debate about guilt was always raised by someone in the audience, who felt that we wanted to make him or her feel guilty in some way. Once, when the issue of guilt dominated a discussion with a high-school audience in a small town near Frankfurt, Erica, one of the Jewish dancers, told the teenagers that they themselves had brought up the issue. "I never mentioned the word "guilt,'" Erica said. "It is you who bring it up. I don't want you to feel guilty. I want you to learn."[7]

At another meeting issues of guilt, anger, and hurt blocked all attempts to communicate. In March 1987 the Jewish-German Dance Theatre arranged a meeting in a Philadelphia church between a group of German students and a Jewish survivor. We, the dancers, intended to talk about the impact of the Holocaust on contemporary Jewish/German relations. We had invited Edith Millman, a survivor of the Warsaw ghetto, because we wanted to give the German students an opportunity to relate to someone who had been victimized simply because she was Jewish. This particular student group had met survivors of Nazi persecution in Germany but not Jewish survivors. The distinction might make little sense to Americans who are used to equating Holocaust survivors with Jewish survivors; in Germany, however, only a few Jewish survivors stayed after the war, and most of them do not talk publicly about their experiences. Survivors in Germany who are willing to talk are mostly non-Jewish political prisoners of the Nazis; the few that are Jewish define themselves along political rather than religious and cultural lines.[8]

The German group visiting Philadelphia belonged to a Protestant campus ministry project. They were traveling through the United States in order to learn about urban poverty and American social policy. They had agreed to meet with us but, as it turned out, their expectations of the evening differed greatly from ours. They wanted to know about Jewish life in America after the war, about the role American Jews play in contemporary politics, and about American publication of neo-Nazi material. These questions, by no means untypical for young Germans, did not deal with the Germans' own personal and emotional involvement in the Shoah, the very thing we had envisioned for the meeting. The German students were uncomfortable in the survivor's presence but listened to her story: Edith had escaped the Warsaw ghetto, survived in hiding with false papers, seen her non-Jewish boyfriend shot in front of her eyes, been reunited with her parents after the war, and studied in Marburg (Germany) for two years before being allowed to emigrate to the United States. As she recounted her years of torment, a few German students went in and out of the room, spreading a nervous energy. When Edith concluded her testimony, several of the German group left the room, never to return. The atmosphere was so tense that Edith decided to leave after she responded to a few questions. It was hard to tell whether she had touched the German students, and if so, how.

Members of the dance company engaged the remaining Germans in a discussion. The ensuing exchange of viewpoints was cautious and seemingly without objective. The tension eventually broke into open confrontation when a German woman suggested that not only Jews but Germans, too, had suffered in the aftermath of the Holocaust. Lisa, one of the Jewish dancers, disagreed fiercely. "How can you say this?" she asked in disbelief. "We lost our history, culture, and family. And what did you lose?" The German student, not expecting such a passionate response, started to cry and left the room. After a moment of uneasy silence, an emotionally charged debate continued long into the night. When we finally parted, the tension was not resolved. I felt depressed and angry, and so did my friends from the dance company.

Only later did we find out that the German group felt similarly frustrated and angry. Dieter, one of the German students, wrote an essay about his impressions of the evening. I quote from it extensively because it represents the viewpoint of many third-generation Germans who have good intentions but no experience with Jews of their age. The essay also shows how Dieter's recollection of the evening differs from mine.

"Does Forgiving Mean Forgetting? A Meeting with Young Jews"

"Perhaps all emotions—anger, rage, strength—are dead. I no longer feel them vis-à-vis Germans. Therefore I can talk to you about my memories of the Warsaw ghetto without blaming you." This is how Edith Millman ended her report on the evening of March 26, 1987, in Philadelphia in front of us twelve students from the Rhein-land. . . . Ms. Millman spoke English although she was obviously capable of speaking German without an accent. How should we Germans react to such a report? Were we supposed to feel guilty again? . . . We had mentioned our list of questions before this evening and repeated them again: How did Jews live in the United States during and after the war? What roles do Jews play in contemporary American society? Who in the States is printing neo-Nazi brochures both in English and German, and how do Americans react to that?

Our questions were not answered during this evening because an aggravating and strained discussion started with the young Jews. They had recorded Millman's story on tape and followed it with such intensity as if they were asked to transform it into internal and external movements. We, too, were touched, but rather stayed in a defensive position. . . .

After one of us made a statement, which aimed at soliciting compassion but might have been insensitively phrased, the debate turned into open aggression. She had said: ". . . We see how difficult it is for you as descendants of victims of Germans to talk to us. But please also acknowledge that it is similarly difficult to live as the descendants of victimizers and to talk to you, especially now that you have arranged this evening in such a way that you make us guilty. But we are not guilty as individuals."

This juxtaposition greatly disconcerted Lisa, one of the Jewish dancers: "I reject such a juxtaposition. This is unacceptable for victims. The problems of victimizers and their children are exclusively yours. . . . Everything has been taken from us by the Germans: history, culture, family. And we still suffer as the second generation. Do you, as young Germans, have similar problems with your identity? How can we talk to you and gain trust if this is your gift in return? . . ."

In this strained situation, we [Germans] experienced that there are situations in which we are forced to be silent. This was difficult since we sensed the underlying accusations. But why talk if that would only worsen the situation and hurt the other even more? . . .

Björn said: I learned in contact with young Jews . . . that the task of coming to terms with the past is never completed. I have to do this with each Jew I encounter. Without mourning there is no hope for trust. But this hope, at least, exists.

This was not easily said: As descendants of victims and victimizers of a racist genocide we are connected, although with different burdens. . . . [During this evening] we experienced how our resistance was provoked because we were blamed, and how a discussion alone might not be very helpful.[9]

Somehow, we had missed each other. We had not been able to listen to and accept the other's confusion, anger, and pain. The German students were extremely sensitive to anything they perceived as inducing guilt or sounding like an accusation. The Jewish dancers were irritated by the students' leaving the room during Edith Millman's talk and their subsequent attempt to compare the suffering of Jews and Germans. And I, as a member of the performance group and a German, was frustrated that we all left misunderstood. In retrospect, I realize that we were all angry because we all felt powerless. It was a disheartening experience. "A discussion alone might not be very helpful," Dieter concluded. I took away the same lesson: when Jews and Germans meet we need to be better prepared for each other. We need to learn how to trust each other so that frustration, anger, and hurt can be expressed without drowning other voices.

Guilt, Hurt, and Anger Among the Third Generation

From the March 1987 meeting I learned that Jewish/German encounters need to be carefully planned because the ethos of guilt and the ethos of remembrance inevitably clash. I got the opportunity to organize such encounters when the Philadelphia Interfaith Council on the Holocaust asked me to help design and then facilitate the summer programs on the Holocaust in 1989, 1991, and 1993. Our goal was to create a protected enclave in which American and German students could explore the intellectual, psychological, personal, and emotional dimensions of Holocaust history and memory. With our German partner organization, the

Berlin Evangelische Akademie, we designed a four-week program, the first half in Philadelphia (with side trips to New York and Washington), the second half in Berlin and Auschwitz. Such an arrangement, we hoped, would allow participants to struggle with differences in day-to-day living and to get to know each other's countries as they struggled with the legacy of the Holocaust. The participants were mostly American Jews and non-Jewish Germans. They gave the program its unique character. But the American group also consisted of Christians, including some minority students (African American, Native American, and Korean American); and the German group included East Germans (after unification), a Dutch woman, and an Afghan student with German citizenship. Each group represented a balanced cross-section of American and German students coming from different religious, ethnic, and national backgrounds with a wide spectrum of academic interests.[10]

Frustrations, anger, and pain emerged regularly during these programs. Despite our careful planning, we sometimes underestimated the strong emotions that emerged from the confrontation of the Jewish and the German ethos. This was true especially for the first program in 1989. The issue of guilt put great strain on the relations of German students (all from West Germany) and the Jewish and Christian American students. It intruded into the discussions, caused friction, and never got fully resolved.

Part of the problem in 1989 was that we facilitators had not reserved enough time to deal with the issue of guilt in the opening phase of the program. We crammed the first three days with tough sessions: we invited Leon Bass, an African American liberator of Buchenwald, to speak; we asked the students to talk about their family histories; three Jewish people talked about their survival in Auschwitz, Siberia, and Hungary; we invited a scholar to lecture on antisemitism; and we encouraged the students to participate in sharing personal experiences with antisemitism and other forms of discrimination. No wonder the students felt overwhelmed. However, the reactions of the American and German students differed greatly. Both groups felt exhausted, but the Germans, in addition, began to rebel against feelings of guilt. Dominant voices in the German group claimed that the program's "hidden agenda" was to make them feel guilty. One student complained that Leon Bass's passionate speech about racism and the American liberation of Buchenwald "was too emotional, came too early, and elicited guilt feelings." Another student said that she did "not feel attacked" by Bass's speech but that his advice about fighting racism was "too trivial." The same student also said that she "was shocked by the description of Arabs and the Catholic Church" by one of the survivors, who, she added, "was no expert on these topics." She also felt that as a young German she was "not in the position to disagree with survivors." Another German student said that only one of the three survivors "did not want us to feel guilty."

In fairness to the speakers, it must be emphasized that they had agreed to share their stories only because they felt it important to reach out to young Germans and Americans alike. "We are not here to make anyone feel guilty," all of them had said during their talks. Many of the German students were unable to hear this message, partly because the program had not paid enough attention to their level of anxiety during the first few days, but mostly because they were not aware of how deeply they were enmeshed in the ethos of guilt. Unfortunately, the students who were most upset and defensive were unable to own their feelings. Instead, they projected them onto the speakers, facilitators, the "hidden agenda" of the program, and their Jewish peers. Regardless of how often they were assured that no one had intended to make them feel guilty, the issue could not be adequately resolved.

Six months after the program had come to an end, every person who participated—the facilitators, organizers, and guest speakers, as well as the students—received a letter signed by five of the German group, in which they voiced their frustration.

> The young Germans [in the program]," they wrote, "were the descen-
> dants of the victimizers, while the young Jewish Americans presented
> themselves as descendants of victims. These roles had to block any
> form of criticism. . . . Were we [Germans] not degraded to demon-
> stration objects? We were supposed to represent 'the Germans,' while
> at the same time, we were presented as exceptions because of our
> interest in the Holocaust.[11]

Clearly, these students felt overwhelmed, defensive, and angry. Feeling that they were unfairly paraded as "descendants of victimizers," muting their criticism, they were uncomfortable in their German identity vis-à-vis the nature of this Holocaust program. Feelings of guilt and anger prevented them from being true to themselves and remaining sensitive to the struggles of their Jewish peers.

Anne Roiphe makes a good point about the effects of guilt and anger. "When Jews insist on recalling the Holocaust," she writes, "when Jews express their anger and their pain about the Holocaust, then they are directly or indirectly accusing others of not being good, and these implicit or explicit accusations cause terrible anger. When people feel guilty they feel vastly uncomfortable and then they become angry with the group or person who has made them feel guilty. . . . [Guilt] can light up the most difficult passions" (1988:27). Roiphe's observations were meant to describe the relationships between Jews and Gentiles in general, but her insights also apply to the specific situation of third-generation Jews and Germans. To address the Holocaust in a heterogeneous group inevitably elicits guilt and anger. Guilt feelings, as well as rebellion against and denial of those feelings, are all part of the same ethos of guilt.

To say that young Germans react to the Shoah with guilt and anger, regardless of the intentions of their Jewish counterparts, is not to say that young American Jews, absorbed in the ethos of remembrance, do not contribute to the emotional tensions. Their emotional vigor sometimes prevents them from listening carefully to what young Germans have to say. Occupying the moral position of being direct or indirect descendants of victims allows them to express their feelings coherently. For Germans, the descendants of victimizers, such emotive and moral coherency is more difficult to achieve.

The Jewish American participants of the summer programs sometimes expressed their anger and agony indirectly, thus hurting their German peers. On the third day into the 1989 program, the students were asked to lie down in a circle, close their eyes, and recall the images they had received of Jews and Germans and whether they had personally witnessed instances of discrimination. Among the many moving and honest recollections, I vividly remember Lucia, a German student, telling us about her first boyfriend, an Israeli. The relationship did not last because she was German. In her boyfriend's family, Lucia said, she was known as "operation Bitburg." There was much pain in Lucia's voice as she recalled this experience, and I empathized with the humiliation she must have felt.

When the group later evaluated this "circle exercise," four Jewish students began telling us why they would never marry a non-Jewish person. At first I heard them voicing their anxiety over assimilation, a concern seemingly unrelated to what had happened in the circle. They argued that intermarriage would lead to the slow death of a minority culture and this was not permissible in the light of the Shoah. We need only recall the injunction "Don't give Hitler a posthumous victory" to recognize the discursive context of their fear. But when the four students kept insisting on this theme I began to wonder what they were discussing. What was at stake? As the talk about intermarriage dragged on, the Germans as well as the Christian American students became increasingly uncomfortable. Eventually, Lucia mustered her strength and said that if one more person talked about marrying only Jews she would scream. A Jewish student completely ignored her signal of despair and continued to attack the idea of intermarriage—at which point Lucia left the room. Wrapped in their anxieties about keeping the Jewish community together, the Jewish students could not acknowledge Lucia's pain and humiliation over the loss of her Israeli boyfriend.

Sadly, indirect expressions of one's emotional attachment to the memory of the Holocaust can hurt people without one's ever realizing it. For both young American Jews and their German counterparts, the emotional stakes are high because their identities are enmeshed in their particular ethos. What might be a perfectly legitimate discourse within one's own community (like the issue of intermarriage) can be a source of pain in a cross-cultural context. The power of one's own attachments to a particular ethos is often less tangible within a homogeneous community than within heterogeneous groups—which is why encounters between Jews and Germans of the third generation can be so explosive and laborious, yet also enlightening and liberating.

Sometimes indirect communication in heterogeneous groups can cause immediate visceral reactions. At the end of the third week of the 1991 program, when the group was already in Germany, we returned from a day trip to Halberstadt, a German town (formerly in East Germany) with a medieval Jewish quarter. In the evening my co-facilitator and I admitted to the group that our translations of the remarks of the local historian, who had given us a tour of Halberstadt's Jewish cemetery that morning, did not always convey the latent insensitivity toward Jews that his language had betrayed. Some of the Jewish American students reacted strongly; they felt that we facilitators had undermined their trust since they were dependent on proper translations and that we had robbed them of the possibility of challenging the historian. We apologized and explained the difficulty of translating ambiguous syntax, which Germans, sensitive to latently anti-Jewish remarks, were able to decode instantaneously while non-German speakers would have been at a loss without a lengthy explanation. We also admitted that we may have inadvertently smoothed over some of the speaker's latent hostilities in order to avoid an embarrassing situation. To no avail: our explanations did not reduce the mistrust and anger the Americans voiced against the facilitators. Eventually, a German student jumped to our defense. "Of course they eased the translations," she said, turning to her American Jewish peers, "because we know *you* people!" The student did not explain what she meant by "*you* people," but from her intonation one could infer that she perceived the American complaints as Jewish hypersensitivity. When no one challenged her on that issue a Jewish student got so upset that she rushed out of the room and threw up in the restroom.

Another example of the indirect expression of anger occurred during the 1993 program when Beth, a Jewish American student, made contemptuous remarks about the assorted cold meat served for dinner in a German retreat center. The group had just returned from Auschwitz and was still feeling upset. Beth took slices of the meat, lifted them in the air, shouted (with a smile), "Who wants to eat this shit anyway?" and threw them across the table onto the floor. Most people laughed and no one challenged her behavior. But her message was clear: by attacking what Germans eat she expressed her anger against them. If people eat shit, they are shit.

I could add other incidents demonstrating similarly charged encounters between third-generation Jews and Germans. But by now the point should be clear: The ethos of each community has left the third generation with an abundance of powerful and unresolved emotions which emerge indirectly if they are not addressed directly. It is important, therefore, to raise these unacknowledged emotions from latency to consciousness.

One way of breaking patterns of nondirect communication is to address prejudices head on, an approach we tried with the students of the Holocaust programs as well as in the Jewish-German Dance Theatre. We collected stereotypes, wrote them on large pieces of paper, pinned them to a wall and read them aloud. Germans were, to name only a few, "cold, efficient, rigid, authoritarian, cultured, obedient, disciplined, enlightened, cruel, compulsive, blond, blue-eyed, sausage eaters, beer drinkers." Jews were "rich, stingy, exclusive, sticking together, patriarchal, hypocritical, intellectual, physically weak, pale, nervous, Woody Allen types, with curly hair and bent noses." Americans were "loud, wealthy, capitalist, ignorant, power-hungry, without culture, and always wear shorts."

The plethora of distortions and mixed messages is astounding. If Jews and Germans of the third generation never meet, these images can easily turn into solid fictionalizations of the "other." This explains, for example, how antisemitism can exist without Jews. Germans who do not personally know any Jews cannot compare their culture's distorted images of Jews with the realities of contemporary Jewish life. Similarly, American Jews fictionalize "the German" in the absence of real Germans. Their fictionalizations differ, perhaps, in that Jewish suspicions of Germans are grounded in the memory of the Shoah rather than in the irrational and passionate hostility that so often characterizes antisemitism. To expel the ghosts, however, is a task both Jews and Germans must undertake.

To confront prejudices directly helps to bring them into the open. But such self-conscious exercises as pinning stereotypes to a board have only limited effect. It is easy to distance oneself from stereotypes of the "cold and cruel" German, the "ugly and wealthy" Jew, or the "loud and uncultured American." Prejudicial attitudes do not really hurt until they are voiced by a person one has learned to trust and respect. When, for example, the German student addressed her Jewish peers as "*you* people," she conveyed an unspoken assumption ("Jews are hypersensitive") that hit home. Prejudices that leak out under stress are less censored but more painful. To work with emotional reactions to prejudices effectively, a safe environment has to be created where people can own up to their biases. Prejudices can be undone and changed when a group is strong enough to tolerate the embarrassment and shame that accompany their unwitting revelation. "I've always thought of Germany as an efficient and formal society—unemotional and heartless," one Jewish student stated halfway into one of the summer programs. Another Jewish student wrote, "I expected the Germans would be very difficult to talk to, especially about the Holocaust. Also, for some reason, it doesn't seem to bother me as much to hear Jews tell their prejudices about Germans as it does to hear them talk about me. I'm not sure this is right."

German students took similar risks. After a crisis in the 1991 program, in which the group established levels of trust, some Germans started to talk about the admonitions they had received from family members before embarking for the United States. "Why do you need to study the Holocaust with those Jews? Won't they ever leave you alone and let you stop feeling guilty?" an aunt asked a student. And a mother instructed her daughter at the airport, "Don't let them make you feel guilty for something you did not do." Other German students admitted that they had talked about the program in evasive terms in order to avoid unwelcome comments from friends and family. Others reported that their parents and friends had consistently referred to the "American" rather than "Holocaust" program. American students related similar situations in which friends and acquaintances openly belittled their intention to participate in this "antiquated" program when there are more urgent and contemporary problems to cope with.

During these and similar moments of trust and intimacy, I was surprised by the heavy burdens third-generation Jews and Germans bring to these meetings. They are afraid of their own emotions, afraid of each other, and afraid of social ostracism. They have grown up with ritualized discursive practices that did little to prepare them for meeting each other; and once they do encounter each other, they go through a painful realization of their deep entanglement in the ethos of their respective communities, a process that makes them vulnerable and defensive. Reconciliation is no easy task.

3 Communitas

Envisioning Transformation

Children of persecuted and of persecutors . . . may have a mission to rehabilitate their parents and undo the past.
—**Judith Kestenberg**

Behind the [German] fear . . . to question analysts and psychoanalysis was not the fear of opening the door to the parents' bedroom and witnessing its 'primal scene,' but rather the fear of opening the door to the gas chamber.
—**Sammy Speier**

The term "reconciliation" has a bad reputation. Different people have used it for different political agendas. Furthermore, reconciliation can be easily confused with the kind of forgiveness the postwar German psyche desires. As I argued in the previous chapter, the German ethos is hopelessly entangled in a circular pattern of guilt and forgiveness, which makes it difficult for Germans to come to terms with the Holocaust and to reach out to Jewish people.

This chapter probes further the concept of reconciliation. Is Jewish/German reconciliation as ill-fated as its critics suggest? Can the idea of reconciliation be redeemed in a post-Shoah context? The term has been manipulated so often that we tend to forget that reconciliation means, at its core, the overcoming of distrust and animosity. To overcome the deep-seated distrust between Jews and Germans we need to create environments in which together they regain confidence in their relations.

What kind of transformative and healing processes will work? Does individual psychotherapy achieve effective changes between third-generation Jews and Germans? Traditional therapeutic settings have their own blind spots as regards the Holocaust: both clients and therapists may have accepted certain behaviors as normal or have failed to ask certain questions because of cultural taboos. Individual therapy has at times overlooked collective pathologies caused by the injurious memory of the Holocaust.

What does a renewed understanding of reconciliation require? Can we conceive of processes in which Jews and Germans together try to transform their cultures' discourses and ethos? In the last part of this chapter, I suggest that the third generation does not need individual psychotherapy in order to impose Jewish/German relations. Rather, they need a cross-cultural, experiential, and creative environment that incorporates some therapeutic elements. In this environment, or *communitas*, Jews and Germans undergo what may be called a cultural therapy.

Transforming the Negative Symbiosis

Can the idea of reconciliation be redeemed? Two prominent intellectuals, Gershom Scholem and Theodor Adorno, would have opposed my premise that meetings between Jews and Germans of the third generation might break the general stalemate of Jewish/German relations. Both Scholem and Adorno, for different reasons, discarded the idea that post-Shoah dialogues would be beneficial for establishing communal identity and for combating antisemitism. Adorno, who regarded antisemitism as "primarily a product of the objective social conditions, and only secondarily of anti-Semites," did not "believe that too much is accomplished by social gatherings, encounters between young Germans and young Israelis, and other such organized acts of friendship, however desirable contact may be" (1986:127f). Scholem advocated a separation of Jewish culture from German society. The highly praised Jewish/German symbiosis of the past, he claimed, was "never anything else than a fiction"; therefore, it would be premature to engage in German/Jewish dialogue after Auschwitz.[1]

The criticisms of Adorno and Scholem remind us of problems inherent in all attempts to renew Jewish/German relations. For one, antisemitism is not just an individual problem, and there are limits to what encounters between Jews and Germans can achieve. I agree with Adorno that "social gatherings" are in themselves not effective since they will not attract or change a staunch antisemite, and may even have no effect on a person of good intentions. Whoever has participated in Jewish/German dialogues in Germany knows of the convolutions, spontaneous mood changes, self-deceptions, and perfidies that characterize these meetings. What starts as a friendly and restrained conversation can suddenly turn into a passionate argument against Zionists, Israelis, the Jewish lobby in America, or other Jewish "misdemeanors." Henryk Broder, a Jew who left Germany for Israel because he became disillusioned with the anti-Zionist/antisemitic bent of his left-wing German peers, defined antisemitism as an "emotion," a passion that can explode at any moment.[2]

To present but one example of those passionate, albeit convoluted, situations, I recall a discussion after a performance of the Jewish-German Dance Theatre during its tour of Germany in 1988. We performers had invited the audience in Hanau, near Frankfurt, to talk to us after the show. Although there was nothing very dramatic or unusual about the ensuing discussion, my journal entry for that day gives a taste of the typical twists of Jewish/German conversations:

> After the performance, we have a discussion which does not go too well. First, it takes the people a long time to get seated, even though we are already sitting and waiting. Then the discussion begins, though sluggishly. Many people are honest and friendly . . . but the ignorance is often so great that their comments and questions sound unintelligible to Jewish ears, and are meaningful only to those familiar with the naivete that characterizes the German situation. The conversation is also difficult because it needs only one or two hostile people to poison the climate, and we seem to manage to find these two wherever we go. Of course, they always talk, and probably do not perceive themselves as being antisemitic. . . .
>
> The confusion and emotionality of the discussion increases when a woman in the audience tries to separate Israelis from Jews. Jews, she says, are religious and international; Israelis are a nation and a government. "All Germans have problems with Israeli politics," she concludes. "*All* Germans?" Erica [one of the Jewish American dancers] interjects agitatedly, and it is not clear whether she asks a question or comments cynically. Then there is a question to Lisa [another Jewish American dancer]: "Are you still angry at us, the young generation?" Lisa responds by recalling a past meeting in which young Germans compared the suffering of Jews to the suffering of Germans, and how angry she had been at this kind of com-

parison. "I have occasional nightmares after our performances," Lisa says. Her anger is not very well received by the audience. A woman who is visibly upset says, "In your performance, you were able to show that reconciliation is possible, but now the trenches are 'thrown up' again [*der Graben ist wieder aufgeschüttet*]."

With passion and vigor, images about Jews surfaced in the discussion: Jews are international and religious, Israelis are national and secular; Jews are acceptable, Israelis are not; a suffering Jew is acceptable but not an angry one. I was particularly struck by the awkward image of "thrown-up" trenches. The German woman wanted to convey her indignation at the angry young Jews who, in her words, made reconciliation impossible. She desired forgiveness, but Jewish anger was too high a price to pay. To her, reconciliation and anger were mutually exclusive categories. But how can Germans and Jews talk to each other after the Shoah if anger is not part of the conversation?

Countless examples of miscommunication seem to support Adorno's skepticism about the utility of "social gatherings." However, they do not preclude all prospects of Jewish/German reconciliation. There are Germans whose gestures of caring and understanding are so genuine that they complement the emotional intensity their compatriots channel into defensive mechanisms. When, for example, the Jewish-German Dance Theatre got a rude review in a major German newspaper, an audience member wrote to the editor: "The critic talks of 'images of admonishing dread.' Was he so insensitive as not to perceive the tenderness reflected in the images of despairing memory? Did he not see the faces of the young Jewish dancers in which grief and the joy for being alive were combined? . . . For the first time, we witnessed how children of victimizers and children of victims were able to embrace each other."[3] Reconciliation, this writer understood, requires a good deal of agonizing work. Grief, anger, and tenderness are not mutually exclusive reactions but belong together. "There is no so highly charged issue in Germany, loaded with mines, traps and poison, as the issue of Germans and Jews," the German novelist Peter Schneider said at a recent conference on German/Jewish reconciliation. "And yet there's no way out. We must offer each other a minimum of confidence."[4] Encounters between Jews and Germans, I believe, can offer "a minimum of confidence" if participants are willing to question their particular ethos and surmount a repetitive,

stale discourse. If reconciliation is a ritual praxis striving toward transformation, then Jews and Germans must meet each other in an environment that provides protection and creates a sense of communal
bonding. Because good intentions alone do not have the power to overcome the full weight of a culture's discursive patterns, as Adorno correctly pointed out, Jewish/German reconciliation must be practiced in
communal and, preferably, cross-cultural settings. In such temporary
communities, I will argue later, participants are encouraged to explore
the depth and ambiguity of their ties to the Shoah and to each other.

Scholem's observation that the German/Jewish symbiosis has been
"one-sided and unreciprocated" (1976:86) recalls another problem of
reconciliation. Jews who lived in Germany before and during the Nazi
era and strove to assimilate paid a high price for that desire, and the few
Jews who decided to live in Germany after 1945 have often found themselves rejected by both German society and other Jewish communities
(cf. Brumlik et al. 1986; 1991). Why, then, would Jews be interested in
mending fences? Is German/Jewish dialogue of interest only to the small
Jewish community in Germany and not to Jewish communities outside
Germany?

There is another aspect of this problem that makes me wary. Many
Germans today—especially liberal, well-educated Germans and among
church groups—are eager to enter into Jewish/German and Jewish/Chris-
tian dialogue. Ironically, these dialogues often take place in the absence
of Jews (the number of Jews living in Germany today is estimated to be
about fifty thousand). Does the desire for dialogue reflect Germans' need
of Jews to secure their own emotional stability and their country's good
international reputation? The Shoah has perhaps inverted their relationship: before the Holocaust, Jews needed Germans; today, Germans
need Jews. Post-Shoah Germany might be as dependent on Jews for its
vindication as pre-1933 Jewry had been dependent on Germany for its
assimilation. Scholem's somber verdict on the German/Jewish symbiosis
should prompt people to ponder their motives carefully before calling
for renewed relations between Jews and Germans. However, I do not
read Scholem's verdict as a final judgment.

Adorno is known for having revised his famous dictum that poetry
cannot be written after Auschwitz. "Perhaps it was wrong," he admitted
in his *Negative Dialectics*, "[to say] that after Auschwitz no poem can be
written" (1966:355). If poems can be written after Auschwitz, then Jews

and Germans may be capable of renewing their relationships after Auschwitz as well. Efforts to rehabilitate these relationships would not imitate the *fiction* of a prewar German/Jewish symbiosis. Rather, they would always have to account for the *friction* that the Shoah has caused. Dan Diner, a second-generation Jew living in Germany, has called this awareness of friction in Jewish/German relations a "negative symbiosis." The Shoah, he said, has tied the two group identities to a common history, to "a kind of antagonistic common ground" which "determines the relations to each other for generations to come" (1986:243). The history of the Holocaust separates Jews and Germans but, strangely enough, also unites them.

This antagonistic common ground—the defining feature of a negative symbiosis—speaks through the following personal stories of a child of Jewish survivors and a child of a Nazi family. Do they both solicit our compassion? Does only one story evoke compassion while the other evokes anger? Our responses to the child of survivors and the child of Nazis may be different because of our moral and emotional understanding of their place in history. Yet, their stories also resemble each other because both children experienced their parents as troubled, secretive, and incapable of talking about the past.

The child of survivors recalls how she learned about her parents' past:

> I thought I knew a lot about their experiences. But only recently, I found out my father had a family before the war. They kept it a secret from me. I found out from my cousin who casually mentioned it in passing. He assumed I knew. When I asked my father why he didn't tell me he said my mother didn't want to think about it and out of respect for her he didn't tell us. It was very shocking for me to find out he had a wife and son. My mother tells me that the last few years he talks about his lost son a lot. The older my parents get, the more they talk about it. They want people to know about it before they die. . . . It's made me wonder what else they have kept from me. (Quoted in Hass 1990:73)

The child of a Nazi war criminal recounts how he learned about his parents' past:

> [My mother] told me my father had taken his life because he was a Nazi . . . [He] held certain positions in the Nazi regime, but she

didn't know about anything in detail, she hadn't been interested, because all that had been before she had met him. But she told me quite clearly that he was a Nazi. . . . Now, I don't want to exaggerate, but she presented his death to me as a just punishment. Maybe that is an exaggeration, but, well, she didn't have any pity for him, let's put it that way. Rather, she described it to me quite objectively, unemotionally, and I never associated any emotion with it. For me, right from the very beginning, my father was my father. There were certain secrets spun around him, but he was never present. . . . He was a nonperson. So the matter was addressed quite openly, in a very cool and objective manner I'd almost say, like a legal brief (Bar-On 1989:48).

Both children carry the burden of their parents' past, though these burdens are different. The child of Nazis portrays a family struggling to stay detached from past events. Pain is hidden behind a wall of objectivity. A similar secrecy is spun around the father's past in the Jewish survivor family, yet that situation strikes me as more tender. Pain is muted out of respect.

Are the experiences of children of victims and victimizers similar? In both families, secrets have caused incomplete family histories and eroded parent-child intimacy. After years of silence, how would I have reacted to learning that my father had had another wife and son who were killed in the Shoah? How would I relate to a father who had been a Nazi and committed suicide? There are "startling behavioral similarities between [Germans of] my generation and some of my Jewish peers," observed Sabine Reichel. "The inability of both groups of parents, in my case an entire nation, to speak about the past—one because of pain, the other because of guilt—caused similar symptoms for their offspring" (1989:144).

To say that the experiences of second- and third-generation Jews and Germans are similar is problematic because it threatens to blur the moral and political distinctions between victim and victimizer. Is it legitimate to compare the suffering of Jews and Germans? Would not such comparisons cloud the difference between victims and victimizers (a question that underlay the Bitburg controversy)? The issue of the comparability of suffering has often encumbered attempts at Jewish/German reconciliation, as examples in the previous chapters have already demonstrated. We would be best advised, I believe, if we learned to listen to different stories with our critical minds intact but without falling into the trap of comparing the levels of suffering—a highly unproductive activity since it always results in a competition. To enter into such a competition is to descend on a downward spiral, with nothing but hate at the bottom.

I find Diner's notion of the negative symbiosis appealing because it prevents such downward spiraling from occurring. Instead of comparing suffering, and instead of stating the question of difference and resemblance antithetically, the negative symbiosis conceives of Jews and Germans as two peoples tied to different memories about the same injurious past: the Shoah. Third-generation Jews and Germans, like their parents and grandparents, are tied to memories of this antagonistic common ground. When they meet, they do not come empty-handed but bring whatever their families and larger social units have taught them, or failed to teach them. Third-generation Jews and Germans cannot be blamed for the ethos and discourse with which they have grown up. But together they can look at how injurious memory has shaped their identities and they can begin to mend their broken relations. "Germans and Jews are intrinsically, emotionally enmeshed with each other, and will be for a long time," writes Sabine Reichel. "Whenever a Jew meets a German, the millions of dead between them take up lot of space. The German thinks, 'I wonder whether he lost a relative in a concentration camp.' The Jew thinks, 'I wonder whether her father, uncle, or grandfather killed any of us.' Both hope for the best, but this spectrum of unsettling, agonizing, unresolved feelings does not make for amicable, trusting, or relaxed friendships" (Reichel 1989:142).

Yet, the antagonistic common ground, which clearly speaks through this passage, is not the only feature of the negative symbiosis. A simultaneous pull toward attraction and rejection, curiosity and suspicion, also characterizes negative symbiotic relationships. Reichel describes how she experienced meeting Jews in New York:

> I would discover that almost all Germans who had spent time in America, especially in New York, had been influenced by their strong and inspiring relationships with Jews, be they troubling and angry encounters or love affairs that sometimes led to marriage. We would even discuss occasionally the ambiguous attraction between Jews and

> Germans, without dependable scientific results. But we all agreed
> that meeting face to face with the people who wouldn't be alive at all
> if our parents' generation had had its way fifty years ago was one of
> the most significant experiences in our lives, one which the Germans
> at home could neither match nor fully understand (1989:143).

Reichel's observations apply equally to the second and the third generation. When Jews and Germans meet, much of their conversation will
revolve around whether or not their respective families were directly
involved in or affected by the Shoah. They have to ask themselves
whether their own interactions today are, at least in part, a symbolic
reenactment of the victim/victimizer dichotomy and the ethos of guilt
and remembrance.

The concept of negative symbiosis describes well the current state of
Jewish/German relations, but it is not flawless. It is no accident that it
was conceived in the context of contemporary German Jewry. Perhaps
young Jews living in Germany feel most strongly caught in a negative
symbiosis of their two selves— Jewish and German. To my knowledge,
the term has been used primarily, if not exclusively, within the geographic and social boundaries of Germany, and it is questionable how
well it can be applied to Jewish/German relations outside Germany. Are
relations between Germans and Israeli Jews, American Jews, or Russian
Jews also characterized by a negative symbiosis? I believe so.[5] Certainly
young American Jews continue to be tied to Germany. They know "Germans," if only as the fictionalized "other," because they have grown up
in a discursive environment and an ethos that rely on the victim/victim-
izer dichotomy. Young Germans, too, are tied to American Jews on the
basis of an antagonistic common ground, which is additionally strained
by the anti-American sentiments so prevalent among Europeans.

There is another flaw. Even if Jews and Germans are to a large extent
entangled in a negative symbiotic relationship, it is not clear whether
this reflects a desirable condition. The term "symbiosis" indicates,
according to *Webster's*, a "relationship of two or more different organ-
isms in a close association that may be but is not necessarily of benefit to
each."[6] In a symbiotic relationship, boundaries are not clearly drawn and
the need for separate identities not established. I sense something static
about a negative symbiosis, a self-enclosed, circular movement. In my
worst fantasy, Jewish and German post-Holocaust generations are

caught in this circular relationship and continue to operate with exaggerated and prejudicial images of the "other," even to act on these images.

The goal of working with the third generation is to help them break with unhealthy ritualizations. Do Germans and Jews therefore have to liberate themselves from a negative symbiotic relationship? It depends. If people want to deny the antagonistic common ground caused by antisemitism and the Shoah, then we need to affirm the negative symbiosis as an accurate description of past and present Jewish/German relations. The concept of a negative symbiosis is perhaps most valuable when used as a tool for assessing the current situation and least fruitful when, as in the case of the victim/victimizer discourse, it prescribes certain roles and behaviors. Third-generation Jews and Germans should not consider the negative symbiosis as their only option. It is possible, I believe, to take the static aspects of the negative symbiosis and transform them into a dynamic and more affirmative relationship, a process which has the potential for healing.

From Individual Therapy . . .

Is it permissible to speak of healing, or even call for a "season for healing" (Roiphe 1988), in the context of the Holocaust? Can the wounds of the victims be healed? Can victimizers be healed, and if so, of what? Can memory be healed? Does the negative symbiotic relationship of third-generation Jews and Germans require healing?

The word "healing" is in vogue, and I use it only hesitantly in the context of the Shoah. Not only does the reality of Auschwitz defy quick answers about what we can learn from the Holocaust; it is still too early to tell what Jewish/German efforts at reconciliation may achieve. This is not to say that healing is impossible or undesirable. Certainly, individual therapy has stabilized many Jewish survivor families and helped them to cope with their pain. But not all stabilization is healing. Postwar Germany, for example, was an antitherapeutic culture at least until the 1970s, with the result that German families have avoided psychotherapy. Still, Germans found psychological mechanisms to stabilize their post-Holocaust identities. Whether these mechanisms were curative or simply allowed people to transfer individual pathologies onto the culture at large is another question.

Because psychotherapy treats injurious memory as an individual psychodynamic problem, does it neglect collective pathologies because therapists themselves operate on certain cultural assumptions? Therapy may heal the individual member of a particular community, but does it support reconciliation between Jews and Germans? To answer these questions, it is important to look first at each culture's attitude toward individual therapy. Since twentieth-century American culture has embraced therapy as a space for treating individual pain, many Holocaust survivors and their children have benefited from therapeutic and psychiatric services. The psychological, psychoanalytic, and psychiatric literature is full of reports of treatments of Jewish survivor families. Psychologists have found that survivors have difficulties in establishing intimate relationships and tolerating emotional responses, present diverse psychosomatic symptoms and depression, harbor intense anger, and suffer from so-called survivor guilt. Similar problems have been observed in children of survivors; the parents, these studies suggest, have transmitted their emotional insufficiencies and psychopathologies, and the children suffer from mistrust, anger, guilt, self-denial, and cynicism.[7]

Reading this literature, which most often operates within a psychoanalytic framework and focuses on individual case studies, I am overwhelmed by the evidence of the pain among survivor families. Jewish survivors, according to these reports, are still suffering from the Holocaust, are still victims, even in the second and third generations. The Christian world at large, and specifically Germans, can learn from these reports that Jewish communities have been thoroughly traumatized by genocidal antisemitism. It explains why they respond so quickly when confronted with latent antisemitism today. Individual case studies also raise the troubling question of whether a person can ever recover from total victimization. "If you could lick my heart, it would poison you," a survivor said during an interview with Claude Lanzmann (1985:196). Jean Amery expressed a similar sentiment: "He who has suffered torment can no longer find his place in the world. Faith in humanity— cracked by the first slap across the face, then demolished by torture— can never be recovered" (Quoted in Hass 1990:7).

Jean Amery, Paul Celan, and Primo Levi, to name just a few, did not recover and later committed suicide. For survivors, "Holocaust memory is an insomniac faculty, whose mental eyes have never slept" (Langer

1991:xv). But many survivors somehow adjusted to the changed circumstances after their liberation. It was not easy. When the war ended,
they found themselves in a world that was not eager to hear their stories
of suffering and survival. "The most pervasive consequence of [society's]
silence for survivors," writes the psychotherapist Yael Danieli, "has been
a profound sense of isolation and alienation" (1980:356). Many had been
dislodged from their native countries and were now living in foreign
lands. Rather than shape their social environment they had to adjust to
it. For a long time, their anxieties as well as a lack of interest in their new
surroundings discouraged survivors from talking. They kept silent and
channeled their energies into reconstructing their lives. Many survivors
feared that telling their stories could be misunderstood as begging for
pity.

The ensuing suppression of painful memories had its effect on family life. Survivors were afraid of recounting the torments they had suffered, and their children were afraid of lifting the lid off their parents'
past, for the disclosure might elicit a host of unwelcome feelings: anger,
guilt, depression, anxiety, horror, sadness. Nevertheless, the children,
Aaron Hass writes, "all had a sense of being aware, from a very early
age, that they were, indeed, children of survivors." However, "not one
person I interviewed could relate a full chronology of their parents' war
years, and, after probing somewhat, it became apparent that even those
who believed they were quite knowledgeable had failed to learn significant details—such as the name of the concentration camp in which their
parents were incarcerated" (1990:69). A child of survivors recalls, "For a
long time I kept forgetting details and needed to keep asking [my par-
ents] to refresh my memory. Also, for a long time, I deliberately didn't
want to know anything. In my home there was constant talk about the
Holocaust and there was a great deal of hysterical rehashing of the
events, which bothered me a great deal" (Hass 1990:81).

To break out of the suppression of injurious memory, which often led
to dysfunctional parent-child relations, some survivor families sought
professional help. In therapy, they could talk about problems resulting
from the Holocaust without running the risk of social embarrassment.
Psychotherapy was a place of safety from which an antagonistic public
was excluded (although the public gaze was reintroduced through the
publication of case reports).

However, an exclusive focus on individual case studies can also lead to contorted and less empathetic conclusions. Readers unfamiliar with the diversity of contemporary Jewish culture, as is the case with most Germans, might be swayed to believe that survivor families are generally dysfunctional and debilitated, and in need of therapeutic and charitable assistance. To combat this perception, survivors and children of survivors have criticized psychological studies for their emphasis on the so-called survivor syndrome.[8] Psychologists have studied the survivors' emotional and psychological impairment but rarely their remarkable capacity for social readjustment. After all the survivors went through, should the world not marvel at their ability to make a normal living and to raise and educate children? "We might fruitfully investigate the resilience of survivors," Hass wrote, "instead of simply focusing on their debilitation. Given the horrors and degradation to which they were exposed, how did they go on and function in a *relatively* normal manner?" (1990:23; cf. Helmreich 1992).

It should not come as a surprise that the total victimization to which survivors were subjected has left indelible scars that have been passed on to the next generation. What should impress us is the survivors' and their children's ability to meet the demands of the post-Shoah world, despite their scars. Hillel Klein, a psychiatrist who has treated survivors in Israel, has concluded, "We can no longer speak of the transmission of psychopathology from one generation to the next, but rather of the transmission of common motifs, mythologies, issues, sensitivities within families and between the generations" (1983:127). I believe this a perceptive and sensitive definition because it moves away from psychoanalytic and medical terminology, which some survivors and their children have experienced as demeaning, and introduces the notion of the intergenerational transmission of painful memories. Defining Holocaust memories as the intergenerational transmission of common motifs and sensitivities rather than of psychopathologies also takes into account that the majority of third-generation American Jews are not direct descendants of survivors. At the same time, it does not ignore the ongoing influence of injurious memory on the ethos of remembrance and on Jewish discursive practices.

The extensive psychological literature on Jewish survivors and their children has no counterpart in Germany. There are almost no psychological profiles of Nazi perpetrators gleaned from direct therapeutic treatment,[9] and little is known about the psychopathology and psychotherapeutic treatment of children from Nazi families. Nazi perpetrators did not seek psychotherapeutic treatment after the war; and if their children decided to do so, the medical and therapeutic professions generally failed to make the intergenerational transmission of the Holocaust trauma a part of their diagnosis. Holocaust memory did not appear as a significant factor in the treatment of individual pathologies. "Various schools of psychotherapy . . . overlook how profoundly the Nazi ideology and the Nazi feeling-world continue to permeate our daily reality," write the editors of a volume on German therapy's neglect of the Holocaust (Heimannsberg and Schmidt 1993:5).[10] Only since the mid-1980s has an awareness of these diagnostic shortcomings slowly emerged. Interviews with second- and third-generation Germans by the Austrian-Jewish author Peter Sichrovsky (1988), the Israeli psychologist Dan Bar-On (1989, 1990), and the German, non-Jewish journalist Dötte von Westernhagen (1987) have begun to fill this gap. Still, as late as 1986 the German psychoanalyst F. W. Eickhoff (1986:34) wrote of the "painful dilemma" that he knew no "direct psychotherapeutic or psychoanalytical situation" with Nazi persecutors, whereas so many Jewish survivors and their children have become "psychoanalytical patients," psychoanalysts themselves, or at least "the subject of published psychoanalytical reports."

The discrepancy between the abundance of psychological literature on the Jewish survivor syndrome and the lack of studies on the transmission of pathologies in German families of victimizers calls for an explanation. The pain of survivors, we might surmise, is so intense that it needs psychological attention. The perpetrators, on the other hand, seem to have experienced their psychological damage as less painful, for they did not seek therapeutic treatment. But another reason may have to do with problems within the psychological profession itself. Sammy Speier, an Israeli-born psychoanalyst who works in Germany, criticizes German psychoanalysis for its neglect of history. "Psychoanalytic practices in Germany are full of patients who are the children of the persecutors, accomplices, witnesses, and bystanders; this state of affairs is, however, collectively denied" (1993:64). Perhaps it was easier for therapists to focus on the victim's trauma than to face the victimizer's cruelty and emotional dysfunction. The analyst Judith Kestenberg has reminded her European colleagues who have worked with children of Nazis of the importance of "undergoing a new analysis, a self-analysis, as they conquer what can be generally subsumed under the heading of 'counter-transference'" (Bergmann and Jucovy 1990:163).[11] A few German psychotherapists have admitted that they unconsciously shied away from certain questions and issues, thus buying into the German conspiracy of silence (cf. Heimannsberg and Schmidt 1993).

The social conditions of postwar Germany permitted the perpetrators to readjust to a new life and repress the past. After the first wave of war trials ended, and after it had become evident that most convicted Nazi criminals would serve only short prison terms, the immediate fear of being punished subsided. Ralph Giordano (1990) and Jörg Friedrich (1985) showed how Nazi bureaucrats, functionaries, ideologues, and criminals were re-integrated into their respective professions in West Germany. Social integration, however, did not solve the affective repercussions of injurious memory. Feelings of guilt, fear of retribution, and the inability to mourn remained collective phenomena and became accepted norms of German society. Although guilt, fear, and the inability to mourn were "a consequence of the denial of complicity" (Eickhoff 1986:35), they were not perceived as individual impairments requiring therapeutic counseling. In fact, to undergo psychotherapeutic treatment would have broken the silence that postwar Germany prescribed as a tranquilizer for itself and have stirred up unwelcome memories and emotions. The few attempts of family therapy with German perpetrators confirmed this resistance. The first generation in particular was not ready to confront the past. "Instead of activating their memory they manipulated or clouded it and thus rendered innocuous their roles as former Nazi activists, sympathizers, or supporters," writes Helm Stierlin about family therapy in Germany (1993:150). As a result, psychological dysfunctions occasioned by injurious memories remained largely unacknowledged in postwar German families; likewise, the intergenerational transmission of these impairments was not recognized.

But emotional confusion lingers just beneath the surface of German families and forcefully emerges as soon as issues related to the Shoah and family history are addressed. The many interviews that Bar-On conducted with children of Nazi families amply demonstrate this confusion. In an interview with Manfred, born in 1947, the son of a Nazi official who killed himself shortly after the war, Bar-On asked whether it was hard to live with the knowledge of his father's crimes and suicide. Manfred's response revealed his rigidity and turmoil: "Yes, well, that's a difficult question, very difficult. [*Long pause*] It's difficult to live if you constantly think about these things in rational terms. Basically you have to stop—this is my view—at some point you have to stop thinking about them. Because when you think about them, then things are difficult. And you can go on and on in your thoughts, and then it gets very difficult indeed" (1989:51).

In another interview Bar-On talked to Helmuth, whose father had been involved in the Nazi "Racial Hygiene Committee." Both Helmuth's father and his son committed suicide.

> H[elmuth]: . . . I try to live in peace with my parents. And somehow, actually, what I feel toward them is mainly love, toward my father as well. Although it was only later on, after his death—and through his tragic, his terrible, fateful entanglement, so to speak—that I learned to love and respect him. I mean, I don't have any need to settle accounts with my father. . . .
>
> [Bar-On]: Why did he shoot himself?
>
> H: Because he believed that he himself would be brought to trial, that the Allies wanted to have revenge on the Nazis. . . . I believe that all of us bear a structural guilt, or let me put it more modestly, for me as a child of our times, our guilt is not less than that of my father. I haven't, thank God, become a perpetrator, a victimizer. I am not guilty of the death of others, though I must utter these words with caution: my son committed suicide.
>
> B: That's a frightening connection you made just now. . . . Where there any specific reasons?
>
> H: He was a very political person. He was living among so-called squatters in Berlin. He was an anarchist. . . . I said he didn't have to commit an illegal, albeit socially motivated act in order to live somewhere. And his reply was, "A person can also participate out of a sense of solidarity with others. Besides, I'm doing what you write." I felt proud when he said that. He was very close to me. . . .
>
> B: It must be very difficult to have to live between a father and a son who . . .
>
> H: Yes, I feel hemmed in, weighed down . . . by both of them. (Bar-On 1989:73, 77)

It took Helmuth the encouragement and active listening skills of an Israeli psychologist to connect the deaths of his father and his son.

Precious little work has been done on how injurious memory is transmitted.[12] The silence that has engulfed German families as well as the therapeutic profession has stabilized a whole culture—not only those who lived through the Nazi regime but also their children and grandchildren. "What would I have done," a participant asked during a German conference on the impact of the past on family therapy, "if my father confessed to me, in tears, that he had killed a Jew. . . . His silence also stabilizes me" (quoted in Von Westernhagen 1987:202). Silence stabilizes but it does not heal. "The goal of [the] work of remembrance is not to veil the contradictions harmoniously" (Heimannsberg 1993:169). In Germany, a false sense of harmony masquerades as silence. Once this silence is accepted as normative behavior, people have less of a chance to become aware of individual dysfunctions. Silence as cultural pathology ultimately destroys trust and intimacy between the generations.[13]

Let me briefly summarize the different attitudes of post-Shoah Jews and Germans toward individual therapy. The German rejection of therapy has largely operated on the (unconscious) assumption that repressing memory (*Verdrängung*) and suppressing emotions (*Unterdrückung*) would stabilize their identities. An ethos of guilt soon informed a whole society, discouraging therapeutic assistance on individual as well as communal levels. Therapy, many Germans erroneously believe, would offset the "stabilizing" effects of the conspiracy of silence. Jewish survivor families, on the other hand, could not escape painful memories. Even if they tried, they experienced their suppression as destabilizing. For them, especially in the United States and Israel, therapy became a real option for countering the destabilizing effects of the Shoah. Psychotherapy achieved for individual Jewish survivor families what the ethos of remembrance accomplished for the Jewish community at large: individuals learned to cope with the disruption the Shoah had caused in their lives, and the ethos of remembrance stabilized the community by integrating a traumatic past into the present by pointing to a better future.

. . . to "Spontaneous Communitas"

Individual therapy is a respectable choice. It is particularly advisable for Germans of all ages who have so badly neglected it in the last decades.

Like some of their Jewish American counterparts who have taken advantage of professional help, Germans would certainly profit from psychotherapeutic sessions that emphasize the intergenerational transmission of injurious memory. However, individual psychotherapy, which may have been helpful for the first and second generations, is not what is most helpful to third-generation Jews and Germans. For them, a different model of reconciliation is needed, one that is geared toward overcoming distrust and animosity in a communal and cross-cultural setting. With the growing temporal distance, Holocaust memory has fewer incapacitating effects on them than on their parents and grandparents. But the third generation also holds on to what their communities perceive as indispensable for stabilizing cultural and national identity. Some of these stabilizing mechanisms may be useful short-term solutions, but others are dysfunctional and cannot be considered healing. As we have seen, collective silence, for example, can stabilize and protect a family for some time but eventually destroys trust between the generations. Third-generation Jews and Germans deserve better. They should be given a chance to transcend their cultures' limitations and break out of negative symbiotic relationships. "[H]ealing from a prolonged silence," the Gestalt therapist Cynthia Harris writes, "take[s] place more readily in an interactive rather than in an analytical therapy" (1993:230). Young Jews and Germans need interactive environments that help them find a stronger sense of who they are in a post-Shoah world.

My vision of creative, reconciliatory rituals leaves the realm of individual therapy and moves toward a concept in which heterogeneous groups are willing to change their attitudes toward injurious memory. Klein's suggestion to move from the concept of individual psychopathology toward the transmission of common mythologies is a step in the right direction. Klein was specifically thinking of the Jewish community, but his insight also can apply to German society, which likewise is shaped by common motifs and sensitivities about the history and memory of the Shoah. But my argument goes even further: to study those motifs and sensitivities, we do not have to look at family systems solely within the confines of one culture. The intergenerational transmission of injurious memory can be also explored in cross-cultural settings. There, third-generation Jews and Germans not only get to know the "other" but also learn to see themselves through the "other" as they negotiate differences in their discursive practices and beliefs.

Because Jews and Germans no longer live together in one community (with the exception of the small number of Jews in Germany), cross-
cultural encounters do not happen by themselves. They need to be
orchestrated. Insights from the field of ritual studies can assist in the task
of conceiving environments in which personal and social transformations occur. I am thinking particularly of those scholars who perceive
ritual as serving communitarian, creative, and transformative needs. Rituals do not have to be static and conservative; they can be "flowing,
processual, subversive," and "invented" (Grimes 1992:22f). Students of
ritual have also turned their attention to the creative (rather than normative) aspects of rituals and to the active (rather than passive and prescribed) roles of participants. The purpose of modeling a creative and
active ritual environment for third-generation Jews and Germans is not
to reinforce a ritualized public discourse but to probe and transform it.
Third-generation Jews and Germans cannot be passive recipients of
information about the Holocaust but must become an active community
of people propelled to strengthen human bonds. As the theologian Tom
Driver has put it, rituals are communal events that "not only bring people together in physical assembly but also tend to unite them emotionally" (1991:152).

The shift to viewing rituals as transformative and communitarian
rather than static and conservative has been prepared by the anthropologist Victor Turner. According to Bobby Alexander, a thorough inter-
preter of Turner's theory, "ritual's primary purpose is social change in
the direction of communitarian needs" (1991:46). That rituals achieve
this purpose is due to what Turner calls "liminality" and "communitas."
These terms describe social conditions in which participants are encouraged to probe, transgress, invert, condense, and transform cultural values. The "liminal mode," according to Turner, is highly creative and yet
ambiguous, marginal and yet essential, protected and yet dangerous,
revitalizing and yet transgressive. Individuals or societies can be sent to
the "limen" (the Latin word for threshold), an ambiguous state in which
they go through transitions from one stage, status, role, or level of consciousness to another. These "liminal phases" are often experienced as a
time of crisis, though the crisis is highly creative and necessary for
growth (Turner 1982:24ff; cf. Krondorfer 1992b).

The notion of communitas guides our attention to the communal
dimension of liminality. Whereas "liminality may imply solitude rather

than social intercourse" (Alexander 1991:35), communitas emphasizes that rituals are relational; they take place among and between people. Turner uses "communitas" rather than "community" in order to differentiate a "modality of social intercourse" (communitas) from a geographically defined place of common living (community) (34). Human bonding is the main feature of communitas.

Turner further distinguishes between "spontaneous" and "normative" communitas in order to draw a line between transitory situations of direct human bonding and the development of new normative structures that try to preserve the initial experience of spontaneous bonding. I am mainly interested here in spontaneous communitas, communal bonding in its initial and most creative stage. In spontaneous communitas, groups experience themselves in a liminal mode because they have not yet developed normative social structures. "Spontaneous communitas," Turner writes, "is a direct, immediate and total confrontation of human identities," in which "a high value [is placed] on personal honesty, openness, and lack of pretentions. . . . We feel that it is most important to relate directly to another person as he presents himself in the here-and-now" (1982:47f). Whenever I speak of communitas in this book, I have Turner's description of spontaneous communitas in mind.

Human bonding and direct, open relations are relevant to creating cross-cultural environments in which third-generation Jews and Germans probe reconciliation. The summer programs on the Holocaust as well as the performance work of the Jewish-German Dance Theatre can be understood as spontaneous communitas. In both instances, young Jews and Germans entered into a transitory and protected environment where they were permitted to separate themselves temporarily from the norms of their cultures. They transcended dominant discursive practices, probed their deep beliefs, and unlearned fictionalized images of each other. They were allowed to question, rearrange, invert, and transform that which they had previously perceived as true about their identities and their culture's memorialization of the Shoah.

It is now time to describe and examine in more detail reconciliatory efforts between Jews and Germans of the third generation. Specific examples from the student programs on the Holocaust, the Jewish-German Dance Theatre, and other Jewish/German encounters will illustrate how communal environments and ritual approaches help to reconcile and transform two peoples tied to an antagonistic common ground.[14]

These reconciliatory practices often border on cultural therapy, which is neither therapy for the masses (treatment prescribed for a whole culture) nor individual therapy, where a single person, with only the help of a therapist, tries to exorcise the demons and ghosts of his or her culture. Cultural therapy happens in a communitas of people from different cultural backgrounds who are flexible enough to become aware of their collective and personal identities as they are faced with people from a different culture. In these settings, third-generation Jews and Germans can learn about themselves and each other. They also learn about the aptness, limitation, and pathology of their culture's ethos and discourse regarding the Holocaust. As a communitas, they are temporarily released from their ordinary duties for the sole purpose of learning how to relate to each other in the light of a legacy that has defined them as grandchildren of victims and victimizers. They can free themselves from a rhetoric that is mainly concerned with self-preservation and are encouraged to become vulnerable without being threatened by their separate yet connected quests for cultural identity. This is, I believe, a key to opening up new ways of relating and caring.

II   Reconciliatory Practices

In this part of the book, I examine typical problems that arise in encounters between third-generation Jews and Germans. I look at strategies that work toward and against reconciliatory practices and evaluate the success of creating a communitas in which young Jews and Germans probe experiential approaches to reconciliation.

The reader may occasionally wonder why I consider some of the described processes successful, especially if they stir up anger and confusion between and among young Germans and Jews. Why call it reconciliation if people get angry, defensive, and hurt? The emergence of strong emotions, I will argue, is an essential part of reconciliatory practices. "The healing process begins with the acknowledgment of anger and the helplessness it engenders," Anne Roiphe writes in her reflections on the Holocaust (1988:217). I agree. Genuine transformations occur only if third-generation Jews and Germans together confront injurious memory and become vulnerable in each other's presence.

The emergence of strong emotions does not disqualify reconciliatory efforts. We should expect that reconciliatory practices will at times be frustrating and that third-generation Jews and Germans will respond to those frustrations by temporarily reverting to the security of cultural biases and learned discourses. Only when, at the end of a process, Jews and Germans have barricaded themselves behind the safety of defensive positions can we say that such a process has been ineffective.

In the following chapters, I introduce a few examples in which Jews and Germans remained in the safety of defensive positions. I suggest that the reader carefully distinguish between a defensiveness that is hostile to all reconciliation and frustrations that occur inevitably in the course of experiential processes. Frustrations, resistance, and protectiveness become counterproductive only if they prevent people from becoming vulnerable and honest. Otherwise, they are unavoidable stumbling blocks on a journey toward mending the broken relations between Jews and Germans.

Three basic premises undergird successful reconciliatory practices. First, the personal and cultural identities of third-generation Jews and Germans are at stake when they confront the history and memory of the Shoah. Jews and Germans are often unaware of how this memory has been inscribed in their identities and do not know how to transform their estranged relations. Increasing their awareness is essential for reconciliatory practices. Second, Jews and Germans of the third generation can help each other in their search for identity when together they confront the history and memory of the Holocaust. Homogeneous groups often fail to transcend their culturally biased experiences and perceptions. A cross-cultural communitas, on the other hand, has the power to break up repetitive discourses and to help third-generation Jews and Germans to see who they are, who the other is, and why they have previously misconceived the other. Third, Jews and Germans cannot restrict themselves to intellectual cognition if they want to understand the legacy of the Shoah. They must integrate personal, emotional, and body-conscious approaches. Talking and debating are important tools of knowledge, for we have to find a language that helps us to conceptualize the problems. However, the mind also rationalizes and resists the emergence of emotions. Creative and experiential processes, on the other hand, work actively and consciously with feelings and lower levels of resistance. Social and individual transformations occur when Jews and Germans work through emotional resistance caused by injurious memory.

4 Skeletons in the Closet

German Family Histories

> In the house of the hangman you don't mention the noose.
> —**Theodor Adorno**

> How can we regard a house as our own and settle down comfortably in it when we know there is a corpse in the cellar?
> —**Barbara Heimannsberg and Christoph Schmidt**

Family histories are a good starting point for studying reconciliatory practices. In families, third-generation Jews and Germans have learned about themselves and history and have acquired fictionalized images of the "other." They are deeply rooted in the transmitted beliefs of their families but are not hopelessly shackled to them. They do have opportunities to break out of a restrictive, harmful, or dysfunctional cultural consensus.

The plight of German family histories will be foregrounded in this chapter for two reasons. First, having grown up in Germany, I have a better feel for the dilemmas in which German families are entangled. Second, many case studies on Jewish survivor families are already available, but there is less material on families of perpetrators. To scrutinize relations between German grandparents, parents, and children fills a void. Third-generation Germans, caught in the biases of their own culture, have little incentive to research their family histories, for their inquiry is met with silence and resistance. In a communitas like the summer programs for Jewish and German students, however, we can expect that Jewish participants will react to their Germans peers' lack of such knowledge. As we will see, cross-cultural encounters can assist young Germans in their efforts to discover skeletons in their closets.

The Conspiracy of Silence

Five decades after the liberation of the death camps, most young Germans still do not know much about their families' connections to the Nazi past. They might know a limited number of "safe" stories about their parents and grandparents that circulate in each family, but only rarely do they realize the extent of family involvement or the degree to which information is withheld and distorted. The polished and censored stories represent a highly regulated repertoire.

It is difficult for third-generation Germans to establish emotional ties to a past that lacks coherence and has numerous gaps and inconsistencies. There is a conspiracy of silence among the older generation, and the third generation lacks the skills to break through this silence.[1] When I flew home in 1987 for a family gathering in celebration of my maternal grandmother's eighty-fifth birthday, the speeches delivered in her honor ingeniously avoided the Nazi period. The speakers talked extensively about my grandmother's childhood, her years spent preparing for her doctoral degree, and her motherhood in eastern Prussia. When it came to those "irritating" years from 1933 on, the speakers mentioned only the early death of her husband in the Wehrmacht and her escape from the advancing Soviet army in 1945, and then quickly proceeded to her postwar efforts to rebuild her life in West Germany. It was obvious that troublesome details and memories had been glossed over, but none of the many grandchildren present that day protested. I, too, lacked the courage to intervene and risk a family fight. Besides, without any evidence, what would I ask or say? I was left with the suspicion that some things could not be revealed in my family.

I speak of a conspiracy of silence because of the tacit consensus among the older generations not to talk. Those who were adults and teenagers during the Nazi regime actively perpetuated and still perpetuate this silence. For example, I never heard my grandmother talk about this time; nor do my parents, who grew up during the Nazi regime, easily volunteer information. These two generations are particularly reluctant to provide a full and uncensored account of their lives. One of my in-laws, who was eighteen when the war ended, replied when asked about his past: "European history has to be written without me." He made this curious remark in the mid-1980s—forty years had passed and he still refused to tell his story! Why? Does he consider his experience to be of no significance for European history? Does he feel that his story would defile European history? Does he secretly hope that without his experience historiography will be incomplete? Is he hiding something that might alter history?

As a teenager, this man had been deployed as a soldier in the Soviet Union. After the war he vowed never to touch a gun again. What happened to him and his generation? Are these former soldiers silent because they are unable to verbalize experiences too large to control or comprehend? Are they at a loss for words because they feel humiliated, or guilty, or ashamed? Were these young adults disillusioned after the war? Did they resent the Allied victory? Are they afraid, and if so, of what? Is their silence a reaction and protection against (real and imagined) accusations?

My in-law's statement that European history has to be written without him is as rebellious as it is disheartening. Like so many others of his generation, he not only continues to deny a part of himself but also withholds his experience from his children. Silence and denial are thus passed on from one generation to the next. "Too many fathers and grandfathers, mothers and grandmothers would rather tell their children nothing of the experiences that were decisive for them," observes the psychoanalyst Sammy Speier (1993:67). What the older generations repress becomes a missing link in their children's construction of memory and identity. The unwillingness of the parents to talk becomes the ignorance of the children. One of the fundamental questions of life, "Where do we come from?" has not been fully answered for the third generation. "What is erased reappears in the children . . . as emptiness, identity confusion, bewilderment, and confusion" (Speier 1993:67).

Germany is certainly not the only country in which communication between parents and children is difficult. A certain degree of miscommunication is part of the social fabric of nuclear families in modern industrialized societies. And we can assume that the more agonizing and intimate a particular experience has been, the less willing parents are to share it with their children. Americans whose fathers and mothers fought in World War II, Korea, or Vietnam also know little about their parents' lives during this time. In that sense, Germany is no exception. What makes Germany different is the fact that the unwillingness to talk has been woven into the nation's social fabric. In countries less traumatized by fear and shame, there are always opportunities to trace one's family history: if parents do not talk, children can turn to grandparents, relatives, teachers, or other adults. In Germany, turning to these sources is fruitless, since "the transmission of experience from one generation to another has been effectively shattered" (Speier 1993:65). The search for one's roots is met by silence, gaps, insinuations, half-truths, and sometimes outright lies. Even to young Germans, the Germans of the past remain faceless figures, detached from any family they personally know.[2]

A typical example of such detachment appears in one of Dan Bar-On's interviews conducted in the mid-1980s. Peter, the son of an SS physician from Auschwitz, is the subject.

> B[ar-On]: Among your circle of friends, do you know whose father did what during the war?

> P[eter]: I don't know a single person whose father was a Nazi.

> B: There's no discussion about this?

> P: I don't know anyone among my schoolmates or my other friends who says that his father was a Nazi or a member of the SS or whatever. There's a lot of talk now about how this one or that one was such a monster, but, as I said, in my circle of friends, it's never discussed. Never. And I don't say that my father was in Auschwitz. OK, quite recently there have been programs on TV, and then they sometimes ask me if that was my father, and I say, "Yes, sure." But nobody expects any further discussion, and nothing more is said. Nothing more is asked either. (Bar-On 1989:33)

Peter, by the way, learned of his father's past only through a television program, when he was already a young adult. His parents had never before told him about his father's deeds in Auschwitz. "My parents did not tell me anything at all as far as I know, nothing at all" (Bar-On:33).

Confronted with such a legacy of silence, the third generation grows up with ambiguous attachments. Since the German of the past has no face, the blank spot can assume any features. Since nobody admits his or her implication in the Nazi crimes, everybody could be a victimizer — even one's father or grandmother. What the older generations fail to realize is that their silence makes the third generation insecure and suspicious. Not knowing anybody who admits his or her involvement is the same as suspecting that everybody is hiding something.

The conspiracy of silence has to be blamed primarily on the tacit consensus of the older generations not to talk. But blaming the grandparents and parents will not motivate them to talk; on the contrary, they will likely maintain a defensive silence. Once already in West German history a confrontation with the Nazi past has led to a serious crisis. The student revolt in 1968 exposed a large number of Nazis who had been reintegrated in West German society. "Accusations leveled against the parents, especially for their silence, . . . sharpened the desire of younger intellectuals to discover the truth about a Nazism they identified with the generation of their parents," Saul Friedländer (1986:29) observed. The students looked everywhere and anywhere for the remains of the Nazi past: in the economic and political structures, in school curricula and linguistics, in social relations and biographies of politicians, judges, and the military. They inflated the concept of fascism, tended to overgeneralize, and accused the whole society of being fascist. They forced West Germany to rethink its relation to the past and to redefine its national identity. At the same time, the students "effectively immunized [themselves] against any confrontation with Nazism" as they shifted "their moral outrage from their parents' deeds to America's policies in Vietnam or Israeli policies vis-à-vis the Palestinians." "This 'rebellion,'" Friedländer wrote, "also created fresh mythologies and displacements and established new barriers between the second generation and the crimes of National Socialism" (1986:29; cf. Fichter 1984). In other words, the students succeeded in unearthing the skeletons in the nation's closet but, by and large, the skeletons in their family closets remained undiscovered.[3]

The generations who had lived through the Nazi era understood that their children's slogan, "Don't trust anyone over thirty," was directed against them. Since these generations had not (and still have not) resolved their feelings regarding the Holocaust, their defensiveness grew as suspicions and accusations were leveled against them. German people are able to offer a variety of reasonable and polemical explanations about the past, but their contrived "objectivity," detachment, and defensiveness have either discouraged the young from pursuing further discussions or angered them so much that they have resorted to confrontational behavior. Confrontations, however, only increase the need for protection, and protective mechanisms, in turn, fuel the anger and indifference of the young. The student rebellion certainly did not succeed in reducing the mistrust characteristic of intergenerational patterns of communication. At a meeting of family therapists in 1986 in Giessen, Germany, participants looked at family conflicts over the Nazi past. They discovered that the "silence between the generations, the inability to ask the parents, or the aggressive and accusatory questioning, which in turn silences the parents," were a result of fear, prohibitions, and pressure to conform (Von Westernhagen 1987:201). So many of the intergenerational discussions on issues relating to the past operate on this frustrating circular pattern of repression, suspicion, anger, fear, and defensiveness.

There would be no conspiracy of silence if the third generation had no part in it. Even two decades after the student rebellion, the children and grandchildren have not yet fully examined their own emotional investment in the legacy of silence. They too know how to obey the conspiratorial rules. Acting out their anger and then patting themselves on the back for having fulfilled their duty ("I asked my parents, but they did not respond") is no recipe for breaking through the silence. In reality, accusations achieve little more than creating a distance from parents and grandparents. Blaming can be used as a device for ignoring one's own emotional investment in keeping the skeletons in the closet. There is no "unilateral case of paternal silence," Bar-On discovered in his interviews. Rather, there is an interaction between parents and children which he called the "double-wall phenomenon." Both parents and children have erected a wall around their feelings: "if those on one side try to find an opening, they encounter the wall on the other side" (Bar-On 1989:328; cf. 1990, 1993).

What makes the legacy of silence a conspiracy is the fact that all age groups participate in it, consciously or not. Those who do not talk and those who do not ask form an interdependent system. The third generation's inability to ask the right questions is as much a part of the conspiracy of silence as the stonewalling of parents and grandparents. "It was never talked about," said Peter, the son of a former Auschwitz physician, "and let me add that I never asked about it either" (Bar-On 1989:29). Out of fear that, upon asking questions, children and grandchildren might be "suddenly overwhelmed by the flood of . . . memories in their families . . . [they] take pains to protect their parents from such sudden explosions of old memories," writes the German family therapist Margarete Hecker. "By not posing questions, they support the process of repression" (1993:89).

There are probably as many young Germans who are thoroughly uninterested in breaking through this conspiracy as there are those who want to break it but do not know how. But younger generations have generally displayed less negative attitudes toward Jews and toward the need to remember the Holocaust than the older population.[4] "Each German generation since the end of the war," Friedländer observed, "feels at some point a weariness regarding the Nazi past" (1986:38). Educators report, however, that the number of young Germans who say that they have heard enough about the Holocaust has been growing in the 1980s. In a survey conducted in October 1990 by the American Jewish Committee, 65 percent of West Germans agreed that "it is time to put the memory of the Holocaust behind us"; and in a similar survey conducted in 1994 by the committee, 39 percent of Germans agreed with the statement "Jews are exploiting the Holocaust for their own purposes."

This defiant attitude seems to indicate a lack of interest in taking a responsible stand on the Holocaust. But there is reason to believe that young Germans are overloaded with visual evidence, factual data, and moral appeals, which leave them feeling bombarded by the Nazi past. This feeling does not necessarily reflect indifference. It can also be interpreted as the failure of an educational system that offers factual information but rarely emotional guidance. Parents, teachers, politicians, and ministers are often poorly prepared to teach their children, students, constituents, and parishioners. Ambivalent about the past themselves, they cannot inspire new generations to look into their closets, actively reach out to Jews, and come to terms with Jewish/German relations.

It does not help to bemoan the third generation's lassitude toward remembering the past or inability to break through the conspiracy of silence. What counts is that efforts can be made to spark interest among the third-generation Germans and to help them formulate the right questions. Asking grandparents and parents about their particular experiences is a first step toward breaking the conspiracy, but asking the right questions is not as easy as it first appears. "We complain about the silence and speechlessness among the generations," a German participant in a therapeutic session on family conflicts reported, "but when we imagined our parents to be willing to answer, we didn't know what questions we wanted to ask" (quoted in Von Westernhagen 1987:200). Part of the difficulty in asking the right questions is that the third generation does not expect gratifying responses. Rather than getting information, asking questions seems only to lead to family fights. The past is a nuisance, and one is better off keeping it under wraps.

If the conspiracy of silence has indeed become part of Germany's social fabric, then certain questions might not be asked within the culture, or only in a way that deters responses. In the absence of Jews and the presence of an active suppression, little seems to depend on finding out what one's parents and grandparents knew about the Holocaust and what they had felt toward Jews. Facilitated, cross-cultural settings, however, can provide incentives for asking the right questions. If young Germans do not know their family histories, and their Jewish peers call them on this lack of knowledge, their relationship is suddenly at stake. In an interactive environment, or communitas, an essential aspect of learning and communicating is the building of meaningful relationships, and the breakdown of communication is experienced as personal crisis. In short, when young Germans meet with their Jewish peers over an extended period of time, they are dependent on making themselves understood, and knowing one's family background is crucial in establishing trust.

The "Swiss Cheese" Approach to Family Histories

During the one month of living together, the Jewish American and German participants in the summer programs on the Holocaust learned that asking and answering the right questions had a direct impact on relations between them. A session on reconstructing family history effectively demonstrated that this interactive and cross-cultural environment was capable of unraveling cultural assumptions: the American Jewish and Christian students were astounded by the ubiquity of the conspiracy of silence their German peers had experienced in their families; and the East and West German students came to realize how deeply they themselves were invested in that conspiracy.

The first day of the program was devoted to family histories.[5] We had asked students to bring photographs and other memorabilia to document their families' past. The visual evidence, we hoped, would be an incentive to share stories of their lives and cultures.

The twenty students split into four mixed groups, where they had a chance to explain their memorabilia as they pinned them to a panel. At the end of the day, we assembled all four panels in a room (where they remained for the duration of the program) and gathered there to listen

to each other's stories. The students thus had an opportunity to introduce themselves and their families, first in a more intimate setting and
then in the larger group. As facilitators, we hoped this exercise would
reveal some of the cultural differences in understanding the function of
memory in the construction of identity.

The memorabilia and stories each had a unique charm and distinct
style. There were snapshots of recent family gatherings; pictures showing the students as babies, and at baptisms and bar mitzvahs; photos with
worn edges depicting smiling grandparents in old-fashioned clothing;
birth certificates; immigration papers; the shoes of a doll; old passport
photos. The students, it seemed, had done their homework, enjoyed the
opportunity to talk about their families, and were able to appreciate each
contribution. But as we listened to the stories, especially later in the large
group, the distinctiveness of each story began to fade, and we began to
notice recurrent patterns and real differences between the German and
the American participants. To put it bluntly, the American students were
much better prepared than their German peers; they had plenty of
memorabilia at hand, had talked to their parents and grandparents, and
occasionally had discovered material hitherto unknown to them. The
Germans, on the other hand, had not pressed their parents for information, were cautious in their presentations, and were content with presenting a few photographs (but sometimes not even that). In one case, a
student refused to talk about his family altogether.

Many American stories focused on presenting family members and
their ethnic origins. Amid the numerous family idiosyncrasies, the immi-
grant and "melting pot" experience (or "salad bar" experience, as one
student called it) stood out as shared cultural background. There were
also a few differences between the Jewish and Christian American presentations. The non-Jewish American students presented their immediate family members in much detail ("This is my Irish grandfather, German mother, Native American grandmother, etc."), but rarely recalled a
particular incident that would link them to the European upheavals of
the 1930s and 1940s. Their families, it seemed, were only peripherally
concerned with the tragedies across the Atlantic. American isolationism
and obliviousness to foreign affairs were somewhat reflected in these
presentations, especially when the students pointed out each relative in
a particular photo without telling the group more about them than". . .
and this is my aunt and my uncle; my aunt is the sister of my father who

is also in this picture; and this is . . .". The non-Jewish American presentations mirrored, at least in part, America's depreciation of history as an identity-building agent. Many Americans, the historian Charles Maier observed, do not see why history should have an impact on the formation of their individual identities, "for almost all discussions of American identity revolve around the question of the American character or personality." Commenting wryly on his countrymen's view of history, Maier added, "Why should so abstract an inquiry matter?" (1988:151).

The Jewish American students conveyed a greater historical sensibility (as did a Black student, who talked about slavery and instances of discrimination his family had experienced). Jewish memorabilia traced the roots of extended families to Russia, Poland, or Germany. Events, people, places, or immigration circumstances were organized around the central date of the Shoah: relatives immigrated either before or after the Holocaust; this side of the family did or did not lose someone in the Holocaust; this photo was taken in Germany in the 1930s, and those relatives escaped to Palestine during the war. The Holocaust was present even if the memorabilia were unrelated to the genocide itself. Listening to these stories, I was reminded of Alvin Rosenfeld's observation that the Shoah figures as a prominent reference point in Jewish post-Holocaust literature. The Holocaust, he writes, "as central to our common awareness now as it is inescapable, casts its shadow backwards as well as forwards" (1980:68). In our session, the Shoah functioned similarly as an organizing principle for the way Jewish students told their family histories and how they placed them within the larger construction of communal memory.[6]

The different styles of the Christian and Jewish American students were due in part to differences between the American majority and minority cultures and in part to the different religious frameworks imposed on history (Christian salvation as forgiveness and Jewish redemption as remembrance). But these differences were slight compared to the discrepancy between the American group as a whole and the German students. Anna, an American student (who is a child of a Christian German and a Polish Jew), recalled:

> In order to get acquainted, we began the program by sharing our family histories. This forced us to face each other and ourselves as well. It was remarkable to watch the Germans as the Jewish students

told of the suffering and hardship of their relatives during the Nazi era. Just as moving was the struggle that the German students went through as they realized the holes which exist in their family histories. Very few of them knew what their grandparents had been doing during the Nazi years. Some of the Germans had asked but received no answers, and some had never asked at all. I felt myself torn between the two groups. . . . Like the German students, I had never asked my German grandfather directly about his experience in Nazi Germany. On the other hand, I could sympathize with the Jewish students who had lost family in the Shoah. . . . [M]y father's family had been targeted too. (Krondorfer and Staffa 1992:22f)

The German students brought two types of photographs: pictures taken during the Third Reich and snapshots of recent family gatherings. Almost none of the memorabilia predated the 1930s; everyone seemed to assume that the session on family history referred to the Nazi era and postwar Germany but not to an earlier time. If I now think about this unself-conscious consensus (in which I fully participated), I am stunned by how strongly third-generation Germans assume that family history applies primarily to the Nazi and postwar era. Interestingly, this assumption was shared by the students from (the former) East Germany as well. Although their specific recollections differed from those of the West Germans, they had selected similar photos and felt similar emotional constraints when talking about their families.

From what I observed, the German students' selection of photographs from the Nazi and postwar periods was not based on a deliberate decision to exclude earlier years. Rather, their choice seemed to express an unself-conscious desire to conjoin their present lives with the Nazi past, to establish some kind of relation between now and then. There were, for example, several pictures of fathers, uncles, and grandfathers in Wehrmacht uniforms. The German students did not bring these photos because they were seeking a confrontation with their American peers, but because they wanted to understand what it was that related them to these relatives in uniform. In fact, prior to the session on family histories, the German participants did not fully realize that Jewish students might react strongly to these photos. Did they not think about their Jewish peers? Or did they instinctively comply with the presumption that only memorabilia of the Nazi era and postwar Germany were adequate for a session on family histories? Regardless of what the motivation might have been, in the context of this interactive and cross-cultural program the German students suddenly realized that the act of pinning a photograph of a family member in Nazi uniform to the panel amounted to public exposure. Now it was visually evident that they were the grandchildren of victimizers, that they were not the victims but the heirs of this past, and that their recollections were clashing with Jewish memories.

Not every German student was able to take the risk of public exposure, and as a result various forms of censorship were practiced. I noticed that a few photographs "disappeared": they had been passed around in the small groups but were withheld from the whole group. One German student, for example, did not put up any photos on the first day but pinned a few to the board a few days later, after a heated discussion on Germany's legacy of silence. Another student from East Germany showed a picture of her grandmother and revealed to the small group, in a faltering voice, that she had been a Nazi and had been present at a local deportation ramp when Jews were loaded into cattle cars. The student pinned a photo of her grandmother to the panel but never related her story to the large group. Another student did not bring any pictures and simply put his name tag on the board. Yet another hinted at some family secrets but refused to talk about them despite the encouragement of both his peers and the facilitators. A remarkably creative response was from a student who did not bring any memorabilia. He pinned a drawing to the board depicting a white circle with black holes, which, in his words, represented the holes in his family history. A Jewish student later called the drawing "Swiss cheese." Nearly all Germans, from East and West, said that their parents and grandparents did not talk about "it"—"it" referring to a blend of issues relating to the Holocaust, Jews, the Nazi past, and family history.

At first, many of the American students empathized with their German peers, who seemed unable to break through their families' conspiracy of silence. Some expressed surprise at this Swiss-cheese approach to history but gave the Germans the benefit of the doubt. After all, they had just arrived in a foreign country, and the group as a whole was still in the process of consolidating. But a crisis was in the making. A Jewish student recalled in her journal:

On that very first day in Bryn Mawr we all were asking, Why? In the back of my mind was: "Was your grandfather a SS guard? Your grandmother a Nazi?" . . . And so we sat there that first day, looking at all the great black-and-white photos of great-grandparents, grandparents, parents and siblings, and listening to funny anecdotes and family stories. But most of the talk came from the Americans. The German students did not have very much to say. At first, I chalked it up to their fatigue of traveling . . . and especially to their being uncomfortable speaking in a foreign language. And then I thought that perhaps it was too soon and too fast to get so involved. I mean, we had all just met each other . . . and had not yet time to build trust. In any event, the family histories of many of the Germans were full of holes—one of the students even went so far as to substitute the family photos that he lacked with a picture of what looked like Swiss cheese to represent all the holes and missing information in his family past. (cf. Krondorfer and Staffa 1992:41f)

German students noticed the difference as well. Torsten, a student from East Germany, wrote about his fear once he became aware of those gaps: "But I was also afraid. What should I expect as a German, a grandchild of a former German soldier? I have read a lot about the Holocaust, but would my intellectual approach prepare me for what might happen within myself? I became aware of how little I knew and how few details I knew about the history of my family and their involvements in the crimes."

Both German and American students were bewildered by the gaps in German family histories, but their expectations differed widely. The Germans assumed that acknowledging these gaps was all that could be expected from them. Their parents' silence would have to be accepted as a reasonable excuse for not knowing more about the family. The Americans, on the other hand, expected that at some point the Germans would fill the holes in the Swiss cheese and tell more. When it became apparent that this would not happen, their initial sympathy turned to anger.

During the 1991 program, the anger came to the fore a few days after the session on family histories. It was prompted by the showing of a German documentary called *Now . . . After All These Years*.[7] The film portrays Rhina, a German village that had a large Jewish population before the war. In the 1980s, the filmmakers went to Rhina and asked the inhabitants what they remembered about their Jewish neighbors and how they explained their disappearance. They then interviewed Jewish survivors of Rhina now living in New York City. Juxtaposing these two "remembrances" made it evident how much the German population had repressed, distorted, and denied. It was painful to watch the effects of the conspiracy of silence among the villagers, especially the persistence of anti-Jewish stereotypes.

In the ensuing discussion of the film, the students became very emotional. Both Germans and Americans were deeply disturbed by the denial and persistence of antisemitism. Halfway into the discussion, they began to make connections between the villagers' silence and their own session on family history. The American students challenged the ignorance of their German peers; they no longer accepted lack of knowledge as a valid excuse and now perceived it as a continuation of their grandparents' and parents' silence. Had the German students really made an effort to escape this legacy, or did their Swiss-cheese approach to history betray their acquiescence in this silence? The following excerpts from the discussion show how the students discussed the issue of the responsibility of third-generation Germans.

Anna (American Christian): "This [film] made it real to me—about Germany not facing its past."

Torsten (East German): "I felt helplessness and shame."

Julie (Jewish American): "I felt so de-legitimated. At least before now, we've all been functioning on the assumption that the Holocaust did happen. . . ."

Anne (East German): "The ideology in West Germany after the war was just to start over, work hard, and make something new."

Iris (West German): "We can't help the old people, it's just necessary that they die. We need to reach the youth."

Miriam (West German): "Remember this village is . . . not the whole story or whole situation." To which Jennifer, a Jewish American student, angrily replies: "How can you say that? Every single one of you [German students] said that your parents wouldn't talk about it. What else are we to expect?"

Steven (Jewish American): "I almost wished just one of the Germans would've stood up when we talked about our family histories and said, 'Yes, my grandfather killed Jews.' At least that would show they can admit what happened."

Kay (East German): "I am so angry! I hope when I go back I won't forget this anger. Why couldn't I ask more questions? It's not the problem [of parents]. It's my problem that I didn't pursue it harder." (Cf. Krondorfer and Staffa 1992:74f)

The students' discontent and emotionality are quite apparent in these statements. The Americans felt cheated: "I still feel that the Germans did not tell the whole story," said Steven, expressing a sentiment shared by his compatriots. "You knew you were going on this program, so why didn't you solicit more information?" The German students, on the other hand, wavered between explaining German society and admitting their own responsibility. But they were dumbfounded when the Americans suddenly turned against them, realizing that their excuse was no longer acceptable. They had arrived in the United States largely unprepared, and it was now difficult to ask for sympathy.

The next morning, when I passed by the photos and memorabilia, I noticed that the drawing of the white circle with black holes was crumpled up—but still pinned to the panel.

A Third Guilt?

The learning and understanding that took place in the session on family history and the subsequent discussion of German responsibility could not have taken place without Jews' and Germans' interacting with each other. The intergroup dynamics were able to elicit questions and responses that intragroup meetings would have ignored. Without the presence of Jewish and Christian Americans, the German students would not have understood that their ignorance was not simply a lack of knowledge but a substantive loss of part of their identity. Had we conducted the session on family histories only among third-generation Germans, no one would have considered the lack of knowledge a tacit compliance with the conspiracy of silence. Young Germans might have lamented this legacy, but would have accepted it as a fait accompli. In the context of Jewish/German encounters, however, their ignorance had a direct impact on intergroup relations. Would a Jewish student be able to trust Germans who did not know their history? Did the German students really not know, or were they afraid of sharing what they already knew? And if they were afraid, were they afraid of (imagined) chastisement by their families or of judgments by Jewish students? And if they were afraid of the Jewish students, was their fear prompted by mistrust?

The argument of third-generation Germans that they could not break through their families' silence has an element of self-pity. Young Germans see themselves as victims of this legacy. They also believe that their dissimilarity to their parents and grandparents must be obvious to everybody. A 1987 poll by the Allensbach Research Institute showed that "only 49 percent of West Germans believe they have the same views as their parents on morality, compared with 84 percent in the U.S. and 76 percent in Britain" (quoted in Miller 1990:290). Young Germans do not understand that not to perpetuate this silence requires an active effort on their part. From the outside their ignorance is little different from the silence of older generations: neither grandparents, nor parents, nor children are capable of talking about their family's life during the Nazi regime. But when Germans encounter Jews, their apologies are no longer convincing. Young American Jews see continuity between the ignorance of third-generation Germans and the silence of their parents and grandparents. Germans, by contrast, presume discontinuity between themselves and older generations.

The failure of third-generation Germans to put more effort into understanding their own investment in perpetuating the conspiracy of silence can be called a "third guilt." A third guilt presumes, of course, a second and a first guilt. The first guilt refers to the crimes committed in Nazi Germany. It is the legal guilt of victimizers and the historic guilt of a society that allowed the genocide to occur. The second guilt has political and ethical connotations. It refers to what Ralph Giordano (1990:11) described as the "grande peace with the victimizers," that is, the suppression and denial of Nazi crimes in postwar Germany and the reintegration of former Nazi officials in West German society. It is political because the restoration and "normalization" of postwar Germany followed administrative and ideological decisions; it is ethical because the repression of memory led to an "inability to mourn" (Mitscherlich 1988) and a failure to educate new generations adequately.

The third guilt has to do with those generations who grew up in postwar Germany and learned about the Holocaust in school and through books, films, and occasional family stories. Peter Sichrovsky must have followed a similar idea when he entitled his book of interviews with young Germans *Born Guilty* (1988). Unlike the first guilt, the third guilt has no legal connotation because the third generation and all subsequent generations are not legally or morally responsible for the crimes of their forebears—unless one believes in collective guilt. Neither is the third generation responsible for the "grande peace with the victimizers," since the restoration of Germany was already accomplished before third-generation Germans had political power. The concept of third guilt does not imply that third-generation Germans are "closet Nazis" simply because they participate in Germany's collective silence. Rather, it refers to the failure of post-Shoah generations to establish personal relationships with Jews and other victims of the Nazi regime; the failure to break through the conspiracy of silence; the failure to understand their own cultural assumptions and emotional investments in regard to antisemitism, Jews, and the Holocaust; and the failure to motivate themselves and their families to discover the skeletons in their own closets. What distinguishes the third guilt from previous legal, historical, and political culpabilities is its relational quality. It signifies the degree to which post-Shoah German generations are willing and able to establish meaningful relationships with people and issues concerning to the Holocaust.

The response of the East German student Torsten to his first visit to a Jewish American home illustrates this relational quality:

> When I recalled that my own grandfather was a German soldier in Lithuania, I was for the first time shocked and bewildered about my personal ties to the Shoah and the past of my host family. In this moment I fully realized why I participated in this exchange program, and I fully understood the meaning of the third guilt. This is the guilt of German grandchildren of my age, who put so little effort in trying to understand the Shoah and, instead, continued to repress German history by avoiding to know more about their own grandparents. I realized that I have always treated the Shoah as an intellectual topic and that I did not resist the tabooization of the Holocaust because I was subconsciously afraid of confronting my family. (cf. Krondorfer and Staffa 1992:36)

In a communitas of Jews and Germans, the debate about knowing or not knowing one's past is no longer an intellectual topic but becomes an issue of emotional and personal concern. Neither guilty of Nazi crimes in a legal sense nor politically responsible for the restoration of postwar Germany, third-generation Germans are nonetheless liable for what they know—and do not know—about their family histories, the Holocaust, and Judaism in general. They are also liable for examining their own emotional investment in the repression of memory and for the efforts they make in reaching out to Jews.

During the summer programs of 1989, 1991, and 1993, the sessions on family histories first activated anger, fear, and suspicion but later strengthened the bonds among the students. Living with one another for four weeks provided ample opportunities for mutual appreciation despite frustration and disappointments over cultural differences. Sharing bathrooms, playing games together, and eating together allowed bonding experiences that transcended the difficulties caused by an antagonistic common ground. At the end of the emotional debate about the film *Now . . . After All These Years,* Sam, a Jewish student, said, "I almost wished I would not have known you [the Germans]. Then it would be easier for me to close the chapter on Germany. It would be so easy to make a blanket statement and say, 'I hate all Germans and I hate Germany, and I never want to go there.' But because I know you, I can't."

Asking the Right Questions: The Quest for Specificity

Kay, an East German, had said that he hoped he would not forget his anger over his complicity in Germany's silence, for that anger would motivate him to ask more questions. Several German students expressed similar thoughts, wishing that the summer program on the Holocaust would give them enough strength to reexamine their past after returning to their families. Their worry about losing motivation to probe their family histories is understandable considering the few incentives German culture offers for such a task. "It takes a great deal of courage for individual[s] . . . to confront their parents' repressed emotions, to bring into consciousness their parents' failures, mistakes, and active participation in the Nazi regime, and at the same time to accept themselves as members of this particular family" (Hecker 1993:91). Another East German student, for example, recalled that her parents said before she went on the program: "It is tasteless to talk about it [the Holocaust]." Confronted with such vigorous resistance, would third-generation Germans be able to keep asking questions, or would the conspiracy of silence eventually prove to be more powerful?

It is difficult but not impossible to break through the conspiracy of silence and actively resist the third guilt's pull to passivity. To tackle this task requires active research, patience, persistence, a certain amount of courage, and, above all, an interest in specificity. Without this interest, the gaps in family histories will remain open. Unfortunately, third-generation Germans tend to skip the quest for specificity and proceed quickly to the lessons of the Holocaust, which are applied to a wide array of political agendas. By skipping specificity, they also skip opportunities for understanding their own historic roots and cultural presumptions.

The enormity of the crimes committed during the Holocaust, as well as the limitless list of current human-rights violations, has led to a drastic and momentous depreciation of specificity. Because there are too many details to know and to remember (how often can you cry over the killing of yet another victim?), meaning can get lost in the immensity of gruesome details. Hence, we look to the larger picture in order to hold onto some reasonable explanations. We point to the failure of economic systems, identify political scapegoats, compare cruelties and genocides, or lament the evil in human nature. Though these are all legitimate attempts to assert meaning, the habit of always moving to the next-larger frame neglects specificity. Applied to the Holocaust, this move bypasses the details of the mass murder of Jews and treats the Shoah summarily as a paradigm for human evil. For example, we may refer to Auschwitz as a symbol of evil but not study the daily camp routines; we may see Auschwitz as the model camp but be unaware of its satellite camps; we may know about Jewish resistance only from the Warsaw ghetto revolt but be ignorant about Jewish partisans in Byelorussia; we lament the plight of the six million but have never listened to the story of a single survivor; we may take the Holocaust as a paradigm for all genocides but not understand the specific mechanisms of antisemitism; we question how a just God could have allowed mass murders but do not examine the structure of the RSHA (Reich Security Main Office). The larger the picture, the more meaning we hope to retrieve.

This generalizing and universalizing tendency allows people to draw lessons from the Holocaust and apply them to political agendas as diverse as supporting either Palestinian or Israeli policies, curbing or expanding the right of free speech, and restricting or endorsing arms sales to various countries. Without an interest in specificity, however, the "lessons" might very well be misunderstood or misapplied. Especially in the context of Germany's conspiracy of silence and the third guilt of postwar generations, the lack of interest in specificity has adverse effects. For example, third-generation Germans learned about Nazi Germany but not about their own family backgrounds. They learned about Auschwitz but never met a Jewish survivor. Without specificity, the Holocaust has no human face.

When I once asked my father why he never did any research on the places where he was stationed as a teenage soldier between 1943 and 1945, he responded: "What would I learn from that? I know what horrible and tragic things the Germans inflicted on Jews and other people. What could possibly be added to that?" To know the specifics of places and events he had witnessed would not enable him, he argued, to improve his understanding of the Holocaust. He forgot to add that his ignorance would prevent me, his son, from asking specific questions. As long as I could put my questions only in general terms, his answers could remain on a general level, too.

Dötte von Westernhagen reported a similar conversation in her book on children of Nazi victimizers. In an interview, Rainer, the son of a former SS member, explained why he had never asked his father about his specific duties in the death camp of Majdanek: "I knew already enough about it through literature and films, in abstract terms so to speak, so that it was no longer important to me to know what he actually did, whether he worked on the selection ramp, or whether he was only responsible for the heating, for the procurement of fuel or of seeds for the garden. I was not particularly interested in that. . . . The moral outrage was so great that I didn't care what specifically happened there" (1988:141f).

"Blurring eases. Specificity pains," Cynthia Ozick once remarked. The avoidance of pain might explain why Germans like to generalize issues related to the Holocaust. "The more narrowly we look into the perplexing lens of Auschwitz, the more painful will the perception be," Ozick said. "[I]t is moral ease to slide from the particular to the abstract" (1976:153). By adopting the always larger framework, the always greater explanation, the always more encompassing paradigm, we dismiss the painful detail in favor of the belief in abstract principles and historical coherence. We gloss over details in order to arrive at some intelligible and coherent patterns. The Holocaust, however, might just as well be composed of "multiple paradoxes," as Anne Roiphe suggested, of "unresolvable contradictions that hold truth in opposites" (1988:21). When we generalize and universalize the Holocaust, it seems that we are driven by an ideal of historical coherence, which Michel Foucault severely criticized as the drive to resolve "the greatest possible number of contradictions . . . by the simplest means" (1972:149).

Claude Lanzmann's documentary film *Shoah* has demonstrated how painful and revealing the quest for specificity can be. Sitting through the nine-hour film (and physically experiencing the resulting lower back pain), one cannot but notice Lanzmann's persistent focus on details as he interviews survivors, bystanders, and perpetrators. By meticulously unpacking what people stored in their memories, he turned the Holocaust from a paradigmatic and abstract concept into a series of gruesome details. Here is an example of Lanzmann's emotionally excruciating but brilliant interviewing technique.

Lanzmann: How was it possible in Treblinka in peak days to "process" eighteen thousand people?

Franz Suchomel (SS-Unterscharführer): Eighteen thousand is too high.

L: But I read that figure in the court reports.

Sure.

L: To "process" eighteen thousand people, to liquidate them . . .

Mr. Lanzmann, that's an exaggeration. Believe me.

L: How many?

Twelve thousand to fifteen thousand. But we had to spend half the night at it. In January the trains started arriving at 6 A.M.

L: Always at 6 A.M.?

Not always. Often. The schedules were erratic. Sometimes one came at 6 A.M., then another at noon, maybe another late in the evening. You see?

L: So a train arrived. I'd like you to describe in detail the whole process during the peak period.

The trains left Malkinia station for Treblinka station. It was about six miles. . . . (Lanzmann 1985:105)

By persistently focusing on detailed information, Lanzmann succeeded in getting victimizers, bystanders, and survivors to talk. Those interviewed became intrigued by the precision of their memories and were unwittingly thrown back into a past world, a phenomenon that Lawrence Langer has called "deep memory" (1991). By asking for the exact time, the clothing they wore, the weather, the color, the smell, Lanzmann led them to recount their stories in such vivid detail that the film became an auditory rather than a visual assault. Lanzmann abstained from any overt moral and political commentary, and the interviews were emotionally strenuous precisely because of their specificity.

Lanzmann's film demonstrated that Germans, including those who were camp guards, are perfectly capable of remembering details when asked the right questions. Under normal circumstances, there would be no need to emphasize so obvious a point. Yet since the war, perpetrators, accomplices, and bystanders have time and again claimed that they do not remember details. Indeed, the conspiracy of silence seems to have reached the proportions of a social amnesia so deeply penetrating the German discourse that we are sometimes led to believe that all memory has been erased. Hence, the third generation's task to ask the right questions is doubly impeded: young Germans are discouraged from asking because nobody seems to remember details or else people belittle the significance of specificity; and, in spite of the temporal distance, the third generation continues to be afraid of the pain of specificity and of the emotions that might emerge if they pierced the darkness of their families' past.

When my younger brother visited me in Philadelphia in 1991, we got into an argument over our father's past. I said it would be important to know how our father grew up during the Nazi era and what exactly he did when he joined the Hitler Youth and later the Wehrmacht. My brother got very upset and accused me of mistrusting our parents. "Do you want to find out whether our dad was in a concentration camp, or what?" he asked. I was perplexed by his anger, particularly because I know my brother to be a very conscientious person when it comes to

Germany's fascist past and neofascist trends. He has even risked personal harm by speaking out against neo-Nazis and other right-wing extremists. His question was even more surprising because I did not imply at any point that I suspected our father of having been a camp guard. My brother and I have trusted him in this respect and, in any case, knew enough about his life during the late 1940s to rule out any such possibility. Why, then, was my brother so incensed?

We were not able then to get to the roots of our conflict (which was also about shifting loyalties within our family), but I think my brother's distress had to do with fearing specificity. He, too, believed that there was nothing worthwhile left to explore in our family history; and yet, as soon as I suggested that we look for skeletons in our closets, he feared the worst—that our father may have been a camp guard.

His question expressed a fear that has plagued many of the third generation. Not knowing anyone who admits their compliance with the Nazi regime, as I said earlier, means suspecting everybody—even a grandparent or parent. The prospect of discovering the unexpected curbs the third generation's interest in pursuing research: fear and suspicion are greater than the desire to acquire a realistic picture. Though most families have rather ordinary stories to tell, there is always the possibility of turning up troublesome news. The third generation needs to realize that the point of family history is not to unearth an SS guard in one's family (albeit such an outcome is possible) but to know the specifics of how close people have been to the centers of destruction, what they have witnessed, how they responded, why they acted as they did and not differently, what tasks they fulfilled, how they felt, and what questions they did or did not ask.

Piercing the Darkness: Research and Coincidence

Third-generation Germans must have an interest in specificity if they are serious about breaking through the conspiracy of silence. But good intentions alone might not yield the desired results. Sometimes it may take years before rays of light penetrate the darkness of family closets, and often we may not get as far as we wish. Young Germans "may despair in the attempt to find and to shape a meaningful continuity between the generations, or, perhaps better, a continuity which creates meaning," writes Helm Stierlin (1993:160). The quest for specificity might be tedious work, requiring much patience, but it is also gratifying once the details about people, places, and events interconnect and forge personally meaningful wholes.

In my experience, the quest for specificity is best put into practice by actively pursuing research and, at the same time, hoping for coincidental occurrences that can draw meaning from the collected stories and data. Sometimes a particular incident leads to more research; at other times previous research makes an incidental encounter intelligible. The combination of research and coincidence is a fruitful way of piecing together one's family history, and it is most effective if pursued on several levels. It is important for Germans of the third generation to familiarize themselves with the historic, political, social, and geographic landscape of Europe; it is also important to be patient with family members, to allow family patterns to change, and to hope that over time resistance to inquiry into the past will wane. Sometimes it is necessary to challenge the repression of memory directly and to acquire information through impersonal sources (like archives); it is also important to accumulate piecemeal information and hope for a coincidence that will consolidate the pile of unconnected items.

There are numerous autobiographical and literary works of second- and third-generation Germans that deal with the Nazi past of the authors' families. Do autobiographical and fictionalized reports reveal how information was obtained? Was it obtained through deliberate research, or as a result of changing family patterns (such as the death of a family member) or pure coincidence? What was needed to break through the repression of memory and to assemble a family mosaic? As important as it would be to trace these questions in "literary testimonies" and "fictional memoirs" (Young 1990:16ff) of second- and third-generation Germans, such a study would clearly exceed the limits of this book, for even a random sampling of titles reveals the abundance of available material.[8]

Two episodes involving my own family illustrate the effectiveness of blending active research and coincidental occurrences. The first involves my wife's effort to uncover her great-uncle's role in the Holocaust. Her story speaks to the necessity of conducting archival research in order to break through a family's suppression of information. Since Katharina has written elsewhere about her story (Von Kellenbach 1990), I can limit myself to summarizing the events leading to her decision to consult archival material.

During a family gathering, when Katharina was still a young girl, one of her uncles surreptitiously showed her a newspaper clipping in which her great-uncle was accused of war crimes. Apparently, the article was a report on his trial before a German court. Many years later, during a Yom Ha-Shoah observance in Philadelphia, she recalled the incident. She decided to contact the uncle who had shown her the article, but he never responded to her written request for more information. Instead, he forwarded the letter to her father, who called her and said there was nothing more to know about this story. Her inquiry, it seemed, had collapsed before it had even started.

Over the next few months, however, rumors started to circulate in the family. Some said that the great-uncle accused of war crimes (who had died in the meantime) had been working for the railroad in Russia; others claimed that he had been in a camp in Romania; and still others emphasized that he had not been convicted of any crimes. Since the information was haphazard at best, Katharina finally decided to try to gain access to the trial records. After a long odyssey through the German bureaucracy (most of the archives containing files on Nazi crimes and criminals are still closed to the public), she eventually received copies of the indictment from the prosecutor's office. All names on the copies except for her great-uncle's were neatly and tidily obliterated. Here is what Katharina recalled when reading the files:

> My sense of victory over "their" conspiracy of silence faded quickly when I started to read the charges against him. As the "vice commissioner" and "specialist for Jewish affairs" in Pinsk, Soviet Union, my [great-]uncle was charged with "several hundred cases of malicious and cruel murder." Among his crimes are the shooting of two men because they carried a stick of butter into the ghetto; the shooting of 40 sick and retarded Jews from the hospital in Pinsk; the murder of a five year old Jewish girl from Zapole; the killing of 280 Jewish women and men. . . . 157 witnesses testified during [my great-uncle's] trial. He was not convicted . . . [and the] trial was discontinued in 1978 because of his heart condition. (Von Kellenbach 1990:11)

Katharina's story is not unusual. It never dawned on her that members of her extended family could have been actively engaged in the Holocaust and that her immediate family would undertake a consolidated effort to repress this knowledge after the war. In 1959 her great-uncle was best man at her parents' wedding. Twenty years later his trial, like thousands of other trials, ended without a conviction.[9]

But why was the newspaper clipping shown to Katharina when she was still a young girl? Was this an unintended leak in her family's conspiracy of silence? Today, Katharina understands this incident as her relative's attempt to make her part of the conspiracy. "Unwittingly," she wrote, "I was nursed on antisemitism" (1990:11). She would be privy to some dangerous knowledge that was meant to remain obscure. She would know and yet not know, thus participating in the repression of memory. The breach of the family conspiracy was not her uncle's revelation of the article to Katharina but her decision to follow up on this information.

Similar stories are reported about other daughters struggling with the Nazi heritage of their families. Dan Bar-On interviewed a woman who had tried for years to get access to a suitcase full of documents of her father that was literally locked away in her brother's attic; and another had searched for information by checking the indexes of books and relentlessly questioning her mother, who refused to talk (Bar-On 1989:245–290). A German psychotherapist reported a client's effort at reconstructing the historical data about her father, only to discover that during his "first tour of duty in the Polish city, 10,000 Jews had been murdered" (Behrendt 1993:14). As in Katharina's case, the women's persistence and active research yielded the desired albeit devastating information. Specificity indeed pains. But not always do the children have the courage to break with their family's conspiracy. During her father's fatal illness, a woman therapist was drawn "into the abyss of [his] memories." She wrote: "[You] confided one more secret that you had carried for over forty years. At the same time you extracted a promise from me never to speak of it again. As of this moment I still feel bound by that promise" (Anhalt 1993:48).

The second episode is about my father and demonstrates how piecemeal information can suddenly coalesce with chance encounters and engender meaning in unexpected ways. For years I have asked my father to talk about his past, and he almost always has offered me political commentary or repeated a certain set of stories dealing with his ambiguous relationship to the Hitler Youth movement and his defiant attitude toward the Wehrmacht. His many stories somehow boiled down to two issues: his strong Catholic upbringing, which conflicted with Nazi ideals, and his small rebellious acts against the army (such as clandestinely listening to radio broadcasts of the Allies). His disillusionment with the Nazis, he said, began rather early and grew stronger after he overheard a neighbor boasting about killings on the Eastern front. From these stories, I distilled an image of my father as a conflicted young boy growing up in a small Czechoslovakian town far away from the atrocities of the Nazis. In my father's recollections, Jews never appeared.

When I moved to the United States in 1983 and began to learn about Jewish culture, I had many chances to talk with survivors, and when I occasionally visited Germany, I wanted to retell their stories to my family and friends. But my inability to convey my belief that Germans ought to listen to their stories was frustrating. When I talked to my family, I often had to resort to political and moral arguments in order to account for the importance of my experience. To them, it was not self-evident that their lives were in some ways bound up in present-day Jewish culture. My frustrations perhaps explain why I was so perplexed when my brother asked me if I wanted to find out whether our father was in a concentration camp. Unlike my brother, I was convinced that my German identity was linked to my quest to understand Jewish life in and after the Holocaust, and that my past was somehow tied to the stories of survivors.

In the summer of 1991 we invited Ed Gastfriend, a Jewish Polish survivor, to the Holocaust program to talk to the American and German students about his imprisonment in Auschwitz-Birkenau and his enslavement in a satellite camp of Auschwitz called Blechhammer. In Blechhammer (Blachownia in Polish) the Nazis had built a chemical factory that was surrounded by a dense network of camps for prisoners of war, Polish civilian prisoners, and Jewish slave laborers (cf. Piper 1967). Mr. Gastfriend recalled the brutal treatment, the harsh conditions, the beatings, the punishments, the small crematory. He wept after he finished his story.

Six months later, in January 1992, my parents came to visit my wife and me in the United States. One evening, my father volunteered to talk about the past, and again he told me some of the old familiar stories. I cautiously asked for more details: How and why was he drafted into the army? What were his military duties? How had he, as an eighteen-year-old, perceived the end of the war? At one point, my father mentioned almost in passing that he was stationed in Blechhammer. Immediately all my senses perked up. Did he say Blechhammer? Indeed he did. He was stationed there for several months, until November 1944, and was assigned to an anti-aircraft battalion that was to protect the chemical factory from Allied bombings. I asked him if he knew then of the slave-labor camp. He said he knew of the camps for POWs and Polish prisoners but had no knowledge of the existence of the Jewish labor camp. His platoon was stationed in the woods surrounding the factory, and he never came near any of the camps.

I then told my father that I had met a Jewish survivor from Blech-hammer. At first, my father did not know how to respond. He got very nervous, almost frightened. He then started to ask me about conditions in the Jewish camp and wanted to know everything Ed Gastfriend had told me. As I recounted what I remembered from Ed's story, my father recalled a day when his platoon had passed a column of emaciated prisoners in striped uniforms on their way to the factory. "Did you talk about this with your friends?" I asked him. No, he did not. No one talked about it. When I showed my father a recent picture of Ed Gastfriend, he studied it for a long time. He was clearly shaken and confused. He also began sharing other memories he had never mentioned before. He answered all my questions honestly. But I, too, was shaken. I had not imagined that my father had been so close to the center of destruction. I now found myself in the middle of two people I admired and for whom I felt a deep compassion: the survivor and my father, both of whom had been at the same place at the same time, but on opposite sides of the fence.

At the end of the evening, I handed my father an article on Blech-hammer that I had copied the previous summer in the archives of Auschwitz. He read it overnight; the next morning, he was pale and still shaken, and expressed anguish over the fact that he had not known about the existence of and conditions in the Jewish slave-labor camp. He was particularly distressed by the fact that Blechhammer possessed a crematory. For the first time he seemed to realize how close he had been to the cruelest aspect of the Nazi regime. Why did he not ask questions, I wondered. Did he comply with the general silence and with the prohibition against asking? Perhaps he believed more in Nazi ideology than he was able to admit today; perhaps he disbelieved the reality he saw, too frightened to admit to himself the extent of the cruelties. "In order to understand what I myself had experienced," a Jewish survivor of Sachsenhausen wrote, "I had to see it, so to speak, objectified on paper"

(Fackenheim 1975:27). The article on Blechhammer must have affected my father similarly. He did not understand the full scale of the Nazi camp system until he began reading about it. Had I not been familiar with Blechhammer, my father and I would not have had this conversation. I would not have associated anything with this place. I would not have interrupted my father's story, and the evening would have been quickly forgotten. A small crack in my father's story soon widened into an opening to the past, and for a few hours we had a candid but intimate conversation. I was not angry at my father. On the contrary, his vulnerability elicited my sadness. His story also gave me a sense of gratification and closure because it allowed me to make a personal connection between my family history and the history of Jewish survivors, a link I had been missing for so many years.

Eventually, though, I did get angry. A few days later I was struck that it was only a coincidence that had allowed us to retrieve those agonizing aspects of my father's past. Had I not known Blechhammer, my father's story would have simply remained lost—to himself, to me, and to others. I asked my father why he had never bothered to learn more about Blechhammer during the forty years since the war. "Isn't it ironic," I asked him, "that I do the work you should have done? Why do I have to tell you that there was a Jewish slave-labor camp in Blechhammer when it is really your task to tell me about your history?" "What is there to learn from my stories?" he responded. "There is nothing we can do about it today."

My anger could not override my feeling of sadness. I also hoped for a new beginning. My father took a copy of the article on Blechhammer back to Germany, intending to show it to his fellows from the anti-aircraft battalion, with whom he has been in contact sporadically. "Would you consider writing a letter to Ed Gastfriend?" I asked him. He declined, feeling that this would exceed his emotional strength. I wonder, though, whether one day it might be possible that people who have been on opposite sides of the fence will be able to show their faces to each other—and weep together.

In retrospect, I think my father and I gained trust during this evening, maybe because I caught him by surprise and left him vulnerable and insecure. But the story also reveals a number of betrayals. I realize that in a way I am standing in for my father whenever I talk to Jewish survivors. Ed Gastfriend should not have to talk to me, not knowing where to place his anger and depression; and I should not have to stand in for my father, not knowing where to place my vulnerability and feelings of shame. For him, listening to what I have learned from my encounters with Jewish survivors is easier than revealing his face. Not only am I replacing my father, I am also protecting him, for he can hide behind me. I am exposed; he is not. In a sense, my father's generation has refused to grow up; and we, the second and third generations, now have to decide whether we will follow in the our parents' and grandparents' footsteps or are willing to confront the legacy of our past.

Making this story about my father public does not come easy. On the one hand, I am somewhat embarrassed about admitting it to my Jewish friends. I eventually shared this incident with Ed Gastfriend himself, who responded with exceptional kindness and warmth. "There is no reason in the world," he wrote in a letter, "you should think that your father's revelation about his war years could possibly affect our friendship and relation."

On the other hand, there is my father. Would I betray our shared moment of intimacy and vulnerability by turning his personal revelation into a public narrative? Would he feel betrayed and, therefore, be more cautious about sharing his experiences in the future? Or would he understand that his past continues to influence the life of his son?

I am not sure that I know the answer to these questions. That it was my father, however, who first broached the issue of the past when he visited me in America gives me the hope that he, too, might be willing to find answers to the past. I sometimes wonder whether he is actually looking for someone who understands the context of his experience, someone who does not blame him but neither brushes aside the gravity of the moral failure of Nazi Germany.[10]

I conclude with Torsten, the East German student, who, during the same weekend that he visited a Jewish American family, happened to learn something that induced a new interest in his family history:

> One of the most intense experiences was my stay with a Jewish survivor family over Shabbat. Before the program, I was almost exclusively interested in the rise of antisemitism, racism and neo-fascism, especially in East Germany. . . . I had more of an intellectual connection to topics related to the Shoah and the German past, but I had

never had any personal contact with Jewish people. During my stay with the survivor family, I learned how deeply the events of the Shoah are ingrained in the Jewish community even after 50 years. I learned about the pain, and how much I am part of it as well. . . .

[My host family] welcomed us, and as I learned about the life of an American Jewish family, I noticed many similarities to my family. We talked intensely about our family histories, and we experienced the pain, grief and helplessness when confronted with the Shoah, affecting not only the parents but also their children, who have to live with their stress and despair. Even little details reminded me of the Shoah. For example, I never thought about the feelings of a child growing up without an extended family. What would it mean to get only a convoluted answer, or no answer at all, when asking the parents about the whereabouts of grandparents, uncles and aunts?

One of the most painful moments was my conversation with the mother of Ms. H. [his host]. This talk, I believe, changed me more than any of the books, articles, and documents I read. Ms. H.'s mother was born in Lithuania and lived before the fascist regime in Kaunas, close to the capital of Vilna. Lithuania was occupied by the Soviet Union after the Hitler-Stalin treaty. After the attack of Nazi Germany, Lithuanian Jews were persecuted and annihilated. With tears in her eyes, and a voice which betrayed despair and helplessness, she talked about the past, and how a German soldier had brutally murdered her child in front of her eyes. When I recalled that my own grandfather was a German soldier in Lithuania, I was for the first time shocked and bewildered about my personal ties to the Shoah and the past of my host family. (Krondorfer and Staffa 1992:34–38)

Asking the right questions, being intrigued by details, waiting for family patterns to change, hoping for incidental occurrences, steadfastly pursuing some type of research—those and similar strategies are capable of piercing the darkness that enfolds German family histories. By these means third-generation Germans can acknowledge their complicity in the conspiracy of silence and actively resist the third guilt.

The probing of old relationships to family members and the risking of new relationships with Jews changes the stalemate of public discourse, the social amnesia, and the negative symbiosis that characterize German attitudes toward Jewish/German relations and the memory of the Shoah. Only upon encountering their Jewish peers did the German students of the summer programs realize their emotional investment in the legacy of their families' silence. My wife, Katharina, remembered the newspaper article because she attended a Yom Ha-Shoah service in Philadelphia; thereafter she began to investigate her family's involvement in protecting a Nazi war criminal. My acquaintance with a Jewish survivor opened a door to my father's past and prompted a painful but intimate moment between my father and me. Torsten reassessed his grandfather's role as a German soldier in Lithuania after meeting a Jewish survivor from the same country. These and many other examples speak of the transformative power of cross-cultural encounters between Jews and Germans born after the Shoah.

5　From Generation
　　to Generation

History can't hurt because it's already past.
—A German historian, the son of a Nazi war criminal

I've never been able to tell my parents about any of my problems. I'm afraid of causing them any more pain. They have no
idea who I really am.
—A child of Jewish survivors

Injurious memory burdens the relations between the generations. The statement above, from a German historian whose
father stood trial in 1965, expresses the unself-conscious desire
of the children of perpetrators to repress their pain. But the
claim that history cannot hurt only reveals how painful the
memory must actually be to this man. The child of survivors,
on the other hand, is well aware of his active suppression, for
he does not want to hurt his parents.[1] Yet there are similarities:
both children are marked by injurious memory; both had been
prevented from sharing their growing pains with their parents
(survivors' children because of the overwhelming trauma of
their parents, German children because the war generation had
no patience for their "petty grievances"); and both developed
mechanisms to quell expressions of pain in their families.

The dysfunctions between first and second generations have
been transmitted to the third generation as well; they need to be
corrected if we want to heal the scars of Holocaust memory. To
do that, Jews and Germans can separately begin the process of
working through the legacy of silence and through feelings of
fear, mistrust, anger, and guilt. Each family, within the limits of
its cultural environment, can mend the intergenerational bonds
by improving communication skills or seeking therapeutic assistance. "Those in the second generation," Aaron Hass concluded
in his study on Jewish survivors' families, "might benefit from a

closer examination of their relationships with their survivor parents. Many children describe intense but superficial ties. . . . Greater communication, I believe, by parents about their past experiences and the continuing effects of those experiences . . . usually not only produces greater intimacy between parents and children but also provides a greater recognition of the strength of survivors" (1990:166). German families would benefit from the same advice.

But to seek a cure only within one's own culture can inadvertently repeat self-referential discursive practices and, in the worst scenario, stabilize collective pathologies. Jewish survivors may be too caught up in pain, and Germans in denial, to overcome intergenerational dysfunctions. A communitas of Jews and Germans, on the other hand, has the power to transform the stalemate of two people caught in the limitations of their cultural assumptions. In the previous chapter, I addressed the issue of the third generation's confronting personal memories within their own culture and showed how difficult it has been, especially for Germans, to uncover secrets of their family histories. But we also saw that the probing of family histories profited from cross-cultural encounters. In this chapter, I pick up a related theme and ask what happens when third-generation Jews and Germans are confronted with personal memories of Jewish survivors or German perpetrators.

The Appellplatz

The greatest similarity between the "children of persecuted and of persecutors . . . [is] a mission to rehabilitate their parents and undo the past," the psychoanalyst Judith Kestenberg cautiously concluded in a comparative study of the second generation (quoted in Bergmann and Jucovy 1990:165). Part of the rehabilitating mission of Jews and Germans of the second and third generations is to take up what the first generation has been unable to do: to meet, to talk, and to struggle with the legacy of the past across generational, cultural, and national boundaries. Because younger generations are further removed from the Shoah, they can seize opportunities to break away from the silence and instability of their parents and grandparents. "Since I have temporal distance and am privileged to study, I can rely on different means for thinking about the Nazi regime," wrote Iris, a West German student, in her reflections on the 1991 Holocaust program. Post-Shoah generations have the power to initiate transformation. Yet, as individuals we are often overwhelmed by the task of challenging our families' attitudes, where progress is often measured in painfully small steps. Collective efforts, however, stand a better chance of succeeding to break the biases of one's cultural environment. During the summer programs, I witnessed several cross-generational encounters in which people of different ages and backgrounds were able to establish affectionate bonds. The most remarkable occurred in the summer of 1991, when Ed Gastfriend, the survivor of Auschwitz-Birkenau, and Anne, a nineteen-year-old East German student, were able to reveal their agony and vulnerability in each other's presence. During a session on testimonies by survivors, both Anne and Ed took the risk of facing the pain in themselves and of facing the other and thus surmounted the invisible walls separating Jewish survivors from the grandchildren of victimizers. For a moment, Anne and Ed were able to transcend the roles history had imposed on them.

We had invited Ed to speak on the third day of the 1991 program. He told us that he grew up in a small town in Silesia. After Germany's occupation of Poland in 1939, his family, like all other Jews, was rounded up, humiliated, beaten, and conscripted for manual labor in their hometown. As a young boy, Ed helped to organize food for his family. Eventually, he was arrested by the Germans and sent to Auschwitz, where he was put into a quarantine barracks next to a special barracks for children selected for "medical" experimentation. To escape this fate, Ed followed the advice of a priest and fellow inmate and volunteered for slave labor at the first opportunity. He was sent to various slave-labor camps but stayed longest in Blechhammer, which was evacuated in 1945 when the Soviet army advanced. The Nazis, trying to erase all evidence of their extermination program, forced the inmates to march westward to the German Reich, territory still under Nazi control. During these death marches, Ed was driven from camp to camp and eventually ended up at Buchenwald, near the (former) East German town of Weimar. There he was liberated.

Recalling the horrors he had faced, Ed used short German phrases he had picked up from the camp guards. *Appellplatz,* the place for roll calls in the camps, was one of the words Ed repeatedly used. After he finished talking, Ed rushed out of the room and cried. Many of the German and American students cried as well. We took a break.

When we reassembled, Anne was still sobbing. Earlier in the program, during our session on family history, Anne had talked about her conflicted attachment to her grandmother, whom she loved dearly but who had been a Nazi and had been present at a deportation ramp. Now Anne could not control her tears after listening to Ed's story. She said it was especially painful to hear his use of the word *Appellplatz* because that had been the name applied to her school yard in the former East Germany. She and her fellow students had to gather regularly at the *Appellplatz* to listen to political speeches. Ed's use of the word made her aware, more than ever before, of how much her life was still tied to her country's past.

Ed Gastfriend listened to her, then got up from his chair, walked across the room, and embraced her. Anne, still in tears, was confused by his embrace but reluctantly accepted it. "It is wrong to be comforted by you because you were a victim of my grandparents' generation," she argued. But Ed disregarded her argument and stayed close to her until she calmed down. It was a touching and revealing moment because both Anne and Ed had dared to become vulnerable and share a moment of intimacy. To me, the Jewish survivor's embrace of a German grandchild of victimizers symbolized an acknowledgement as well as a triumph over the past: no longer defined simply as victim, Ed Gastfriend was able to reach out to the third generation and, by offering comfort to Anne, empowered himself.

Auschwitz was no longer an abstract concept, a metaphor. Rather, it had become a place connected to a human face, a human story. From the pain of specificity something new and unexpected can emerge.

Survivors: "The Difference between Heart and Head"

A week later Anne had another heart-wrenching encounter with a survivor. We had sent pairs of American and German students to stay for a weekend at the American homes of families of Jewish survivors or children of survivors. They got a glimpse of Jewish home life and celebrated the Sabbath, for most Germans for the first time.

Anne had a particularly memorable experience. Her host's mother, a survivor, visited on Friday night and brought a torn piece of fabric from her camp uniform to show to the German guest. Anne wanted to touch it but the mother panicked and shouted "No!" Frightened, Anne quickly withdrew her hand. At the intervention of Anne's host, the survivor eventually allowed Anne to touch the piece. But immediately afterward she insisted that Anne wash her hands. She even accompanied Anne to the bathroom and watched her clean her hands.

Anne's experience reminded me of the contaminating power of the memory of the Shoah. Memory, or even objects that recall the Shoah, like the piece of fabric from the camp uniform, can poison. Memories defile those who come into too close contact with them. In turn, memories can be defiled by those who approach them too casually. Injurious memory can assume negative sacred power.[2]

In his study of oral Holocaust testimonies, Lawrence Langer noted that the fear of trivialization informs a large part of the survivors' anguish over telling their stories. "People just won't understand," survivors often say. They fear that their memory may be defiled by the lack of understanding and indifference of outsiders. But the memory also threatens to consume the survivors and their listeners. "The Holocaust threatens to be a permanent hole in the ozone layer of history," Langer wrote in his introduction, "through which infiltrate the memories of a potentially crippling past" (1991:xv). When Anne wanted to touch the camp uniform, the survivor panicked, perhaps driven by the fear that a German might defile her past. But one can also interpret her gesture of quickly withdrawing the fabric as a protective, gentle act. She may have wanted to protect Anne from being contaminated by her anguished past, for she insisted that Anne wash her hands after she had touched the fabric. The survivor, I believe, was acting out a strongly felt, internal ambivalence: she took fright when Anne, a German, threatened to defile the fabric; but she may have also felt compassion for the young German, who was in danger of being "defiled" by this relic of terror.

If asked about her reactions, the survivor might have come up with a perfectly reasonable explanation of why Anne had to wash her hands. Her reactions to Anne, however, were too spontaneous to admit of rational motivation. The struggle between subliminal, visceral reactions and rational justifications befalls many Jewish survivors who meet young Germans. Survivors are wrestling with the discrepancy between what they feel and what they consciously want to convey. They want their stories to be heard, but why should they become vulnerable before Germans again? The general difficulty of talking about one's trauma and survival—which Langer described as being torn between two voices: "you won't understand" and "you must understand" (1991:xiv)—is amplified when Jewish survivors encounter third-generation Germans. Survivors know that the third generation cannot be held responsible for the crimes of their parents and grandparents. Still, the young are often the only Germans they will meet, and it takes an effort not to identify them with the Nazis of the past.

In 1989, the Philadelphia Interfaith Council on the Holocaust tried to arrange a meeting between Jewish survivors and students from the first summer program. The council negotiated with the Philadelphia Association of Jewish Holocaust Survivors about the scheduling of the evening. The planning proceeded slowly. Half of the members of the association wanted the event to take place, and the other half was vehemently opposed to it. Eventually we agreed on the importance of such a gathering and completed the planning. At the same time, the rumor spread that some survivors would picket the event.

As facilitators and organizers, we did not know how much substance there was to the rumor. We feared that a picket line by survivors would greatly antagonize the German and American students who had just begun to open up to each other. Fortunately, nothing happened when the students arrived at the synagogue where the meeting was to be held. On the contrary, nearly two hundred survivors and their families had gathered inside to welcome the students. Adinah, a Jewish-American student, remembered:

> I was expecting the gathering to be formal, forced and polite. (Strained, if anything, because it was probably the first time some of the survivors encountered Germans since the Holocaust.) Instead, it affected me profoundly. First, I was struck by the caring, grandparently way in which the older participants treated us, especially the Germans in our group. . . . The most moving aspect of the evening for me, though, was seeing one of the survivors walk by in front of me, with a number tattooed on his arms. I've seen many survivors with numbers on their arms before, but I'd always seen them in the capacity of speakers on the Holocaust experience. This man and all the other men and women walking around the room with numbers on their arms were just people eating lox and bagels. . . . At that moment it hit me that despite all they've been through, they now have lives just like my grandparents. . . . They have moved on. They have each found a way to deal with the Holocaust. Now it's my turn. (Krondorfer and Schmidt 1990:13)

Adinah expressed her surprise at how modest and pedestrian she found the survivors to be. I was surprised by how smoothly the evening went. Occasional tensions surfaced (at my table, for example, three people avoided all eye contact with me and another German for the entire evening). But the overall mood was unpretentious and friendly. Somewhat suspicious of the idea of Jewish/German reconciliation, the survivors nevertheless mustered enough courage and curiosity to welcome the third generation.

I have often been struck by how eager some survivors are to make contact with young Germans. If I conveyed my willingness to listen to them, they established a human bond, and the meeting often ended with our exchanging addresses. Never has a survivor used a meeting to attack me personally (though I often expected survivors to do exactly that). To be sure, there was always a mixture of anger, frustration, and tension. But mostly, these meetings were precious moments, for they gave us a chance to connect within a relatively safe framework. Perhaps all that Jewish survivors and young Germans can hope for are small gestures of redemption, moments in which meaning emerges out of sharing and listening to injurious memory.

I remember, for example, an evening at the Jewish Community Center in York, Pennsylvania. After a performance by the Jewish-German Dance Theatre, several survivors in the audience surrounded the German members of the company. Standing at the refreshments table in the reception hall, I was beseiged by elderly people who talked all at the same time, some in English, some in German. I could not focus on any particular conversation, and after a while I simply tried not be drowned in the outpouring of attention.

"I am from Mannheim. Do you know Mannheim?"

Yes, I tried to say, but someone else interrupted.

"My husband is from Kassel."

"I am from Düsseldorf. I fled after 1938. First to Palestine. It's just luck that we survived, just luck."

"Wo kommen Sie her?"

"I am from Frankfurt," I responded.

"Ach, Sie kommen aus Frankfurt. Ich kenne Frankfurt."

"You do?" I asked, but before getting an answer someone else urged me to eat.

"You have to taste my *Apfelkuchen*. It is a German recipe. Only the

Schlagsahne [whipped cream] is missing." The old lady giggled at her own German words but was hushed up by others.

"I could not tell my husband that I came to see your performance. He would not have been able to take it. He survived Auschwitz. I was in Bergen-Belsen."

The disjointed conversation did not seem to end. After forty minutes I escaped. I was grateful and tense and sad and overwhelmed—and I never got to taste the *Apfelkuchen*.

During the 1991 program on the Holocaust, the Jewish and Christian American and German students had a chance to talk to Abraham Foxman, the national director of the Anti-Defamation League. Foxman described the survivors' desire to tell their stories and their hesitation. It is like a struggle between head and heart, he said. Foxman, who had survived the Shoah as a child (he had been hidden by a non-Jewish family), delivered a passionate speech directed mainly at the German participants.

> "I try to put myself in your shoes. 'Why are we still talking about the Holocaust?' you think. Why are we still talking about it? . . . We have no choice," said Mr. Foxman, answering his own rhetorical question. "It is part of our heritage. . . . It is important that we talk and I can say to you: I hate the German language. Here," he said pointing to his heart, "but not here," and he pointed to his head.[3]

Foxman's recurring trope, the difference between heart and head, was a fitting description of the inner state of survivors. "You are innocent, yet you take part in the guilt," he said, looking at the German students. What the head knows might be in conflict with what the heart feels, but "we can only grow in our relationship if we allow pain and anger."

The Third Generation: "It Was a Little Harsh Sometimes"

The reactions of the German and American students to Foxman's speech were mixed. Surprisingly, the American Jewish and Christian students criticized him while the German students defended him. The Americans felt that his speech was theatrical and staged. His pointing to his heart and head, they said, was rehearsed and impersonal rather than spontaneous. His trope probably reflected the political agenda of his large organization. They also felt that it was inappropriate to "lay a guilt trip" on the Germans. In short, the Americans wanted to protect their German peers from what they perceived as the insensitivity displayed by a representative of the first generation.

The German students, on the other hand, claimed that Foxman's speech did not offend them. "It was a little harsh sometimes," one German said, "but I have to accept it because I understand the reason he feels that way."[4] The German students were even ready to accept his statement that young Germans although innocent, share in the guilt. "We, that is, Germans, Jews, Americans, and others are all responsible," said Volker, a theology student from West Germany, "but there must be special German responsibility—and perhaps it is guilt."

Among the Jewish American students, only Steven, the son of a survivor, defended Foxman. "I did not agree [with Foxman's opinion]," Steven wrote in his journal, "it was too harsh and unfair. Nonetheless, I was glad he said it because many Jews feel this way (emotionally if not rationally); we [the students] just haven't met any. Many of the Americans felt protective of the Germans at this point, but I did not. It was a viewpoint that needed to be heard" (Krondorfer and Staffa 1992:76).

Given the ethos of remembrance and the ethos of guilt and forgiveness, one would not expect that Jewish American students would criticize Foxman's speech and Germans defend it; rather, Germans would try to defend themselves against induced feelings of guilt, and Jews would welcome Foxman's speech since it tied in with the task of remembrance. That this was not the case accounts for the transformative power of communitas, which effected changes in the students' relationships. American Jews felt protective of their German peers while the German students, in turn, felt protective of survivors.

German students were often curious, surprised, and gentle when meeting Jewish survivors. However, like survivors, they were also ambivalent about cross-generational encounters. Anger, fear, and suspicion characterized some of the reactions of the third generation, especially if the encounters were not facilitated well. We need only recall the nervous energy and discomfort of the German students who had met with the Jewish-German Dance Theatre and Edith Millman, the survivor of the Warsaw ghetto, in a Philadelphia church, or the accusation of German students in the 1989 Holocaust program that the survivors we had invited as speakers tried to make them feel guilty. I also remember Jan, a West German student, who had felt uncomfortable during the weekend stay with a Jewish survivor family. Upon his return, he told the group that his hosts had made him feel uncomfortable because they had geared the discussion toward the issue of collective guilt. They also did not seem to appreciate the German book of paintings he had brought as a gift.

Jan could not put the reactions of his host family into perspective. Speaking from the place of a fragile cultural identity, Jan, like so many others in his generation, displayed a low level of tolerance for the ambivalence of his Jewish hosts toward Germans. Most Germans in the third generation do not know, for example, that a number of Jewish households boycott German products. Unaware of such a possibility, it strikes all the harder if, as in Jan's case, a German gift is not received with gratitude.

Agonizing moments are inevitably part of Jewish/German relations. Some misunderstandings and antagonisms can be eased by preparing Jews and Germans for meeting one another, but they ultimately cannot be prevented. Perhaps one should not even try to prevent those moments of agony, for they also have the power to make people think and change. Jan, for example, eventually got over his initial frustration. At the end of the program, he put together a slide show and introduced different German audiences to Jewish American culture.

East German students were especially fascinated by the personal memories of survivors. In 1991 and 1993, after the fall of the East German government, it was easy to recruit East German students for a program on the Holocaust. They were eager to absorb anything they had not had a chance to experience before. They had also preserved a refreshing emotional directness and innocence with which they responded to human pain. Anne's and Ed's bonding has already illustrated this immediacy. Mina K., a Jewish survivor from Poland, had a similarly strong impact on East Germans. Mina had escaped the German occupation of Poland by seeking refuge in the Soviet Union. She was twice offered Soviet citizenship. She declined and was punished with imprisonment in a Siberian slave-labor camp. The East German students had never before heard of Jews being persecuted in the Soviet Union during the same years when the Nazis waged their genocidal warfare. They had been taught—though they did not necessarily believe it—that the Soviet Union had protected the rights of minority cultures. East Germany took great pride in its antifascist tradition, but it had no diplomatic relations with Israel. Moreover, since few Jews lived in East Germany and the authorities severely restricted the right to travel abroad, most East Germans had never met Jews. "During our program, we had several heated debates about the question of how East Germany had approached the issue of the Holocaust," wrote Kay, an East German student:

> I do not think that it was a taboo. Rather, fascism was an important public subject, discussed in the media, schools and other GDR-institutions. The GDR saw itself as being rooted in the Communist resistance, to which a large part of the government belonged. However, to describe the discussion about the Holocaust is more difficult. In contrast to the exaggerated depiction of the persecution of Communists, the crimes against the Jewish people were not constantly discussed, though they were never denied. These crimes were less usable for propaganda purposes: they prevented you from claiming the status of a victim. . . .
>
> In our art classes, we looked at a painting by Hans Grundig, called "To the victims of fascism." The teacher insisted on the difference between the murder of righteous, communist resistance fighters and Jews, who misunderstood the nature of Nazi persecution. . . . As far as I am concerned, the goal of the education was to keep children ignorant of the responsibility of the German people.
>
> As children we learned that fascism is terrible but we did not conceive of it as part of our own history. When I was 8 or 9 years old, I told my parents that we played "partisans and fascists," and that we defeated the latter. My parents then told me that those fascists were really our grandparents. This was the first time that I understood the complexity of our relationship to the past, which exceeds a simple black and white picture. I had to come to terms with the fact that my grandfathers were soldiers in the German army. (Krondorfer and Staffa 1992:61ff)

Similarities and differences between East and West are apparent in this passage. The historical claim to victimhood legitimated the communist government in East Germany. That communists were victims of the Nazis was so overemphasized that Jewish victims were marginalized and overlooked. As in West Germany, family histories were neglected and Jews ignored. Whether communist or capitalist, German postwar society tried to write Jewish people out of history. The cold war provided both Germanies with an odd opportunity to disregard the Jewish victims of the Shoah. The West accused the East of continuing a dictatorship, and the East accused the West of harboring Nazi war criminals. Young East Germans had been stripped of the opportunity to reach out to the Jewish community, yet West Germans, who had been free to discover post-Shoah Jewish life, were similarly ignorant. The internal restrictions in the West functioned like the external borders in the East, with the result that most young Germans have never met Jewish survivors.

The German students who met Jewish survivors during the summer programs profited greatly from these cross-generational encounters. Unfortunately, the American students had fewer opportunities to experience similarly intense and productive encounters with first-generation Germans in Europe, for it is close to impossible to get former Nazis to talk to third-generation Jews. Thus, the German speakers they came into contact with had been in the political resistance and often had been prisoners in camps themselves. The American Jewish and Christian students rightly complained that they had been robbed of the chance to confront the first generation. They were not exposed to the same challenge and learning experience in Germany that Anne, Jan, and Kay, for example, had had in America. Even the weekend we arranged with German host families in Berlin in the 1989 program, to which pairs of German and American students were sent, turned out to be unproductive. The Americans returned frustrated because nothing happened during their stay at German homes. The families were friendly but remained either unwilling to or uninterested in talking about the Holocaust.

German street life, too, was calm. If American students expected to run into antisemites at every corner, they were disappointed. Nothing dramatic seemed to happen. They noticed the political graffiti on walls, and when they saw swastikas among the graffiti, which usually were crossed out or scribbled over with countermessages from the left, they asked for translations and explanations. Like many previous Jewish American visitors, they were suspicious of elderly Germans. What did these people do fifty years ago? Ben, an American student of Jewish and African descent, articulated his suspicion when sharing his thoughts on an incident in Berlin's subway. An older woman had entered the crowded subway and was looking for a seat. Ben spontaneously got up and offered her his place. Moments later he wondered whether he had offered a seat to someone who, fifty years earlier, had betrayed or persecuted her Jewish neighbors. He had gotten up in respect for his elders, Ben said. But did they really deserve his respect? When Ben later passed an antique shop, a similar thought crossed his mind. Where did the shop get the furniture, the paintings, the silverware, the jewelry? Had these pieces once belonged to a Jewish family?

Once, two Jewish students came across an outspoken antisemite:

Ariane: When we flew from Frankfurt to Berlin, the man who sat between Lena and me said that he was too young at the time, but if he were in the army, Hitler would have won. . . . He said that the Jews controlled the country because money was power and the Jews had most of the money. . . . The man constantly contradicted himself. He had started his argument with: "You all come here to say how bad Germany is! Hitler wasn't even a German. He was an Austrian." He was frustrating to listen to but what an eye opener. I felt almost if Jon [the co-facilitator] had planned to have that man sit next to us to test what we've learned.

Lena: I sat on the plane next to this man whose father fought in Hitler's army. He had defined opinions about Hitler's theories and practices. I was shaking when I got off the plane. We [in the summer program] have created such a microcosm of "idealism." It was weird, upsetting and challenging to see this point of view. (Krondorfer and Schmidt 1990:22)

When Lucia, a German student, heard what had happened on the plane she wrote in her journal how ironic it was that she had enjoyed the flight to Berlin, anticipating the chance to share "the city, my city, with the group." In the meantime, her American Jewish peers had had to endure a person who praised Hitler. "That is the situation," Lucia wrote. "Quite precisely. Turns my stomach."

If the American students did not get their equal share of talking directly to the perpetrators of Nazi crimes, they still met Jewish and non-Jewish survivors in Germany and Poland on several occasions. The survivors talked about their resistance or active work in the underground. This was new for the American participants because many Jewish survivors now living in the United States either were not political activists during the war or did not emphasize their political activities in their testimonies. On the other hand, survivors who had settled in Europe and were willing to talk to the third generation stressed their participation in the resistance.

German students especially appreciated the political context. Kurt Goldstein, a German Jew, had fought with the International Brigades in Spain and was handed over to the Germans by the French because he refused to join the Foreign Legion. He survived Auschwitz. Gad Beck, an assimilated German Jew, hid in Berlin and worked for the underground during the Nazi years. Franz von Hammerstein was connected to the Confessing Church and was later imprisoned in various camps. Sophia Boharecka and Cienciala Stanislaw, non-Jewish Polish survivors of Auschwitz, were active in the Polish resistance. "The political resistance of Sophia Boharecka and Kurt Goldstein showed me," wrote Barbara, a West German student, "that people did actively resist even during the Nazi regime, and they can serve as a model for my generation" (Krondorfer and Staffa 1992:29).

Encounters between the first and third generations in Europe were of valuable political content but stayed on a more intellectual level than those in the United States. The stories of survival and resistance to which the students were exposed in Berlin and Poland did not grab their attention on the same visceral level. It is perhaps easier to listen to survivors who were persecuted for political reasons. Politicized injurious memory facilitates the quest for meaning and is less threatening because it contains a spark of empowerment. Active resistance is straw to grasp at in the otherwise meaningless and disempowering universe of the Shoah. In our fantasy we may want survivors to be heroic resistance fighters (cf. Danieli 1980:366). It is far more terrifying to listen to stories of the persecution of people who were victimized for no other reason than that they were Jewish. The meaninglessness of suffering is hard to bear.

I want to conclude this chapter with a passage from Hartmut's journal about his weekend stay with a Jewish American survivor family. Hartmut was a West German participant in the 1989 program. Though very cerebral and rational in his approach to the Holocaust, in the passage below he acknowledged in a sensitive, nondefensive manner that the deep frictions between Jews and Germans across generations might never be fully overcome.

Flipping through photo albums. Jeanette [a child of survivors] is in touch with a number of relatives in Germany and traveled the Federal Republic as well as the GDR and Berlin some years ago, so she has an idea of what Germany is really like. The frequently mentioned "German-Jewish symbiosis" of pre-Nazi times comes to mind again, the galloping fascination with the "Berlin Jewish spirit" in the German media. Nostalgia, wishful thinking? Jeanette didn't dare to tell her father about the German guest, me. We will never be able to overcome the psychic havoc upon the mind of Holocaust survivors, cannot bridge the gap but must at least recognize the constant pain and understand that this part of German history hasn't passed. (Krondorfer and Schmidt 1990:10)

Indeed, neither pain nor history have died away; both live on as injurious memory. As time passes, anguish and antagonism become less apparent and less consuming—at least on the surface. Still, when third-generation Jews and Germans are confronted with personal memories of the first generation, the young and the old are engaged in the strenuous process of trying to render meaningful the suffering endured during and after the Holocaust. Scratch the surface and potentially crippling memory will invade our relationships and identities.

6 Whose History Is It Anyway?

The hunger for memory has been a remarkable cultural feature of the last decade.
—Charles Maier

The memory of an event is an interpretation of the event.
—Leon Wieseltier

Museums and Communitas

Reconciliation practiced in spontaneous communitas is, one might say, the opposite of museums and memorials. Museums and memorials are public representations of memory in the form of architectural and sculptural structures. By the time they are opened to public view, museums and memorials are already finished products; as such, they represent history as well as cultural and national identity.[1] In communitas, on the other hand, attention is given to process rather than product. Essential to communitas is the flow of social relations and human bonding rather than inflexible aesthetic and representative structures. Museums and memorials are concrete buildings, exhibit halls, sculptures, and other objects in and through which a community may or may not find itself mirrored, represented, and challenged. Going through a museum or standing in front of a sculpture, the public reacts to a solid manifestation of memory—and that is fundamentally a more passive relation than what transpires in spontaneous communitas.

In communitas, Jews and Germans approach questions of biographic and cultural memory by interacting with each other. It is a relational process geared toward a "growing inventory of an active memory" (Maier 1988:121). As a growing inventory, active memory can be continually tested, rearranged, refined, and transformed by a group. Communitas accommodates change: Jews and Germans join reconciliatory processes with

144

whatever (fixed) ideas they may have about memory and identity; but they are permitted and encouraged to revise those ideas as they expand their vision of how to integrate the memory of the Holocaust in their social relations. Museums and memorials are less flexible in that regard. To be sure, the creation of Holocaust museums and memorials is always preceded by public discourse. They undergo a planning phase in which the public (or its representatives) negotiates the continuum of its national identity and argues over its aesthetic and political representation. Once established, however, memorials and museums legitimate the historical representation of the dominant discourse. In Victor Turner's terminology, museums and memorials embody "structure" (1982); they represent and legitimate society. Communitas, on the other hand, embodies "anti-structure." Anti-structural environments are creative and innovative. They can subvert social norms and rejuvenate social relations.

By defining museums as structure and communitas as anti-structure I do not intend to construct an artificial opposition between conservative and innovative forces.[2] Rather I want to point to the different options societies have when approaching questions of memory and identity. In the 1980s, most of the attention and financial assistance was given to museums, and since then there has been a kind of craze to establish museums that memorialize the Holocaust. The U.S. Holocaust Memorial Museum opened in Washington, D.C., in April 1993, fifteen years after President Carter's Commission on the Holocaust recommended an "appropriate national memorial to the victims of the Holocaust" (Berenbaum 1981:7; cf. Miller 1990:220ff). The Beit Ha-Shoah—Museum of Tolerance was opened two months earlier in Los Angeles, and another Holocaust museum is planned for New York. In Germany, there were also plans for constructing a national Holocaust museum, although they were shelved after unification. Germany and America, it seems, have tried to satisfy the decade's "hunger for memory" by building new museums (Maier 1988:149).[3] At the same time, it has been very difficult to find sources to sponsor programs geared toward human encounters in cross-cultural settings.

The choice ought not to be museum or communitas. Both are "modes of human sociality" (Alexander 1991:151). Museums serve a valuable purpose in the task of remembering: they mirror and reflect the political and aesthetic consensus of a community or nation. But communitas pursues a similarly precious goal: there people together can examine how political communities go about the task of remembrance and how public remembrance relates to personal memory and identity. Both museums and communitas are important; the dialectic relationship between them keeps memory an active and growing inventory.

In this chapter, I will look at how and why a communitas of third-generation Jews and Germans plunged into a crisis when confronted with museums. On visits to the Holocaust Memorial Museum in Washington and to the reconstructed Rashi Synagogue and Jewish Museum in Worms, Germany, these young people experienced these sites of memory as painful and troublesome, but important questions and insights concerning the memorialization of the Shoah were generated. Are Americans permitted to appropriate European history? Germans asked. Are Germans allowed to represent Jewish history? American Jews wondered. Confronted with museum sites, young Jews and Germans accused each other of being possessive of "their" history. They were surprised to discover how deeply they were hurt and antagonized by public representations of memory.

A Holocaust Disneyland

Students of the Holocaust program in 1989 visited Washington. During the two-day stay, they took a specially arranged tour of the White House, saw the Vietnam Memorial, talked to a representative of the American Jewish Congress, attended a dinner reception at the German Friedrich Nauman Foundation, and visited the offices of the U.S. Holocaust Memorial Council. Of all these activities, the last provoked the fiercest discussion. It forced the students to confront their beliefs about how the public ought to represent their historic and national identity. They also struggled with the issues of trust and anger that underlay many of their discussions. For a moment, the crisis actually seemed so profound that my co-facilitator and I feared that people might leave the program. In the end, however, the group consolidated again.

When the students visited the offices of the Memorial Council, the Holocaust museum was still at the planning stage. Michael Berenbaum, the project director of the museum, welcomed the students and, using a miniature model, guided them through the exhibition. At the entrance, each visitor would get the passport of a victim, a kind of *curriculum vitae* helping the visitor to identify with a real person. In the elevator, visitors would listen to voices of American liberators. They would arrive at the top floor and begin a downward tour through rooms filled with artifacts, information boards, photographs, and videotapes, all arranged chronologically from the inception of a genocidal policy to its implementation in the death camps. The exhibition would end with the liberation of survivors. Before leaving, visitors would pass through a huge memorial hall in which they might contemplate the experience.

Berenbaum's informative presentation was followed by a slide show by Sarah Blumfield showing the architectural inspiration for the design of the building and technical aspects of the exhibition. In the brief discussion period that followed, the German students began to question the project. Why duplicate the museum in Yad Vashem? Why does it have to be the largest museum in the world? Why a museum that focuses only on victims? Can the Holocaust be understood without putting it into the broader context of German history? Would the museum create anti-German feelings? Why begin the exhibit with American liberators? "However beneficial, courageous and admirable . . . the liberation of the concentration camps by American soldiers [was], [to feature them at the entrance] seemed out of place to me," a German student wrote in her journal. "[This is] a display of national pride rather than a remembrance of what happened to the victims" (Krondorfer and Schmidt 1990:13). By the time the curator, Susan Morgenstein, came in to give the last presentation of the afternoon, tensions had grown among the students. The Germans were suspicious of the museum project as a whole; the Americans appreciated the idea of a national museum on the Holocaust.

The German mistrust of the American museum project came to a peak when Morgenstein made a minor error. Among a few artifacts donated to the museum by survivors from all over the world she presented a school report of a Jewish child. The curator mistranslated and misinterpreted this report, saying that Jewish children got poor grades in their segregated religion classes because the Nazis wanted to demonstrate their inferiority. The school report, however, stated just the opposite: Jews were given poor grades in all classes except religious education. An enclosed letter from the donor noted that "they had always Jewish teachers in their religion classes, and we, of course, got the kind of grades we deserved." When a German student discovered the curator's mistake, there was an uproar and a moment of triumph among the Germans. Her error proved to them that Americans should not be entrusted with the representation of German history; they were bound to make mistakes; they would misappropriate German history because they were guided by national interests. "I am afraid that the museum will become a Holocaust Disneyland," a German remarked angrily.

That evening I jotted down the following notes in my journal.

> Everyone was very emotional; the Americans were puzzled because of the strong outpouring of German emotions which they did not understand—they felt the museum project was a good thing. . . .
>
> My reading of the situation is that much of the German anger is also due to anti-Americanism: "The stupid Americans should not be allowed to talk about European history." There is a feeling of cultural imposition, a taking away of power. Perhaps this is how young Germans reveal their pride.

During an open forum on the following morning—a time when students could voice any of their concerns—they began to quarrel with one another. Instead of addressing the issue of their different reactions to the museum, they fought over the general structure of the program. Some of the Germans voiced their dissatisfaction and suggested that they be allowed to spend more time on their own while in Washington. One German wanted to leave the room; he did not want to participate in this open forum, he said, because the allotted three hours for visiting the National Gallery would not give him enough time. "I need a minimum of four hours for the Gallery," he said, "because I love paintings." Some American students quickly reminded him that the program was not about paintings or general sightseeing but about the Holocaust.

The student stayed, but the dispute dragged on for another hour. When it finally ended, nobody had mentioned the visit to the offices of the Memorial Council. The anger directed against each other and the program in general had diverted from the underlying fear of talking about the strong emotions expressed the previous day. The antagonism raised by the Holocaust museum was still too strong to be discussed. We ended the session with no resolution and, frustrated, the students dispersed in small groups to explore the city on their own. When we regathered in the evening, they at last were ready to talk. They raised important questions about the representation and appropriation of history, argued over the value of Holocaust museums, and compared institutionalized memorialization with their personal forms of remembering. "We had one of the best, if not the best, open forums about the Holocaust museum," a German student wrote in retrospect. Since the discussion was so important, I reconstruct parts of it from my notes.

Matthias, a German student, was the first to broach the issue of the visit. He complained about the poor presentations of the last two speakers; a Jewish student responded, "We all agree on the bad style, but let's talk about content." Jan (German) launched straight into the first substantive argument. The museum is not educational enough, he said. It is an object of prestige, intended to show off. "It would be better to spend the same money on ten groups of students for the next ten years." Jan also felt that the museum would raise anti-German sentiments, and he objected to the fact that American visitors were supposed to identify with the victims: "And afterwards they go to McDonald's."

Two Jewish American students also criticized the museum. Adinah generally approved of the idea of a Holocaust museum in Washington but thought there was a problem with the "American pride of liberation" that was displayed. Keino, an African American, criticized the museum for not focusing on the aftermath of the Holocaust. "It should be more directed toward the future."

"But why is the Holocaust part of American history to begin with?" asked Catherine (German).

"Because survivors live here," Jeremy (Jewish) responded.

Suzanne (Jewish) added, "Because the lessons are about survival."

"Because you need to start somewhere," Lena (Jewish) said.

"But Americans do not know much about European history," Catherine objected. "I also find it inappropriate to identify with victims because suffering is always personal and cannot be understood by outsiders like tourists."

Claudia (German) disagreed with Catherine: "It is the human touch we miss in German history. We learn facts in school but no personal stories."

"But museums should be built where things actually happened," Catherine continued to argue. "A memorial in America, yes—a museum, no."

At this point, Lucia (German) remarked: "I think it is important to have Holocaust education in the United States. But I had a problem with the two women speakers. I agree with Jan's concern that the museum can trigger German-hate, and I particularly disliked one of the women saying that 'this is what Germans always say.' I felt that the women would go form the impression that Germans don't like Holocaust education. I also have problems with bringing objects [of the Holocaust] over to this country. I feel that this is sacrilegious. To put a ramp, a cattle car, an oven in a museum is a cheap kind of symbolism."

Leon (Jewish) responded. "I am surprised by the outpouring of emotions, and I doubt the sincerity of the intellectual criticism. I think there are different reasons for the emotions. I think that there are possessive historical claims on the side of Germans. That upsets me for it prevents me as an American from learning. Why is it inappropriate to present the Holocaust in the United States?" After a brief interruption by Jan and Lucia, he continued: "The victim is central to our understanding of what took place since no one other than victims cared about the victims. Even the stories of survivors are hard to comprehend and to imagine, and the museum would help me to imagine victimization.".

Jan: "But this is a super-subjective attitude which is bound to make mistakes. Just think about the school report, for example."

Leon: "You take this incident as overly symbolic and transfer it to the whole project. That is really not fair."

Suzanne: "And the council is not all Jewish."

Jan: "But all the speakers were Jewish."

A Christian American student interrupted the argument to compare the Holocaust Museum to the Anne Frank House in Amsterdam, which she had visited the year before. "The Anne Frank House," she said, "is also part of a sightseeing tour in Amsterdam but still affects everybody. The same will happen in Washington."

Jan: "The Anne Frank House is pure information. It is not about victimization like the museum here. You can never feel like a victim—because you can't! And you shouldn't."

Leon: "Why shouldn't we try?"

Lucia, in a conciliatory move, agreed with Leon. "What is central to the issue here is the question: How do we learn? For example, the psychology of the SS man is often studied in Germany—that is wrong, because the SS man made a choice. I agree with Leon that listening to victims is important."

Adinah (Jewish) added: "People learn differently: there is cognitive learning, others learn visually or through listening and touching. Not everyone has a chance to go to Auschwitz, but on their way to the National Gallery, they might go to the museum."

"But what can you learn in it?" another German asked. "Would you make the connection to other genocides?"

"Again, there are different ways of learning," Adinah responded. "The Vietnam Memorial today affected me although I didn't learn anything about Vietnam."

"How can we fight antisemitism if there is no knowledge about the Holocaust?" a Christian American student asked, directing her question to the Germans. "The most upsetting thing for me is the talk about objectivity because, I mean, who else speaks out in behalf of the victims?"

"Fear scares you into action," Jeremy commented. "Therefore, it's good to have a museum."

Catherine returned to the issue of victimization. "You cannot identify with somebody who died forty years ago. It's too late for compassion."

Lena disagreed: "In the Holocaust, the personal was lost. Humans became '-isms.' I believe it is important to re-create the personal dimension."

"Perhaps Americans like feelings," Jan responded, "like a movie or a show. Germans like things intellectually."

"It is good to learn not only on an intellectual level," Gisa (German) countered.

"Can I tell you my conclusions?" Hartmut (German) asked. "I think the issue is the trivialization of history. In a museum which focuses on victimization, you can't understand the social background of the victims, and I doubt that American visitors can draw abstract conclusions and fill in the gaps."

"My concern is Jan's opening statement about McDonald's," said Suzanne. "I don't think that's a reality. You have to set a priority list of what you want to achieve if you're visiting Washington. If your emotions are negative, perhaps your priorities are wrong."

Diverse perspectives on how to remember the Holocaust are obvious in this discussion. Should the museum focus on victims and neglect the victimizers? Does such an approach distort history? Do Germans or Jews have a privileged claim to that history? "As a claim upon official memory," Charles Maier writes, "the victim's anguish comes to be seen as a valuable possession" (1988:161). The Holocaust museum in Washington focuses on that anguish, and the German students objected to this. They feared that the museum would distort the suffering and take it out of context by asking visitors to identify with the victims. Ultimately, the victims' suffering would be trivialized: tourists, Jan argued, would get a quick thrill before "going to McDonald's"; and Lucia felt that the museum would descend to a "cheap kind of symbolism."

We could disregard these statements as capricious, angry responses of young Germans had there not been similar opinions voiced by German critics when the museum opened in 1993. Those critics interpreted the American efforts to memorialize the Holocaust as opportunities to divert attention from domestic problems. American Holocaust museums, a German critic said, have "less to do with the German past than with the American present."[4] The magazine *Der Spiegel* published, for example, an article by the journalist Henryk Broder claiming that in a few years the Holocaust would become a trademark of America, like "Mickey Mouse, Coca Cola, and McDonald's" (Broder 1993). Similar concerns were raised by some Americans as well. Recalling Saul Friedländer's criticism of the vulgarization of the Holocaust, Judith Miller (1990:232) wondered whether the museum in Washington was in danger of transforming "Europe's most searing genocide . . . into an American version of kitsch," thus representing a "considerable threat to dignified remembrance." Like the German students, Miller questioned whether the Holocaust can be claimed as an American experience. "While it is now evident that the United States did not do enough to prevent the genocide in Europe or to stop it once it had started, the Holocaust is not an American experience. Americans did not do it, nor were they its targets or victims" (1990:233). Philip Gourevitch, the cultural editor of *Forward*, also has questioned the museum's mission of Americanizing the Holocaust. America lacks a positive metaphor for its history, he argues, and the museum is supposed to fill this void by reminding Americans of the reality of absolute evil—though this evil has been committed not at home but elsewhere (the argument recalls the German students' possessive claim of the Holocaust as European history). Gourevitch furthermore objects to the museum's overabundance of video monitors which show the killing of Jews *ad nauseam*. "Violence and the grotesque," he writes, "are central to the American aesthetic, and the Holocaust museum provides both amply. . . . [O]ne is repeatedly forced into the role of a voyeur of the prurient" (1993:60f).

The Jewish and Christian American students of the 1989 program objected to such criticism. By focusing on victims, they argued, the Washington museum would give their suffering the attention it has long deserved. Visitors would be able to "imagine victimization" and see Jewish victims as human. The museum would help to personalize the abstract figure of six million Jews who perished in the Shoah. Leon Wieseltier (1993:18–20), the editor of *The New Republic,* raised similar concerns in an essay on the museum. It is important, he wrote, to represent the Holocaust by commemorating the "precise pain" of victims and exhibiting the "painful precision" of historians. As a "house of memory *and* history," the museum is a visual assault, "a rape of the eye"; but because the Nazis themselves documented their genocidal program with obsession and voyeuristic pleasure, the visual evidence of the brutal killings is irrevocably part of Holocaust history, memory, and historiography and hence must be displayed in the museum.

I wonder, though, whether the American students brushed off German objections too quickly. Because young Americans have grown up in a multimedia age of instant replays and the constant availability of visual information, they may have overlooked the viable grievance over the museum's catering to American taste, "where the public's attention span is measured in seconds and minutes rather than years and decades . . . [and] where sentimentality replaces insight and empathy" (Miller 1990:232). Robert Alter issued a similar warning in 1981. Criticizing the plans for a multimedia project of the Wiesenthal Center for Holocaust Studies in Los Angeles, he wrote: "Mustering all the riches of American electronic gimmickry, the conceivers of the project above all want to make the Holocaust, as they say, an 'experience,' to sell to millions. The ultimate aim is not to ponder or remember or understand the Holocaust but to simulate it." The aim of this simulation, Alter contended, is "to create what can never be created in this spurious manner, a sense of identity."

Can a museum never create a sense of identity, as Alter claims? Perhaps. But we know that it can at least threaten identity, as the students' debate over the legitimacy of the Holocaust museum has demonstrated. Mistrust informed many of their arguments. The Germans did not trust Americans to represent "their" European history accurately. They felt that Americans lacked the intellectual maturity to cope with the history of the Holocaust and accused them of cheap sentimentality. "You can never feel like a victim . . . and you shouldn't," the German group argued—an argument likely to be misunderstood. Indeed, the Jewish students heard the Germans say that they were unwilling to be compassionate toward the victims (Catherine had said that "it's too late for compassion"). But the German detachment was only part of the story. When the German students argued against identifying with the victims, they also expressed indirectly their own precarious situation. With whom should they identify, the perpetrators or the victims? Third-generation Germans can neither embrace Germany's past, unless they pursue a nationalistic agenda, nor claim the status of victimhood, unless they risk offending the real victims of the Nazi onslaught. That German students thought of themselves as approaching the museum in Washington intellectually ("Germans like things intellectually") reflects the moral and emotional ambiguity with which they struggled when confronted with the question of identity and memory. Their solution to this deeply ambivalent situation—that is, their need to distance themselves from their national past without falsely identifying with the victims—was to intellectualize the problem.[5]

The German intellectual detachment drew strong reactions from the American students, who reproached the Germans for wanting to depersonalize suffering and ignore the perspective of victims. They also felt that the Germans were possessive of the past. What they overlooked, however, was that a Holocaust museum can be accepted more easily if it emphasizes the victimization of one's own history and people. Americans can identify with the liberator and the victim; at worst, they are reproached for their indifference as bystanders. The victimizer, however, is always the "other." But for third-generation Germans, the victimizer is not the "other" but the skeleton in their nation's and their families' closets.

The debate about the Holocaust museum plunged the communitas of students into crisis. The Germans perceived the American version of publicly memorializing the Holocaust as a threat to their identity; Americans defended that version. In only a few days their roles were to be reversed.

At Rashi's Synagogue

Once the students arrived in Germany, the American Jews rejected Germany's memorialization of Jewish history. In Washington, the German students had possessively claimed the Holocaust as "their" history; now, in Germany, the Jewish American students wanted to hold on to "their" Shoah. In the 1989 program, the conflict emerged as early as the second day, when the students visited a medieval synagogue in Worms. I was not surprised, in part because of what had happened in Washington and in part because I had visited the Worms synagogue with Jewish friends before. Actually, I have had the chance to see it three times, each time with a different group. The visits helped me gradually develop a sensitivity toward the pain stored in places in which Jewish life once flourished. Without the presence of Jewish friends, however, I doubt that I would have understood the tremendous loss reverberating in the deserted synagogue.

I went to Worms for the first time in the summer of 1980, when I was still a student of theology and was studying Hebrew at Frankfurt University. Our teacher, an assistant affiliated with a communist student union, took our class to the synagogue in order to introduce us to Jewish life in Germany. The synagogue, the oldest in Germany, was founded in the eleventh century, when the famous rabbi and scholar Rashi lived in the city. The original building was severely damaged during the Crusades, and a new synagogue was erected in the twelfth century. The second building was destroyed during Kristallnacht in 1938. Rebuilt in the early 1960s, the synagogue today remains empty but open to visitors. A museum of Jewish artifacts has been added; it is located in the so-called Rashi House, next to the synagogue.

The place did not impress me particularly on my first visit. Ignorant about Jewish European history, I could not fit a medieval rabbi into my worldview or register the fact this empty building had been peopled with Jews only forty years earlier. I doubt that any of my fellow theology students had a more profound experience; in our conversations we did not link the visit to our efforts to study the Old Testament in Hebrew. The absence of Jews must have been so thoroughly ingrained in our minds that we did not even notice the loss of Jewish culture from our midst.

This indifference changed dramatically when I returned eight years later with my American Jewish friends and fellow artists from the Jewish-German Dance Theatre. It was November 1988, a time when hundreds of events all over the country commemorated the fiftieth anniversary of Kristallnacht.

On our way from a performance in Tübingen to Hanau, we took a detour to visit Worms. We arrived at the synagogue late in the afternoon, shortly before an inhospitable janitor locked the grounds. I remembered the place from my days as a theology student and wanted to show my friends around. But, to my frustration, my Jewish friends wanted to be alone. Their mood was grim. They seemed less impressed by the smell of moisture emanating from the old stairs leading down to the ritual baths, the *mikvah,* than by the absence of Jews. They did not appreciate the medieval building but could only see an empty synagogue. They ignored the art exhibition in the synagogue's women's section and were distressed by the fact that, in lieu of a daily prayer book, only a book for the high holidays was available.

I did not yet understand. When Lisa, one of the dancers, complained that the synagogue did not even have a prayer book, I got defensive and said that this neglect was, after all, the responsibility of the Jewish community. Lisa did not respond. She sat down on a bench and began praying in Hebrew. I immediately felt a knot in my stomach, in part because I was embarrassed, in part because her prayer seemed a theatrical gesture. When Lisa ended her prayer, she abruptly left the synagogue and started sobbing. She refused to be consoled. "I feel German, excluded, and angry," I wrote in my journal on this day.

Later, at dusk, we went to the old Jewish cemetery in Worms. Again everyone went his or her own way, and again I felt isolated and excluded from the grief my Jewish friends experienced. Sheila, another dancer, wept and said she did not want to see any other Jewish cemetery in Germany. "It is too hard on me," she admitted. For me, however, the cemetery had "a calming effect," as I wrote in my journal. "I see less of the terror than I see history, or better, stories of the past eight hundred years, stories of normal and happy lives. It is not the graves that are testimony to the Holocaust. Rather it is the absence of graves after 1942 which gives the Holocaust its presence." I also scribbled a question in my journal: "Why is this place so depressing for Jews while I and my German [male] companions do not have a similar emotional outburst? Is it because I am a man or because I am German? Unfortunately, we do not find time in the group to talk about these issues."

A year later I returned to Worms again, this time with the students of the 1989 program, on their second day in Germany. We were stopping at places of Jewish life in the Rhine Valley. The synagogue in Worms was our first stop. We went directly to the adjunct museum, the Rashi House, where we were supposed to get a tour of the exhibition. The tour guide was friendly and knowledgeable but seemed detached. She offered a historical and "objective" presentation, tracing the history of Jews in Worms and drawing our attention to various religious objects whose purpose she briefly explained. She did not, however, adjust her presentation to the needs of our group. In the context of a group of American Jews and Germans, her detachment was irritating, and small mistakes took on greater significance: she said "Israeli" when speaking of Jews. She did not exactly ignore Nazi history but somehow managed to gloss over uncomfortable details. She mentioned, for example, that at the end of the war Allied bombers had destroyed what was left of the synagogue after it had been set ablaze during Kristallnacht. Although this was true, she did not mention that in 1942 the Nazis had already dynamited the walls that had survived the fire in 1938. There could not have been much left to be destroyed by Allied bombing raids.

As she took us through the museum, we saw seder plates, menorahs, candleholders for Shabbat, and embroidered tablecloths neatly arranged in glass display cases. We looked at pictures of the synagogue before 1938 and its torched ruins afterwards. We saw burned Torah scrolls and prayer shawls behind glass. For the German students, and for myself, there was nothing unusual about the exhibition; it was like many others in Germany. The only thing different was the presence of our Jewish peers, which motivated us to listen more carefully to the tour guide's presentation of German history. But we were not overly distressed by the museum itself. That changed abruptly when we heard the muffled sound of sobbing: two of the American Jewish women were in tears. Lena wrote in her journal:

> For the first time on this trip it really struck me. This museum is the only way in which many people in this community will ever know of Judaism, Jews and Jewish life. The museum is two big rooms, plus basement. Approximately twelve glass cases worth of "artifacts." So little in remembrance of a once thriving community. There are only two Jews left in Worms, . . . not even enough for a *minyan*.
>
> I'm not quite sure what I felt at first on this tour of the Rashi-House. Disgust, hatred, fear, sadness. Then I saw a case which held a Torah and *b'rith* shawls in it. Both were burned. At this point I couldn't help but cry. . . .

> What ran through my head was [a] saying that if the Torah is
> even dropped or the slightest bit torn the whole congregation fasts
> for at least twenty-four hours. . . . And here the documents were
> burned. How it must have destroyed the people of its congregation.
> (Krondorfer and Schmidt 1990:18f)[6]

Noticing the emotional turmoil among the Jewish students I recalled
my own experience a year earlier, when I had been upset and confused
by the reactions of my Jewish colleagues from the dance company.
Whereas the American Jewish students mourned the tangible absence of
their people on the grounds of this former synagogue, the Germans distanced themselves and did not know how to handle the outpouring of
emotion. A humorous moment occurred when Hans, a member of a
German interfaith organization who accompanied the students to
Worms, turned to Lena and asked, with great sincerity and empathy,
whether she was crying because of allergies. The question was so incongruous that I would have smiled if the embarrassment on all sides had
been less contagious.

There was no time in Worms to process the reactions. Three more
visits were scheduled for the day: to the Martin Buber House in Hep-
penheim, the empty synagogue in Helmsbach, which had been a warehouse until recently, and a modern, luxurious synagogue newly erected
in Darmstadt by the city government for its small Jewish community. A
serious discussion of the day's events did not take place until evening.

When the open forum started, everyone was tired. The students
devoted the first half of the session to general complaints about the program instead of sharing their impressions of the day. As in Washington,
the atmosphere grew so tense that my co-facilitator and I feared a major
explosion. And sure enough, a new crisis was in the making. Dominant
voices in the German group accused the facilitators of having a "hidden
agenda" and proposed that we skip the trip to the Central Office for the
Persecution of Nazi War Criminals in Ludwigsburg scheduled for the
next day. In the ensuing discussion, the Americans defended the program, and when the German proposal came to a vote only two participants opposed the trip to Ludwigsburg.

It was 9:30 p.m. when the group finally began to talk about the day's
events. The Jewish students expressed their sorrow over the absence of
Jews in Germany. The empty synagogue in Worms and the display of
religious artifacts in the museum bothered them particularly.

"In the museum I felt like the last Jew in Germany," said Jeremy. "It felt as if I was standing behind the glass."

Lena said she now understood why she could never live in Germany. "I couldn't live here either," Suzanne agreed. "It is a double-edged sword, though. I know that you have to bring Jewish culture back here, but you can't exist here either."

"Hitler's attempt to rid Germany of Jews has been successful," Leon commented, "because everything is behind glass today."

"Will antisemitism rise again because of all the money that is poured into the rebuilding of synagogues?" Isac asked the group.

"I don't even know for whom the museum exists," Suzanne remarked.

Many of the German students were disturbed by the Americans' harsh judgments after only one day in Germany. A few Germans took it upon themselves to refute, defend, and explain each complaint the Jewish students were expressing. It seemed difficult simply to listen. Inevitably, Jews and Germans got stuck in defensive positions. When Leon said he was "surprised how thoroughly Judaism and the Holocaust became history in this country," Jan quickly responded: "And I was surprised to hear survivors speak in the United States and to see that the Holocaust is not history." What could have turned into an intimate sharing of feelings was lost in a general frenzy. People retorted without listening, cut each other short, and reproached each other for not understanding.

The group did not resolve the conflict during this evening. Their journal entries, however, revealed more conciliatory sentiments. In their personal writings, the students were willing to admit ambivalent feelings and give time and attention to other perspectives. Differences remained, but they were far less dramatic than what one would have expected from their positions during the evening's discussion.

Adinah (Jewish): I kept staring out the window [of the bus] at the beautiful scenery we were passing, and felt sick to my stomach: . . . those are the same beautiful trees and blue skies that my ancestors would have seen out the window of the cattle cars that took them to their deaths—*would* have seen if there had been windows out of which to look. I don't know if this is anti-Germanism. I don't feel particularly anti-German, just anti-Germany. Am I able to hold this country itself guilty when I don't feel its current inhabitants are guilty? I don't know what to make of all this. I'm not feeling very open-minded right now. It's a beautiful country whose beauty is hidden from me behind the thick scar tissue of the past.

Jan (German): One of the many discoveries of the trip for me was "my positive feeling" upon our return to Germany after the American part of the program. Just as important was discovering my defensive reaction toward criticism of my home. For instance, I never dreamt it possible that statements like: "I could never live here!" could have been so injurious to me, even considering the history of the Holocaust and its consequences. I became conscious of how much I identify, feel, and define myself as a German. Moreover, I find it difficult to say anything other than: "I don't think I could live anywhere else"—despite the Holocaust.

Lena (Jewish): In our group we discussed whether we could ever as Jews live in Germany. I said I couldn't. How could I choose to raise my children and live my life in a country which historically destroyed millions of breaths?

Gisa (German): It was a shock for me to come back to Germany, the country I am living in, and look at it with the help of Jewish eyes. I realize that Jewish culture is mainly in museums, without community life.

Isac (Jewish): What does it feel like to be in a place that only 50 years ago was a thriving community? . . . Does everything become OK when a synagogue is restored after being a mattress-frame warehouse, or the newest synagogue in the world is built by the government in Darmstadt? . . . Will later generations say: "Hey, Jews, leave us alone, we did enough for you after the war. We rebuilt your synagogues, paid reparations to survivors. It's the past and we're not responsible to you anymore." . . . Why tamper with fire? Why do Israelis want to come here? It is paradoxical. (Krondorfer and Schmidt 1990:16–20)

The journal entries reveal that the students were able to learn from each other although they had been unable to admit this in front of the whole group. Without abandoning their own positions, they acknowledged and included other perspectives. Germany "is a beautiful coun-

try," Adinah was able to say, although the "but" lingered behind her affirmative remark. "I never dreamt it possible that statements like: 'I could
never live here!' could have been so injurious to me," Jan admitted,
although he could not imagine living anywhere else. These were
instances of small transformations. Previously held beliefs about one's
own identity were altered without denying one's cultural roots and communal belonging.

These transformations could not have occurred had third-generation Germans and Jews gone to these places as separate groups. They
occurred because the students visited the museums together and because
together they approached the perplexing issue of public memory. "Advo-
cates of memory cannot have just the memories they want," writes
Charles Maier. "Memory . . . is complex. Like 'historization,' it can be
used, not to confront the past, but to complicate it" (1988:161). The students certainly experienced this complexity. At the Holocaust Memorial Museum in Washington, Germans perceived the emphasis on Germans as victimizers as a threat to their identity. They feared that the
museum would decontextualize the Holocaust and portray them only as
villains. Had the Germans stayed among themselves, they could easily
have trashed the American memorialization of the Shoah as Disneyland
sentimentality, not realizing that their anti-American feelings could be
perceived as a "typical" German insensitivity toward Jews. But faced
with the reactions of Jewish and Christian Americans, their reactions
were turned into an issue of group dynamics that had to be resolved.
The same happened in Worms, where Jewish students objected to the
historization of Jews. The local Jewish museum, they feared, looked at
Jews as a relic of the past, as if they were no longer alive as a people
and culture. Their jumping to the conclusion on the first day that they
"could never live in Germany" as Jews hurt the Germans and pushed
them into a corner.

When these sentiments surfaced, students realized that their visceral
responses and intellectual objections had the power to antagonize and
hurt others. They realized that they could not criticize the museums
without affecting social relationships. But as part of a communitas, the
German and Jewish students were prevented from having a threatening experience turn into lasting hostility. Before a culturally conditioned
perception could degenerate into a prejudice, it became a group-
dynamic issue that called for immediate attention. Initially adverse reac-

tions were transformed into a refined understanding of the complex links between memory and identity.

"How scared we are of going to Auschwitz," Lucia wrote in her journal two days after the visit to Rashi's synagogue. If Washington and Worms elicited such strong emotions, what would Auschwitz do to the group? Would the fragile bonds among the American, Jewish, and German students break again? Indeed, questions of memory and identity, which the students had resolved to a certain extent in their discussions about the museums, forcefully reemerged in Auschwitz. I return to these questions in the last chapter. But before traveling to this landscape of utter evil, I will introduce another dimension of reconciliation: the intersection of memory, body, and performance.

7   Memory Embodied

All of one's past—historical and evolutionary—is contained in
the body.
—**Joseph Chaikin**

To remember, we must be willing to enter the anxiety and
despair that the Holocaust evokes.
—**Alan Rosenberg**

How do we cope with Holocaust memories and images inscribed
into our bodies? How can we access deeply felt beliefs in the
roles we embody as Jews and Germans in a post-Shoah world?
The body remembers, although we are generally oblivious to
how we embody and enact personal and cultural memory. We
may notice embodied memory when we develop psychosomatic
symptoms, and we often count on medical treatment to relieve
the pain. But there is, perhaps, a better cure: to use our bodies
actively and creatively in the task of remembrance and reconciliation. I will argue in this chapter that Jews and Germans
who interact physically and spontaneously in a protective environment become aware of how their bodies have stored and
expressed injurious memory, and that this awareness can help to
transform stale Holocaust discourses into trusting and affirmative relationships.

Body in Pain

The history of the Holocaust contains a multitude of stories
about the physical violation, humiliation, and destruction of
Jews and others. Remembering this history elicits strong bodily
reactions. We know from survivors how physical and anguished
the resuscitation of "deep memory" can be (cf. Langer 1991). In
Claude Lanzmann's monumental documentary *Shoah*, for example, the body language of survivors often betrays the pain they

experience when asked to remember the past. But we also see the stoic faces of perpetrators who shut themselves off from all injurious memory. For the perpetrators, it seems, the repression of memory is desirable, and its resuscitation is not.

Suppressed memory, however, can return with a vengeance. An American Jewish newspaper, for example, carried the story of a man in the West German town of Schermbeck who spoke up during a commemorative service at the fiftieth anniversary of Kristallnacht, to which former Jewish residents had been invited. It was on this occasion that the old man admitted having taken part in the pogrom fifty years earlier. "The next morning," the paper reported, he "was in the hospital. He died soon after." Once he had unburdened himself of his guilt, the report implied, his health abandoned him.[1]

It is the exception, not the rule, that the return of repressed memory results in a fatal psychosomatic reaction. In most cases, injurious memory seeps unnoticed into the family networks of individual perpetrators and social institutions, where it remains latent. Whatever has not been resolved by the first generation—whether it is pain or denial—resurfaces in subsequent generations and affects them not only intellectually but also physically. The students of the Holocaust programs, for example, developed stomach pains and headaches, vomited, and often felt paralyzed. During their visit to Auschwitz, a Jewish American student suffered from severe stomach pains, stopped eating, and withdrew into herself for several days. Her condition improved after I suggested to her that she may be grieving. A striking psychosomatic reaction befell a West German student a day before the trip to the death camps. She woke up with a massive eye inflammation; her eyes and cheeks were so swollen that she could hardly see. (Her condition improved once we arrived in Auschwitz.) Erica, a Jewish member of the Jewish-German Dance Theatre, also developed an allergic inflammation of her eyes when we toured Germany in 1988.

How do we cope with these bodily reactions to Holocaust memory? Should we ignore or acknowledge them? When Anne, an East German student, arrived in Berlin halfway through the 1991 program, she complained of stomach pains and went to a doctor. The doctor could not diagnose any illness, but when he found out that she was participating in a program on the Holocaust, he said simply: "Leave the program. It's too hard on you." His advice could have been that of a caring professional, although it reminded me of the antitherapeutic silence that Germany has prescribed for itself ever since the end of the war. If memory hurts, the physician seemed to suggest, avoid it. But would that really heal the wounds? The body remembers and responds to anguish, even if it is repressed. Remembering is also a bodily experience. "To remember, we must be willing to enter the anxiety and despair that the Holocaust evokes," the philosopher Alan Rosenberg writes. "The process is painful. The pain is inseparable from understanding. The road to understanding passes through anguish" (1988:383). Understanding is more than intellectual cognition: it is becoming vulnerable to experience.

Jews and Germans committed to the task of remembrance and reconciliation do not have to wait until the body sends out psychosomatic signals of stress and anxiety. Rather, a conscious approach to the bodily dimension of remembering the Shoah can be made an integral part of reconciliatory practices. A communitas, which provides zones for exploring "direct, immediate and total confrontation of human identities" (Turner 1982:47), engages participants on all levels of being, including the body. Awareness of the bodily dimension of injurious memory should be as much a part of Jewish/German encounters as political discussions and intellectual reflections. To change the static Jewish/German symbiosis into a more vital and intimate relationship, we had better pay attention to what we can learn from and through our bodies.

Improvisation as Reconciliatory Practice

For me, it was modern dance and experimental theater that offered the possibility of exploring Holocaust memory through creative movements and other body-conscious approaches. I had become disenchanted with the purely verbal communication of Jewish and Christian, and Jewish and German, dialogue groups as well as the public discourse of Holocaust commemorations because they often avoided emotional honesty by hiding behind a safe and stale rhetoric. I wanted Jews and Germans to become vulnerable in each other's presence; talking alone did not serve this goal. I knew that if I could creatively express the bodily tensions I felt in encounters with American Jews, I would better understand the dynamics between us; I assumed the same would be true for Jews. When a few American-Jewish and German artists expressed interest in the same issue, we formed the Jewish-German Dance Theatre in the winter of 1985.[2] It was in this group that I first experienced the power of creative rituals.

For four years, we met regularly for rehearsals. The first months of working together were intense, raw, and alive, but later our rehearsals became more technical due to a demanding performance schedule. We showed our piece "But What About the Holocaust?" to small theaters and Jewish community centers in Philadelphia, Boston, and other locations on the East Coast and, as we became more confident, decided to tour Germany for four weeks during the fiftieth anniversary of Kristallnacht in 1988. We performed our production in seventeen German cities and offered workshops at several occasions. This tour was followed by a series of performances in Pittsburgh, Harrisburg, New York, and other cities and by a second tour of Germany in June 1989. Years of intimately working with each other and a fast-paced year of performing on two sides of the Atlantic had left us emotionally drained, and since each of us also felt the need to get on with other aspects of our lives, we decided to disband.

The dance company is an example of a communitas of Jewish and German artists who consciously employed the body for understanding how their identities were linked to the memory of the Shoah. Coming from different artistic backgrounds—some professionally trained in modern dance, others, like myself, specializing in experimental drama— we used our diverse skills to explore collaboratively issues of personal and cultural memory beyond the narrow frames of official discursive practices. Mostly through improvisation, movement became our primary medium. Improvisatory movement, as one of our members has written, "offered us opportunities to engage in a total experience plumbing the emotional, intellectual and psychological dimensions of our relationships to the Holocaust. Physical expression elucidated the barriers and confrontations between us and at the same time engendered group bonding. . . . [O]ur bodies were a constant common base . . . [that] reminded us of our fundamental equality [and connected] us to forces larger than ourselves" (Green 1992:26). Our improvisations deemphasized intellectual and text-centered approaches and instead focused on emotional and body-centered processes. It was in rehearsals, "the essential ritual action of theatre," (Schechner 1977:132), that we began our journey into the dangerous territory of Holocaust memory, from which we eventually emerged with a performance that challenged American and German audiences.

In the beginning, we did not know what to expect from one another, nor did we anticipate the depth we would reach and the struggles that would ensue. We were stimulated by autobiographical memories, dreams, emotional responses, news items, and a questionnaire about prejudice. We talked to survivors, read books, and viewed selected films together (such as Eli Wiesel's *Night* and Claude Lanzmann's *Shoah*). Our consulting this and other material had but one main purpose: to support our improvisational, body-conscious, movement-oriented approach (cf. Krondorfer 1988, 1989).

I believe that our focus on improvisation was critical for the success of our experiment. To be able to think of our rehearsals as incomplete, fluid, and improvisatory gave us the protection we needed for entering the scary place of direct human encounters. As long as we improvised, we could explore ambiguous feelings without having to formulate definitive positions by which we would be judged. Our rehearsals were "a playing around with reality, a means of examining behavior by reordering, exaggerating, fragmenting, recombining and adumbrating it" (Schechner 1977:60). By "playing around" in this way, we gradually came to embody, experience, and express the pain, anger, fear, confusion, and shame that burdened our relations as American Jews and non-Jewish Germans. We slowly worked our way through layers of accumulated information and misinformation about the Holocaust and about our respective cultures. In this quest, our bodies became vehicles for expressing the frightening reality of the Shoah and for exploring our fragile human bonds.

Physical improvisations have an enormous reconciliatory potential, as the examples below will demonstrate. I will first describe the so-called "circle exercise," which is intended to motivate Jews and Germans to share intimate stories and resuscitate childhood memories, and then the "empty-space improvisation," which required a high level of physical participation. These and similar exercises are most effective with people who are familiar with creative movements or at least not intimidated by them. But they can also be employed in workshops for people less familiar with dance and theater. They may initially raise levels of anxiety and resistance but also an awareness of the complexity of Holocaust memory and Jewish/German relations.

Improvisations allow people to move freely in and out of different situations and roles, blending past and present identities with the result of creating a dense tapestry of cultural and personal memories. In a concluding section, I examine one thread of this tapestry that is particularly pertinent for reconciliatory practices: the issue of role reversals. Is it desirable to encourage Germans and Jews to switch roles, the former temporarily embodying victims and the latter victimizers, so that they develop empathy for each other? Or do such reversals only perpetuate those discourses that confound victim and victimizer for ideological purposes?

The Jewish-German Dance Theatre used the circle exercise early on in its rehearsals because it helped us overcome our initial timidness and dare to reveal our emotions. Following a rather simple but effective technique, the circle exercise led us quickly back to childhood memories and improved our listening skills. We lay on our backs on the floor, heads pointing to the center and touching each other, feet stretched outwards, forming the perimeter of the circle. We closed our eyes and relaxed. After a few minutes, someone would start to talk about a given subject but would be limited to a few sentences or a short narrative, so that others would be able to join. This exchange of short personal statements led us to reach deep into the recesses of personal memory. Sessions lasted anywhere from fifteen minutes to an hour or more.

The first time we introduced the circle exercise we asked ourselves the following question: "When did I hear about the Holocaust for the first time?" Without correcting or interrupting each other, we listened attentively as we were taken back into childhood memories. Martin, a German, remembered how he had painted swastikas on toy airplanes in the fourth grade. When the teacher reproached him for doing this he felt embarrassed but did not understand why. His story reminded me of a similar situation. I was sitting in the back of my parents' car as we passed a column of American tanks on the autobahn. I must have been eleven or twelve years old. I looked at the American soldiers, stretched out my arm, and yelled, "Heil Hitler!" My parents were upset and told me never to do this again. Like Martin, I felt deeply embarrassed without knowing exactly what I had done wrong. Lisa, on the other hand, remembered when her parents explained to her as a young girl what the Holocaust meant to them as Jews. And Sheila, who had thought of herself as having no biases against Germany or Germans, recalled a moment of intense fear when she crossed the German border during her first European vacation in 1968. Some of these memories were later integrated into our performance.

Because we had good experiences with the circle exercise in our rehearsals, we later used it in workshops that the Dance Theatre conducted in the United States and Germany. By relaxing their bodies, Jewish and German participants got in touch with forgotten fears and memories. The memories of Jewish American participants, for example, were often tinged with fear as they recalled dreams in which they were hunted by Nazis or remembered parents, relatives, and teachers portraying Germans as untrustworthy and vicious people. They often voiced their ambivalent feelings about meeting Germans. German participants also talked about fear, though they were less afraid of potential violence directed against them than of embarrassment when first meeting Jews. I remember a German woman recalling her teenage years, when Jews were pointed out to her for the first time. They wore black frocks, black hats, and long beards. They looked strange, foreign, and frightening. "Why frightening?" asked a Jewish participant. The German woman could not say. "Perhaps because they looked awkward," she speculated. "Everyone kept a distance from them." She also admitted that she felt uncomfortable recalling this memory in the presence of Jewish participants.

The circle exercise usually succeeded in creating intimacy and vulnerability. The relaxation, the slowing down of the usual pace of arguments, the physical contact, the warmth of other bodies, the closed eyes—all helped the participants to abandon the rhetoric of learned discourse and focus on emerging memories. The circle exercise became a step toward creating a communitas of people in pain, of people on a "road to understanding [which] passes through anguish" (Rosenberg). Occasionally, however, the generated intimacy overwhelmed participants, who began to resist the exercise and block memories. The two examples below testify to the potential of such "ritual misfiring" (cf. Grimes 1990).

In a workshop in Dinslaken, a city near the industrial center of northwest Germany, we asked the German participants to remember when they had first heard about the Holocaust. Lying on their backs, heads touching each other, the Germans were reluctant to talk. Eventually, we company members began sharing our family histories, hoping that the workshop participants would follow our example. They did not. They only talked about images they remembered from books and films on the Holocaust. When the exercise came to an end, the Jewish ensemble members voiced their disappointment over the Germans' unwillingness to talk. The German participants, in turn, excused themselves by pointing to the silence of their families. "The German silence is agonizing for Jews and embarrassing for Germans," I wrote in my journal. In Dinslaken, the circle exercise failed to retrieve intimate memories but made us aware of how frightening it was to become vulnerable in each other's presence.

I witnessed such resistance to the circle exercise on only one other occasion, when I introduced it to the students of the 1989 summer program. After a series of warm-up exercises, I explained the intention and procedure of the circle exercise. We then lay down on the floor and I asked the students to think about two questions: "When did I first meet a Jew (or a German)? What images did I learn about Jews and Germans when growing up?" With their memories, old pains resurfaced. Some students cried. However, as soon as the session ended, the students began to protect themselves. Many German students dismissed the circle exercise as "dangerous," "infantile," and "pseudo-psychological." During the exercise Lucia, a German woman, had told about losing her Israeli boyfriend (reported in chapter 2). In the subsequent discussion, her Jewish peers voiced disapproval of intermarriage, disregarding Lucia's pain. She could read this only as a personal rejection. It was more than she could bear, and she left the room in anger and frustration.

The circle exercise misfired in these two situations, yet the sessions were not altogether counterproductive. Such misfires also speak to the power of creative rituals: resistance can be a defense against it. In Dinslaken, the resuscitation of injurious memory induced so much fear and mistrust that participants shut down. In the student program, on the other hand, the process did not break down until afterwards. The circle exercise itself opened sources of real pain which many students had not realized before. At the end, however, they became frightened by it. As a result, some refused to see any value in the exercise; others praised it for its success in triggering a real, albeit painful, conversation. Resistance, we can conclude, is a psychological mechanism to which people resort when they get frightened by their physical and emotional vulnerability. Resisting intimacy and vulnerability is part of the journey toward reconciliation.

While the circle exercise was meditative and largely stationary, the "empty-space improvisation" engaged the body in more active and challenging ways. Like most of the improvisations of the Jewish-German Dance Theatre, it relied on spontaneous movements. Borrowing from experimental drama Peter Brook's (1968) concept of the empty space, Joseph Chaikin's (1972) idea of the presence of the actor, and Jerzy Grotowski's (1968) notion of *via negativa,* we used only a minimum of props, costumes, technical equipment, and scripts. Often, we sat in a large circle, created an empty space in our midst, and let our bodies and voices spontaneously respond to material drawn from personal stories, readings, memories, or dreams. Whoever felt compelled to move would get up and improvise a movement sequence, a sound, or a short narrative. Others joined, relating to the first person or creating their own world. We thus began to weave in and out of these "worlds" or transform them. We could also remain at the periphery of the empty space and simply listen and watch for a while.

One of the early empty-space improvisations of the Jewish-German Dance Theatre was stimulated by our reading of Elie Wiesel's *Night,* an autobiographical description of his survival in Auschwitz-Birkenau. Placing the book in the center of our large circle, we began to journey back into the world of the camps. At first we did not move but internally recalled scenes of humiliation, torture, and despair. Eventually, somebody reached out for the book and opened it. Martin entered the circle, picked up the book, closed it, and put it in his pants to hide it. Brigitte, another German, confronted him and demanded the return of the book. When she got it back, she randomly opened a page and began to read aloud. Lisa accompanied Brigitte's reading by beating her fists rhythmically on the floor, and swinging her upper body in full circles, almost touching the floor with her chest. Lisa's movements, stretching sideways and bending backwards, reminded me of a prayer, a desperate prayer, a prayer for the dead. Her rhythmic pounding on the floor incited the whole group to move forward, crawling into the circle, merging in the center, and piling up into a heap of bodies. The weight of our limp bodies was oppressive. We were entrapped. Sheila, somewhere at the bottom of the pile, panicked. We grabbed whatever body parts our hands could hold onto. Someone sank his teeth into Sheila's sweater and bit a hole in it. Lisa started to chant a line from Wiesel's *Night*: "In every stiffened corpse, I saw myself! In every stiffened corpse, I saw myself!" After a moment, Eric, a non-Jewish American, responded: "In every survivor, I saw myself." And as he repeated this phrase, he slowly counted the fingers of his hand, as if to count the dead or the few survivors of the camps.

The pile of bodies disentangled. Lisa began to jump up and down, shouting: "I don't believe it. I don't believe it. I don't believe it." Brigitte and Sheila embraced, clutching each other tightly. A sense of despair slowed down our movements. Some of us sat at the periphery of the circle, paralyzed. Then Eric grabbed Martin and me and urged us to run. "We have to run. Run!" The pace accelerated again. Martin and I were reluctant to move, but Eric dragged our bodies around the room. In retrospect, the scene reminded me of the infamous death marches.[3] As the three men were running, Brigitte and Sheila danced slowly, humming: "It's over, it's over." We men, however, did not listen but continued running in large circles around the room until Lisa stepped into our path to stop us. Eric resisted and carried on until we were able to hold him and press him down to the floor. There, all of us huddled together, exhausted. A few of us cried. The improvisation lasted for almost an hour.

In this as in many similar improvisations we often worked ourselves into a trancelike state in which we lost our ordinary sense of time and space. The sessions had the quality of a liminal experience: we constantly crossed boundaries between present and past, between self and other, between Holocaust images stored in our memories and anguish felt in our bodies. We also inverted roles. Jews slipped into the role of Germans, Germans identified with victims. There was room for experiencing ambiguity, spontaneity, and role confusion. Nobody asked, for example, whether it was legitimate for Germans to join the pile of dead bodies. Nor did anyone ask why a Jewish dancer shouted, "I don't believe it," a phrase which, in a different context, could easily be mistaken for a German revisionist statement. There was no room for defensiveness, explanations, or self-conscious questioning. We were fully present and ready to respond to each new movement and impulse. We embodied and played around with emotions, memories, and images that might have been too uncomfortable to express intellectually.

. For improvisations to be an effective reconciliatory practice, we depended on a protected zone. Without that protection, I believe we would have been unable to make ourselves physically and emotionally vulnerable. The poisonous memory of the Holocaust was too frightening for us to enter it without the safety of a communitas. Within a protective framework, however, we were able to put our bodies at risk: to experience the pain, anger, confusion, and embarrassment. By embodying and enacting cultural memory, we were able to test the self in relation to others, discover unacknowledged parts of ourselves, probe our cultural heritage, and sensitize ourselves to individual and collective fears and desires. Most importantly, by working with our bodies we discovered new ways of relating: we carried, shoved, squeezed, pushed, leaned on, and embraced each other. As a communitas of Jews and Germans, we absorbed each other's frenzy and entrusted our bodies' weight to others. The experience of holding and trusting each other physically soon encompassed emotional and symbolic levels of trust—in spite of the poison.

The Reincarnated Jew

During the improvisations, our role reversals as Jews and Germans, victims and victimizers, liberated us from ossified discourses and from deeply felt beliefs in who we were supposed to be as post-Shoah generations. These spontaneous role reversals occurred during improvisations, that is, during a time for ourselves, for self-contained experimentation not meant to be publicly performed. Had we publicly suggested that reversing roles of victim and victimizer would liberate Jewish/German relations from their stalemate, we might have been accused of trivializing the suffering of the victims and of relativizing issues of victimization and guilt. But trivializing the Shoah was far from our intention. As a performance company, we did not intend to repeat the rhetorical twists and turns of victim/victimizer discourses as practiced, for example, in Bitburg. Why, then, did we experiment with role reversals? What would Jews gain from "understanding" the perpetrator? Why would Germans want to identify with Jewish victims? What would Jews or Germans learn from embodying and identifying with the other? To answer these questions, I need to sketch more fully the ideological abuse of inverting the roles of victim and victimizer. Only when we are aware of some of the detrimental effects of such reversals in the social reality of Jewish and German communities can we appreciate the transformative potential of embodying the other under the protective condition of communitas.

"You can never feel like a victim—because you can't! And you shouldn't!" a German student had said during the discussion about the Holocaust museum in Washington. "Why shouldn't we try?" a Jewish student responded. Because it might degenerate into "a cheap kind of symbolism," some argued. Others countered that to "imagine victimization" would help them understand the Shoah. The students' debate in Washington reflected the volatile nature of the status of victim and victimizer in the minds of Jews and Germans. We can assume, for example, that most Jews would perceive any confusion of victims and victimizers as a threat, for it would trivialize the deaths of six million. In addition, role reversals have always been part of the antisemitic strategy to blame Jews for the injury they suffered at the hands of others: Nazi ideology, for example, legitimated its genocidal program by declaring a Jewish conspiracy to control the world. Even after the Shoah, the notion that Jews as a group are guilty of wrongdoings and deserve whatever punishment they get is still alive. Jews have also been accused of exploiting the Shoah and claiming exclusive rights to victimhood in order to mask their alleged role as "perpetrators" (as, for example, in Israel). "The antisemitic guilt feeling aspires to see victims no longer as victims but as victimizers," wrote Karlheinz Schneider, a Jew living in Germany (1984:136). Certain victimologies have become anti-Jewish weapons.

Wittingly or unwittingly, third-generation Germans often employ antisemitic strategies because they are confused about their roles as regards the victim/victimizer dichotomy. In interviews, children and grandchildren of Nazi families tend to portray themselves as victims. "The [Nazi] parents saw themselves as victims," Peter Sichrovsky writes, "and when they were young the children accepted that view. However, once they became old enough to learn something about the actual role their parents played during the war, the children themselves often became victims—the victims of their parents" (1988:7). As an example, Sichrovsky mentions the son of a concentration camp guard who "referred to himself as the Jew of his family" (1988:11). Claiming the status of victim for themselves, post-Shoah German generations have often

failed to differentiate their social and historical place from that of Jewish
victims. A "ritualized self-stylization as victim . . . is a tasteless and false
identification," writes Dan Diner, chiding the German tendency to use
Holocaust symbols as props and paradigms. "The past seems to be . . .
symbolically inverted and magically beseeched," and an opportunity to
"become aware and work it through is wasted" (1986:248; cf. Rosenthal
and Bar-On 1992; Von Westernhagen 1987:171f; Bornebusch 1993:116).

More harmless signs of inverse symbolic identification include, for
instance, the recent trend among German parents to give their children
Jewish names (like Sara, Jacob, Isaak, Ruben, Rachel, Rebekka).
Another, less subtle inversion is the religious conversion of some Germans to Judaism after the Holocaust. Dan Bar-On interviewed, for example, Menachem, the son of a Nazi family, who became an orthodox rabbi
in Jerusalem. One would expect that a thorough soul-searching must
have preceded Menachem's decision, yet the impression from the interview is of a man who has not fully come to terms with his German identity. In the beginning, Menachem denies that the Holocaust played a
crucial role in his decision. But when Bar-On broaches the topic of Menachem's relation to his father, he touches on a sore spot.

B[ar-On]: Do you talk to [your father] in your imagination, try to
examine things, make them clearer?

M[enachem]: Look, if that had been feasible and would have resulted
in something, perhaps I would have been pleased. Maybe. On the
other hand, I know his background. I know the anti-Semitism he had
grown up with as a child, an entire milieu that was saturated with
anti-Semitism. It didn't start with Hitler. To the point that at his
death—and then at the funeral—I felt nothing at all. Felt as if nothing had happened. In Judaism, we have Yahrzeit, Kaddish, the seven
days of mourning, the thirty-day memorial. But it was as if he were
someone I had no relationship with whatsoever. Somebody had died,
my sister had phoned and asked a favor of me . . . it was really cold,
cold. . . .

B: I think you're very angry with him . . .

M: [*Angrily*] No, no! It doesn't interest me at all! I'm not angry with
him. It's not a significant factor in my life. (1989:177)

Though I do not doubt the sincerity of Menachem's far-reaching choice, his fierce rejection of his father raises questions about his motivation. When reading the above passage, I could not help but think that his conversion to Judaism was motivated by a quest for the moral clarity and emotional intimacy he could not find in his family of origin.

Another bizarre case of symbolic role inversion took place a few years ago, when an acquaintance from Berlin visited my wife and me in Philadelphia. When we began to talk about the Holocaust, our friend said that she considered herself a reincarnated Jew. She had once attended a New Age workshop on reincarnation, she explained, where she unmistakably experienced herself in the body of a Jewish woman who was killed in a concentration camp. Ever since, she said, she was convinced that she had been a Jewish woman in her former life. (Among third-generation American Jews, we sometimes find similarly strange role confusions. In 1992, I talked to a young Jew who was HIV-positive and used the Holocaust as a paradigm to explain his condition. He correctly perceived himself as a victim of the virus; but he was also convinced that he resembled a SS officer because he had the power to spread a deadly disease if he wanted to do so.)

For a German to claim the status of a reincarnated Jew is the ultimate in ritualized self-stylization as victim. In such cases, the admonition that a German should never try to "feel like a victim," as the German students argued in the debate about the Holocaust museum in Washington, seems a healthy response. When the German students insisted on the impossibility of feeling like a victim, they may have overintellectualized the debate on Holocaust memorialization, but they also were trying to distance themselves from false identifications. When young Germans, like my Berlin acquaintance, refer to themselves as Jews, they can do so only on the basis of a fictionalized image of Jews-as-victims and at the expense of not reaching out to Jewish people today. If third-generation Germans talk themselves into believing that they can embody both victims and victimizers, why would they need to get to know Jewish people? Meeting Jews would only disturb their claims to victimhood. A task of reconciliation, then, is to undo false identifications.

Embodying the Other

In a communitas of Jews and Germans, exploring the victim/victimizer roles has the power to transform the impasse that afflicts the Jewish/German negative symbiosis. The aim of such role reversals is not to enter into a competition of suffering or to create permanent inversions, that is, to legitimate undifferentiated and ritualized self-stylizations as victim. Rather, role reversals in protected and controlled environments are meant to be a temporary experience in which Jews and Germans develop an empathetic understanding of the other's anguish and confusion. "If one is told often enough that one cannot understand one eventually stops trying," Andrew Greeley said about listening to survivor testimonies (quoted in Rosenberg 1988:389). Third generation Jews and Germans must slip into each other's shoes, for otherwise each might stop trying to understand the other's struggle with Holocaust memory. By consciously and temporarily switching roles, Jews and Germans can physically experience how each group approaches the Holocaust and justifies the construction of memory.

Ironically, the issue of conscious role reversals was first introduced to the Jewish-German Dance Theatre by an outsider. During our formative phase, in the spring of 1986, the company had asked the sociodramatist Dan Estes to conduct a session with us.[4] At his suggestion we reenacted historic situations from Nazi Germany, such as a confrontation between Jews and the Gestapo or a scene about book burnings. These reenactments, however, were far too artificial and did not touch us deeply. We relied on clichés and did not feel comfortable with our assigned roles. That situation changed dramatically when the director asked the participating Germans to volunteer for the role of Hitler. We, myself included, declined. It would have been easier to play Hitler within a homogeneous group of Germans, but in the presence of Jews such (playful) identification was too scary. What if one of us Germans played the role too convincingly? Would our Jewish fellow artists think that we harbor a secret fascination for fascism? If we acted out Hitler's hostility, would we perhaps be accused of being antisemitic? There was not yet enough trust in the group and in oneself to take such risks.

Eventually Lisa, a Jewish member, volunteered to play Hitler. In her embodiment of Hitler, she confronted us with an outburst of real and unmitigated anger. As a group we felt overwhelmed by her violent gestures and speech. We withdrew into silence, and Lisa's anger was left hanging in the air. Lisa felt abandoned by the group. She had taken the risk of making herself vulnerable, but no one in the group was able to pick up the cue and interact with Lisa-playing-Hitler. I felt that I could have countered her anger only with a similar kind of combative energy. But I did not muster the courage to do so. I also felt a need for a gentler response.

As we unraveled our frustrations I realized that the source of my desire for more gentleness derived from my identification with my father. I voiced my wish to slip into my father's skin in order to confront Hitler, still being played by Lisa. As I tried to embody my father an independent play soon developed. I explored those parts of my father's story I was then aware of (I did not yet know that he had been stationed in the anti-aircraft battalion in Blechhammer, the satellite camp of Auschwitz). I embodied my father in his teenage years when he was torn between the staunch Catholic conviction of his parents and the Nazi ideals of the Hitler Youth movement. Since my grandfather, a conservative Catholic, did not follow Nazi ideology, my father could not move up in the Hitler Youth hierarchy. I imagined him, belittled by his classmates and comrades, to have suffered humiliations as teenager. At one point in my play, the director intervened, handed me a pillow and tennis racket, and asked me to act out my father's and my own frustration. But confused about the convergence of father-son roles and about my anger and compassion, which I experienced simultaneously, I was incapable of acting it out. The session concluded at this point.

It was only by chance, so to speak, that our dance group came across the transformative power of embodied role reversals. Initially, none of the German members felt enough trust to identify with the victimizer in the presence of their Jewish peers. Even when the Jewish dancer acted out her anger in the symbolic role of Hitler, the group as a whole remained paralyzed. But Lisa's enactment set another play in motion: my embodiment of my father's past. Later, as levels of trust increased with each new rehearsal, all company members improved their skills in moving in and out of various victim/victimizer configurations.

When Jews and Germans talk to each other today, they also struggle with the past; and when they talk about the past, they also struggle with their present relations. The two dimensions are inseparable. As a communitas, members of the Jewish-German Dance Theatre had certainly experienced the confluence of these two dimensions. By embodying different roles, we felt emotionally claimed by both past and present. The diffusion of roles set us free temporarily from the psychological strains of our historically and ideologically determined roles. Since we understood that we embodied the other only temporarily, we did not have to worry about the danger of abandoning moral and historical distinctions between victim and victimizer. On the contrary, role reversals often pulled us out of emotional impasses, especially when both Jews and Germans claimed special privileges to pain, as if pain could be possessed as a commodity. Together, we mourned the fate of Jewish victims and survivors, as we likewise tried to empathize with our German parents who had lived through the crumbling Nazi empire as adolescents and young adults.

By temporarily identifying with the other (who could be a person from the past or someone from the ensemble), we learned some intimate truths about the other and, in addition, involuntarily revealed subconscious images of the other. A Jew embodying Hitler and a German playing a camp inmate were less about the accurate portrayal of history than about our perceptions of the past as post-Shoah generations. To distinguish between history and our embodied memories of this history was, I believe, the critical juncture for the effective and transformative use of role reversals as a reconciliatory practice. To experiment with these reversals as a communitas enabled us to discuss and correct our enacted assumptions of each other. When Jews, for example, embodied their image of Nazis, we had to ask whether the Germans saw their parents and grandparents reflected accurately. And we wondered how Jews reacted to Germans embodying Jewish camp inmates. To see the other acting out one's own cultural identity was as irritating as it was sometimes comic. It was infuriating when the portrayal was either grossly distorted or revealed aspects of one's identity that were difficult to admit. On the other hand, role reversals also relieved pressure. To watch Lisa play Hitler propelled me to get in touch with my anger as a German. Though I did not dare to express it during that session, as time went on I took the risk of identifying with the victimizer. Later, in one of the scenes of our performance, I embodied a Goebbels-Hitler configuration and bawled out Nazi speeches, only to be pushed off stage by the furious dance of a Jewish woman.

It is important to realize that playing with roles was not an end in itself. As a matter of fact, role reversals were only one aspect of the work of the Jewish-German Dance Theatre. In most other improvisations we stayed close to our Jewish and German heritage and to our religious, national, and gender identities. When we chose to embody different roles, we aimed at gaining insight into the other's perspective.

I think that a general rule can be formulated from these experiences: in a cross-cultural communitas, role reversals are an effective ritual tool precisely because the confusion of roles has such a powerful social reality outside of its protective walls. Role inversions are a pervasive social phenomenon and are potentially harmful because people remain unaware of them. In the worst case, it is the victimizer who thinks he or she is persecuted as victim. Whoever misnames power relations and misidentifies victim and victimizer takes part in the political and emotional manipulation of Holocaust memory. In a communitas, however, where basic levels of trust have been established, role reversals can foster an empathetic understanding of different perspectives and function as a corrective mechanism for cultural misrepresentations.

One last example: in a workshop that the Jewish-German Dance Theatre offered in Dinslaken, we concluded the afternoon with an empty-space improvisation. Sitting in a circle, we asked the German participants to brainstorm about Jewish/German relations and respond to each statement, either verbally or through movement. It soon became obvious that the Germans shied away from any real contact. Tired of the wavering, Lisa placed herself in the middle, lying with her back on the floor. She said: "I am a Jew. Did you ever touch a Jew?" No one responded at first, until some of us cautiously touched her with our hands.

In the subsequent discussion, Diethelm, a German man in his fifties, admitted that he did not fully participate in the exercise because he was too overwhelmed by the workshop as a whole. "When I came into the room in the beginning," he said, "I did not wear my glasses. Then I saw the face of Anne Frank reflected in the faces of Sheila, Lisa, and Erica" (the Jewish dancers of the company). He could not stop seeing Anne Frank's face for the entire workshop, Diethelm said. "And suddenly, I became afraid for my own daughters. I feared that I might lose my own daughters in similar circumstances." Diethelm spoke softly and was visibly affected by the events. However, there was something overbearing in his compassion: in the faces of young Jews he could only see victims, and seeing victims he would think of his daughters. His mental and emotional leaps were remarkable. The presence of young Jewish women reminded him of the image of Anne Frank, the Jewish victim *par excellence,* which in turn conjured up an imagined victimization of his family. Erica's response brought back a reality that this man, caught in his own world of memories and fears, had failed to grasp: "We are not Anne Frank," Erica said. "We are here. We are alive." Her gentle but clear response drew boundaries between Diethelm's blurred vision of an unresolved past and the reality of a workshop with young American Jews in present-day Germany.

When these kinds of embodied interactions take place, Jewish/German relations begin to change. When Jews and Germans play with roles in the context of Holocaust memory and in the presence of each other, they have an opportunity to recognize social and ideological role confusions for what they are: a fictionalized image of themselves and others. As I have tried to show, moments of such recognition occurred in a communitas where Jews and Germans were permitted to embody and enact memories, images, and roles transmitted through their respective families and cultures. If reconciliation is our aim, we must provide more creative and cross-cultural environments where Jews and Germans can recognize their entanglement in the memory of the Holocaust—and the body cannot be ignored in this task.

8 Reconciliation on Stage

The Public Responds

Will cohesiveness and identity be lost if we should find ourselves in a new place?
—**Anne Roiphe**

Germans need friends who remember.
—**Fritz Stern**

Communitas, Performance, and the Public

When the Jewish-German Dance Theatre arrived in the West German city of Bielefeld on 6 November 1988, we were confronted with the possibility that neo-Nazis would interrupt our performance. Compared to the years following German unification, when a wave of skinhead and neo-Nazi violence swept the country, 1988 was still a calm time. But on this evening, three days before the fiftieth anniversary of Kristallnacht, our ensemble had to address the threat that a group of neo-Nazis which occupied a house in Bielefeld might disrupt our performance. What would we do? Would we leave the stage and let the audience deal with them? Or would we trust in the power of our stage presence and try to calm the interference? I wrote in my journal:

> We talk about what to do if someone tries to interrupt our performance tonight. Lisa surprises me when she shares her understanding of German neo-Nazis. "Germans don't know how to love themselves," she says. Erica asks the people who help us set up the stage: "How can you live with neo-Nazis in Bielefeld? Aren't you afraid as audience?" We finally decide that in case of a disturbance we would stop our performance and ask for the houselights to be switched on. One of us would stay on stage and inform the audience that we would not continue performing until the people disturbing the

peace left the theater. But we are painfully aware of the ineffectiveness of our plan should neo-Nazis really show up.

Police arrive. This is the first time on our German tour that we will perform with police protection. They patrol the building and say that they are able to send reinforcements if necessary. An hour before opening, all doors are locked and we are asked to close all windows, even those in the restrooms. The janitor guards the entrance. He says he knows the neo-Nazis and wouldn't let one in. Erica panics. As a child, she lived for many years in Israel, always alert to possible attacks. Bielefeld reminds her of that fear. She doesn't even go to the restroom alone anymore.

In the end, nothing happens. The performance is a success. A German friend tells us afterwards that he is shamed by the fact that doors had to be locked and that we had to fear a disruption by other Germans. We also overhear a comment from a spectator that he would not have come tonight had he been Jewish [because of the neo-Nazi threat].

A few months after our tour in Germany, the company was invited to perform in a Jewish community center in Greenwich, Connecticut, on the occasion of Yom Ha-Shoah, the annual Holocaust Remembrance Day. The audience consisted mostly of Jews, and we assumed that many of them were survivors or members of survivor families. The performance went reasonably well, but when we began our discussion with the audience after the performance, people were not eager to talk. Unlike other audiences in the United States, the Greenwich audience was reserved. We later found out that many of the attending survivors felt that Yom Ha-Shoah was "their" day, an event commemorating their suffering. They were ambivalent about the idea of sharing it with others, especially Germans. The ice was not broken until someone asked me about my family. What did your parents do during the war? How do they feel about your dancing and performing with Jews in public? I responded as honestly as I could, talking about my parents' past and about their slowly growing interest in my work. I also told them about an argument I had had with my sister, who had once claimed that Jews control the American media. My answers eased some of the tensions. In a private conversation afterwards, a child of survivors told us that the honest remarks about my family had dissolved her skepticism about the evening.

The events in Bielefeld and Greenwich pointed to a dimension of reconciliatory practices I have not yet addressed: encounters between public audiences and a communitas, that is, a public that witnesses the outcome of the struggle of young Jews and Germans with Holocaust memory without actively participating in transformative processes itself. How do audiences react, for example, to a performance in which Jews and Germans publicly stage their artistic version of the intimate and painful process of reconciliation? By watching such a performance, are audiences consumers who remain inactive and untransformed or are they motivated to rethink the effects of injurious memory? Do performances have the power to bond audiences and performers in such a way that transformations occur even in the short span of an evening?

In responding to these questions, I am shifting the focus from communitas to the public. So far, I have mainly described how third-generation Jews and Germans, bound together as a communitas, reacted to public discourse and different forms of memorialization. Now I will look at the public response to the achievements of a communitas, with the work of the Jewish-German Dance Theatre again as guide. In the previous chapter, we saw how rehearsals and workshops permitted participants to explore ambiguities and complexities of their relations to the Shoah, and how guided fantasies, physical improvisations, and embodied role reversals enabled Germans and American Jews to reach levels of intimacy and vulnerability that, despite occasional setbacks, prevailed over defensive attitudes. Performances, however, differ from protected and self-contained rehearsals and workshops in that they are open to the public gaze—a gaze that can be hostile, empathetic, or indifferent. When performing, the Jewish-German Dance Theatre left the protective environment and faced a new challenge: with each audience, we had exactly one evening to earn people's trust and to convince them of the reconciliatory potential of a performance created by a communitas of Germans and Jews born after the Holocaust.[1]

As this chapter will show, audience-performer interactions are sometimes so powerful that they themselves can be interpreted as a reconciliatory practice. When the company staged its artistic version of breaking the paralysis of Jewish/German relations, the performances and ensuing discussions created a forum in which audiences felt encouraged to address a volatile and taboo subject. Since our audiences were mostly self-selected, we expected them to be sympathetic, and in general they were. But we also experienced many difficult and disturbing audience-performer interactions. People were often puzzled, sometimes even intimidated, by seeing young Jews and Germans together approaching the memory of the Shoah through the arts. It sometimes felt as if a motionless, voiceless young Jew on stage would alone be capable of releasing all those unresolved emotions long stored in the German psyche. Sometimes, we met vigorous resistance and the defensiveness of public discourses. In Greenwich, for example, we faced the survivors' reluctance to include new visions in the commemoration of the Holocaust; in Bielefeld, we needed police protection because of potential neo-Nazi violence.

But our performance also enabled audiences to abandon initial skepticism, mistrust, and resistance. The personal honesty we achieved on stage encouraged audiences to leave their defensive positions. Since we used sets, props, and costumes only sparingly, our presence as Jewish and German performers filled the stage and, symbolically, filled the void the Holocaust had left. Therein lay our strength: audiences could see for themselves how deeply Jewish/German relations could change if one took the risk of practicing reconciliation. After the performance in Bielefeld, for example, there was an emerging sense of shame and an openness to listen and change among some German spectators; in Greenwich, we noticed a growing willingness among individual Jews not to exclude others from the commemoration of painful memories.

Our encounters with audiences were, of course, brief, and it was impossible to follow up on what people did with their experience two or three days later. However, the many private conversations, media reviews, and personal impressions on which this chapter is based show how powerful it can be to provide occasions for Jewish and German audiences and performers to interact. Sometimes, these interactions succeeded only in exposing the tremendous tensions of Jewish/German relations; at other times, the interactions truly transformed previously held beliefs and biases.

"And Forgive Us Our Sins": Misnaming Christians and Jews

The most memorable interactions with audiences occurred during the Jewish-German Dance Theatre's tour of Germany in November 1988. On this occasion, the fiftieth anniversary of Kristallnacht, Germany experienced a surge of desire to remember the past.[2] Private and public organizations and commissions staged commemorations all over the country, and as part of this momentum we were able to schedule our performances within the relatively short period of four weeks. We performed for small-town audiences in remote regions as well as sophisticated audiences in cosmopolitan cities. To our knowledge, it was the first time that any group of post-Shoah German and Jewish-American artists had collaborated on a production about Holocaust memory in Germany.[3]

For many spectators, the three Jewish members of the company were the first Jews they had ever met. Because there are only a few Jewish communities scattered around Germany (and these maintain a low profile), many Germans have not had a chance to talk with Jews about the Holocaust. They welcomed our presence and were eager to share their personal stories, memories, and opinions. "The German past has assumed a new, portentous present," Fritz Stern wrote in *Dreams and Delusions*, "and in recent years many [Germans] have felt an even greater political and psychological need to deal with the past; some wish to understand it, others to banish or trivialize it" (1987:19). Many Germans we met expressed their wish to understand by responding sensitively to our performances. They were able to listen to the concerns of the Jewish ensemble members and share their personal experiences without becoming defensive or derisive.

At times, though, it felt as if our performance had opened Pandora's box, and what emerged was frequently not what we wanted to hear. After years of silence and repression, audience reactions ranged from the grotesque to the offensive. Among the recurring controversial issues were questions about Israel, Jewish identity, German guilt, and Christian identity. "Why do you call yourselves the Jewish-German Dance Theatre rather than 'American-German' or 'Jewish-Christian' theatre?" we were asked repeatedly, as if our choice was limited to naming our ensemble along either religious or national lines. This question, like other controversial topics, was fueled by the general German discourse on victim and victimizer and the concurrent ethos of guilt and forgiveness examined in the first part of this book. The contentious issue of Jewish and Christian identity, which emerged repeatedly during our post-performance discussions, deserves attention.

The Protestant congregation of Schramberg, a small town nestled in

the hills of the Black Forest, had invited the company to perform in the
local school. We were scheduled to play on a Sunday evening. We set up
the stage in the morning, rehearsed our piece, and then took a long hike
in the surrounding woods. We climbed up a hill to a castle and enjoyed
a marvelous view. In the distance, the dark edges of a pine forest
stretched along meadows and fields. Beneath, in the valley, the rooftops
of the old village glistened in the warm autumn sun. The scenery was
profoundly peaceful. We wondered: Who would come to our performance? Who, in this small town, would be interested in Jewish/German
issues or, for that matter, in an experimental performance?

About one hundred people showed up for the performance, but
when we finished, the audience did not respond. When we took our first
bow, no one applauded. We took a second bow, and still there was
silence. Finally, as we left the stage, the applause set in, hesitantly. Stefan,
our lighting technician, overheard the complaints of some elderly people
as they were leaving the school. "We didn't understand anything," they
grumbled. A review in a regional newspaper captured the mood of the
evening:

> It was not an easy evening for the audience. . . . [The performance]
> was no entertainment but had to become a painful encounter. The
> few people of Schramberg who exposed themselves to this evening
> were put to a test. The artistic means employed by the dancers are
> not very popular. They rely on the expressive strength of their bod-
> ies, without a stage set, without elaborate costumes, and only with an
> accompanying vibraphone. . . . [T]he barrenness of their images was
> effective. . . .
>
> It is difficult to know whether it was the quality of the performance
> or the special situation of Germans being confronted with the con-
> tent: In any case, moments of shock passed before the audience was
> able to applaud at the end of the performance. That only few of the
> spectators stayed for the discussion afterwards—or should we say,
> had the "courage to stay"?—was symptomatic for the evening. . . . The
> diffidence might have been more painful for some than for others—
> but almost everyone lost the power of speech during the difficult con-
> versation between the descendants of possible victims and possible
> victimizers. The pain is certainly necessary and should not dimin-
> ish—speechlessness is the true evil. The members of the Jewish-Ger-

man Dance Theatre have overcome this silence for themselves but they probably remain the exception. This, too, was demonstrated during this evening in the school hall.[4]

As the critic stated, the conversation after our performance in Schramberg was difficult and tense. I particularly remember a clergyman objecting to a scene in which we had portrayed Christianity's hostility toward Jews. In the clustered group of kneeling people recited parts of the Lord's Prayer in German: "Our Father who art in heaven / Thy kingdom come / Thy will be done / On earth as it is in heaven / And forgive us our sins / Amen." The recitation of these lines increased in ferocity until it suddenly stopped. The kneeling group got up abruptly and marched across stage. The rhythmic pounding of marching feet eventually drowned out the voice of the Jewish woman reciting the Shema. The choreography culminated in the "Christian" group's encircling the Jewish woman and whispering the lines of the Lord's Prayer in an ominous tone. The stage lights dimmed, and, in the dark, the Shabbat candles were extinguished violently.

The clergyman voiced his objection to this scene by criticizing Israel. He charged Israel with being specifically prone to violence, a feature he traced from the conquest of Canaan to Israel's invasion of Lebanon in 1982. "A difficult evening, troublesome for many spectators," wrote another critic about the performance in Schramberg. "The clergy of both confessions [Catholic and Lutheran] in Schramberg had to watch, for example, a harsh scene in which the German Lord's Prayer harasses the traditional Jewish Shabbat rite—an allegory for the entanglement of large parts of the church in the Third Reich and, hence, in the Holocaust."[5] The critic understood well the basic intention of this particular scene. The Jewish-German Dance Theatre wanted to indicate that Nazi antisemitism had historical precedents in the Christian tradition of Jew-hate and that this tradition accounted for the failure of the church to act on behalf of Jews during the Third Reich. As performers, we felt that the symbolism was so embarrassingly obvious that we almost decided to delete this scene from the program. Little did we know that it would provoke controversy in Germany.

Two days before the performance in Schramberg, our choreography about the Lord's Prayer had already sparked controversy in the old university town of Marburg. Several students from the university's department of Protestant theology had attended our performance. In the discussion afterwards, a student remarked that the scene about the Lord's Prayer was "too sarcastic." It did not do justice to Christianity or to Jewish/Christian relations, he said. We replied that church and theology have been latently or overtly antisemitic for many centuries, and that students of theology should confront that heritage. A professor of theology agreed with our assessment of Christian anti-Judaism but criticized our dance for its inconsistency, because, he argued, "the Lord's Prayer is a Jewish prayer." Our Jewish ensemble members were quite puzzled by this remark (and I remember thinking that such a statement can be made only in a culture where people no longer are in contact with Jews on a daily basis). Unfortunately, there was no time to argue with the theologian because a young woman interrupted. She identified herself as a German Jew and addressed Lisa and Erica, the two Jewish dancers who had been part of the group reciting the Lord's Prayer. "As a Jew," the woman said, "I would never recite the Lord's Prayer, not even on stage." Her remarks bewildered the audience and triggered another question from a young German. "Is it true that Jews are defined religiously?" We would hear this question over and over again, and often our audiences would volunteer an answer as well: Jews, they claimed, are defined religiously and are distinct from Israelis, who are defined as a nation. There was no awareness of Jewish self-understanding or of Judaism as a culture, but a need—if not obsession—to define Jews.

A review in Marburg's local newspaper continued the convoluted discussion with the audience. "The forgiveness which the audience expected never took place," wrote the critic in self-revealing terms. "The ensemble had come to demonstrate that they were unwilling ever to forget the Holocaust. Even in moments of deepest religiosity, which characterized the performance, there was no reconciliatory moment. Although the Shabbat prayer and the Lord's Prayer were recited simultaneously, one prayer always tried to drown out the other, and each group remained in the isolation of its own religion."[6]

Caught in the ethos of guilt and forgiveness, this critic missed the point not only about Christian antisemitism but also about reconciliation. Reconciliation to her meant forgiveness, that is, the expectation that the Jewish-German Dance Theatre would somehow forgive German audiences. The notion that reconciliation always requires active effort and that our performance in itself represented an active struggle toward reconciliation escaped her.

We were surprised by the widespread misunderstandings provoked by the dance about the Lord's Prayer. Even Jürgen Moltmann, a well-known liberal German theologian, who had seen the performance in Tübingen, criticized the piece. In a letter to the Jewish-German Dance Theatre, he generally praised our efforts: "That Jewish-American and German dancers do this grief-work together," Moltmann wrote, "evokes hope and creates reconciliation. This grief-work does not cover up the events [in the past] . . . but the shared body language, the shared lamentations, the shared dance make it symbolically possible for understanding to occur. It creates a bonding experience." Moltmann concluded the letter with a remark about the Lord's Prayer: "In the whole program, only the scene 'Vater Unser' remains strangely abstract. There, the numerically stronger group of people reciting the Lord's Prayer ousts the single Jewish woman praying the 'Shema Israel.' This seems to be a reference to the militancy of the Christian mission to the Jews or of the 'Deutsche Christen' [The "German Christians" comprised the majority within the Protestant church under the Third Reich and followed Nazi ideology.] But this piece fails to do justice to the central texts of the Jewish and Christian religion. It does not penetrate their meaning and is difficult to understand."[7]

Why did German audiences resist or misunderstand our choreography about the Lord's Prayer, which seemed to us so blatantly obvious in its intention? Did we offend religious sensibilities? We did not expect such fierce reactions to a dance that symbolically portrayed a triumphant Christianity crushing a Jewish minority, especially since German society has been largely secularized. Compared to Americans, Germans rarely define themselves in religious terms and are not active churchgoers, although the majority are registered members of the Catholic and Protestant churches.[8] Churches are virtually empty on Sundays except for a handful of elderly people and children. What, then, fueled the objections to our artistic rendition of the Lord's Prayer?

Since we kept running into similar misinterpretations, we realized that we had touched a taboo. Even if most Germans identified with secular rather than religious forces, they perceived Christianity, I surmised, as a potential source for redeeming an otherwise troubled German identity. Especially since the bloody stain of Germany's national past was

hard to deny, there existed an even greater need to keep Christian identity—secularized as it might be—free of blemish. It was essential to
regard the cross and the swastika as incongruous symbols: had we only
been better Christians, so the assumption goes, the Holocaust might not
have happened. A stronger Christianity would have objected to the Nazi
desire to annihilate all Jews.

By drawing attention to Christian Jew-hate with our choreography,
we diffused the boundaries between *Kreuz* (cross) and *Hakenkreuz*
(swastika), which irritated Germans who had split an idealized Christian
self from a disillusioned "national" self. At least the "Christian" part of
the German identity, they seemed to feel, was redeemable—albeit at the
expense of disregarding the anti-Jewish legacy of the church. Our dance
about the Lord's Prayer attacked the delusion of a Christian self
unstained by antisemitism. By emphasizing the authoritarian tone of the
prayer and concluding with the line, "And forgive us our sins," we subverted the desire to mend one's shattered (national) self-esteem and to be
forgiven. So many Germans misread our choreography of the Lord's
Prayer because they could tolerate neither Christianity's authoritarian
side nor the ironic play on the line on forgiveness. It is "too sarcastic," a
theology student said. The clergyman in Schramberg objected to it on
the grounds of Israel's supposed liking for violence. "There was no reconciliatory moment," the critic in Marburg complained. The scene was
"difficult to understand," Moltmann remarked. Forgiveness, we need to
recall, has been held dear in the psyche of postwar Germans, although it
is inextricably linked to unresolved feelings of guilt. As a circular and
self-referential system, the ethos of guilt and forgiveness has resisted the
notion that reconciliation is a practice that must be continuously
rehearsed in community with others.

From the Black Forest to Berlin

Questions of Jewish, Christian, and German identity dominated many
of our discussions in Germany but did not exhaust the political complexity and emotional range of audience responses to our performances.
In many respects, each interaction between ensemble and audience was
different. The opening lines of the poem "Todesfuge" (Death Fugue) by
Paul Celan, a Romanian-born survivor of the Holocaust, reflect what I
often felt during our 1988 tour of Germany: "Black milk of daybreak we

drink it at sundown / we drink it at noon in the morning we drink it at night / we drink and we drink it." The poem captures the despair over the merciless perseverance of the Holocaust trauma. Black milk is poison and paradox. So many of the reactions, opinions, and memories summoned by the performance of the Jewish-German Dance Theatre remained helplessly tangled in contradiction. I often despaired of the little we were able to achieve in a culture nursed on and saturated with "black milk." And yet, our performances also unlocked doors to injurious memory, setting in motion the arduous process of transformation.

In order to give the reader a sense of the directness and urgency we experienced when performing for German audiences, I will quote extensively from the journal I kept of the 1988 tour. The reader will again become witness to the perplexing degree of ritualization with which Jewish/German relations are afflicted: sometimes, our audiences remained stuck in a stale discourse; sometimes, we, as a communitas of Jewish and German artists, could not handle the intensity of public responses; and yet we frequently observed genuine attempts by German audiences to heal their broken relations to Jews and vice versa.

> October 5, 1988: Philadelphia. . . . After almost two years of waiting, anticipating, and preparing, the tour of Germany with The Jewish-German Dance Theatre is about to begin. . . . My fears are manifold: to be accused of being a *Nestbeschmutzer* [one who fouls the nest]; the fear of misrepresenting Germany and offending my German friends; the fear of being caught in between my Jewish and German friends and having to defend either; the fear of internal company conflicts; the fear of being ignored by German audiences; and, above all, the fear of performing my solo dance about my father in his presence. Surely, one night he will sit in the audience and watch me perform the piece in which I accuse him of not talking, of taking his silence and suffering to the grave, never sharing it with me. This piece must upset him, and I am afraid of performing it. Is this journey to my *fatherland* also about my father? And yet, I do not understand my solo performance—despite its anger—as an attack. I look at it as a love poem, because I try to slip into my father's skin, to understand him from inside. And yet, it will upset him because he perceives himself differently, that is, he thinks he has come to terms with the past.
>
> October 19: Oberursel. Our first, albeit condensed, performance,

takes place in my former high school. It is strange to be back. . . .
The school has sold 250 tickets, and more students are waiting outside to get in. Not even standing room is left. There is no stage, and
we quickly have to adjust our choreography to the limitations of the
space. . . . After the performance, questions of the students revolve
around the issue of guilt. "Should we feel guilty?" they ask in so
many different ways. . . .

When we clean up and pack, I am approached by Mr. Gupa, who
works for a local newspaper. He is very nervous and admits that he
was unable to take notes during the performance. He was born in
1925 in Berlin, he tells me. Since he is of German and Indian descent,
the Nazis considered him a full-blooded Aryan. He also mentions
that he had been briefly in the SS. One day during the war, he says,
he met Count Hans Hasso von Keltenheim at his castle. The count
told him that he knew a lot about the Nazis (though he wouldn't tell
him any details) and that he wished Germany to be thoroughly
destroyed. At this point, Mr. Gupa is overwhelmed by emerging
memories. Tears well up and he tries to control his emotions.

October 20: Ansbach. A small city in northern Bavaria. . . . We
premiere our full performance for the first time in Germany. We
begin our piece in total darkness. We have placed ourselves among
the audience and begin walking toward the stage, banging stones.
We immediately feel that the audience is with us tonight. . . . At the
end, they applaud after a moment of silence. We have three curtain
calls. When the houselights go up, people are not eager to leave the
theater. Brigitte invites them to stay for a discussion, and about 30
young people take up the offer. . . . We talk for twenty minutes. The
people are touched. Erica asks if there are any Jews in Ansbach or if
they know any Jews. No, no one does. But somebody knows where
the synagogue and the Jewish cemetery are located. "The last Jew
was buried there in 1975," he says. A teenager says that prior to this
evening she did not want to be bothered by this history. "It belongs to
my grandfather, not to me," she says. "But now I look at it differently.
Your performance has changed me. Before, I thought that I am not
German. Now I know that I am German and that I am part of this
history."

October 21: Marburg [where we have a discussion about the
Lord's Prayer and Jewish/Christian relations].

October 23: Schramberg [where a clergyman objects to the scene about the Lord's Prayer].

October 25: Tübingen [where we perform in front of a large audience in the *Landestheater,* and a Protestant theologian dismisses our scene about Christian antisemitism].

October 27: Hanau [where we get into a heated discussion with the audience about whether or not Jews are distinct from Israelis; see chapter 3].

October 29: Dinslaken [where we conduct a workshop in which a German participant imagines the face of Anne Frank reflected in the faces of the Jewish dancers; see chapter 7].

When we arrive in Dinslaken, all of us spontaneously have a strange feeling. Nobody in town, even our host families, seems to know that we are performing here. The only person with information is Rev. S., who is very helpful. We find it difficult to relate to the north Germans. They strike us as awfully repressed. When we meet as a company the next morning, everybody tells the same story: our host families do not talk. At the home where Lisa, Sheila, and I are staying, our hosts invite us to join them in the living room but do not talk. Finally, to break the awkward silence, we ask them:

"How are you connected to Rev. S.?"

"We sing in the choir."

"What do you sing?"

"We sing a Bach cantata."

Pointing to a photograph showing their son holding a violin: "Your son plays an instrument?"

"Yes, he plays the violin."

"Where does he play?"

"In a chamber orchestra."

"Is he a professional musician?"

"No." We continue this staccato conversation for a while until we finally excuse ourselves. . . . Ironically, when we part two days later, our hosts ask us to write a note in their guest book. "We have had this book since we got married 21 years ago," they say, "and our house has always been open to people from different cultures." The guest book is very thin. . . .

When our performance begins we still have an uneasy feeling. About ten minutes before we start, we count only 15 people in the

audience, mostly our host families. At the end, though, there are
about 60 people. In the discussion period afterwards, there is silence,
silence, silence. There are a few unengaged questions. Is the silence
hostility or bewilderment on the part of the audience? We do not
know how to interpret it. The wife of one of our host families
approaches us later and says: *"Sagen Sie, wollen Sie uns eigentlich
beschuldigen?* (Tell us, do you actually want to accuse us?) I was only a
child. I do not feel responsible. I do not even feel ashamed." Her
husband replies: "I see that differently. I am ashamed. But do not
tell this to her"—and he points to Erica, one of the Jewish dancers,
who stays at their home.

November 1: Münster. Still in Dinslaken, we hear that a Molotov
cocktail had been thrown at the synagogue in Münster. Nothing happened because it bounced off the bullet-proof glass. . . .

Erica is afraid today because of the bomb . . . and her performance energy is high and angry. For her, it is not a performance any
more but reality. She cries after the performance. She is emotionally
and physically exhausted (she is plagued by allergies and has already
lost several pounds). Lisa cries briefly during the performance itself
. . . and from the audience, we occasionally hear sobs. After our performance, there is silence again, but it is a different kind of silence.
Silence can be very distinct. Silence speaks. In Dinslaken and other
places it was tense and hostile. Here it seems empathetic and compassionate.

A sensitive review in the local paper reflects the mood in Münster: "Due to the bomb attack on the synagogue of Münster, the guest
performance of the Jewish-German Dance Theatre was unexpectedly confronted with a macabre, unfriendly, and, as far as the host
country is concerned, not very flattering reality. . . . [The perfor-
mance] was an impressive and lasting testimony to performance art
and historical consciousness. The stage was barren, spartan, and as
naked as the mortal agony of Jews in the death camps. . . . With
expressively choreographed gestures and very malleable body language, the four women and two men pursue 'the intention to heal.'
They do so by blending cultural memory and personal experiences
with a necessary search for the past, as painful as that might be."[9]

November 3: Berlin. It is cold and gray in Berlin. We stay here
three days and have time for some rest and sightseeing. We go to the

Wall. . . . We also visit the terrain of the former Gestapo headquarters. Today, it is an empty place. Only a basement is preserved, and it houses a small exhibition. We look at photographs. I am deeply affected by three: In one, I see local Lithuanians clubbing Jews to death, a pogrom initiated by the *Einsatzgruppen*.[10] The second photo shows German *Einsatzgruppen* as they execute civilians. One of the German soldiers laughs while holding his gun to the neck of his victim. The victim is overcome by fear and total disbelief. Those Jews could have been Lisa's family, which has Lithuanian roots. . . . And then there is a third photo from the last days of the Warsaw ghetto. Resistance fighters are rounded up and marched through a street blackened by smoke. In the first row I see a young woman. She looks proud despite the misery, not defeated. She reminds me of Lisa: proud, angry, and sad. In our performance, Lisa gets off the stage and defiantly addresses the German audience: "I am afraid of you. And you are afraid of me. But it takes both of us to be here. . . ."

We perform in a church in Steglitz [a district of Berlin]. During our dress rehearsal in the afternoon, we get an unannounced visit from CBS. The camera crew is tired; we are their last assignment for the day. They do not want to interrupt our rehearsal, they say, and will film just for a few moments, then leave. We are in the process of rehearsing the Lord's Prayer. "This is powerful stuff," the American cameraman says. And Elliot Bernstein, the director, decides to come back in the evening to film our performance. They stay until midnight. . . .

"What do you want to achieve with this piece?" is the first question we are asked after our performance. We are somewhat unnerved by this question and do not really respond. We later find out that the questioner is a member of the Berlin Jewish community. A Jewish colleague of his explains: "As Jews, we do not need any more information about the Holocaust. We also do not need any reconciliation. What we want to know is what [non-Jewish] Germans do with it." Later in the discussion, a German woman admits that she has been inspired by the solo about my father, in which I portray his unwillingness to talk. She says she will now go to the archives and search for documents about her own father, who has recently died. The only thing she knows about him, she says, is "that he was a follower of Hitler [*daß er mit Hitler mitgelaufen ist*]." "That is exactly what we want to hear," replies the man from the Jewish community.

November 5: Herne. Back to the northwestern part of Germany. After all the attention we got in Berlin, the performance in Herne is disappointing. Only 30 people show up and we do not communicate. Technically, the performance is okay, but the audience does not respond. . . .

November 6: Bielefeld [where we get police protection because of the threat that neo-Nazis may interrupt our performance].

November 7: Herford. On this day fifty years ago, Hershel Grynszpan entered the German embassy in Paris and shot Ernst vom Rath, a secretary. Two days later, the pogroms of the so-called Reichskristallnacht began, which left about 100 Jews dead, synagogues burned, Jewish shops looted and destroyed, and 20,000 Jews deported. . . .

As we are putting on our makeup, we hear that the small theater is almost sold out. And survivors are in the audience! Klotho, a neighboring town, has invited former Jewish residents for the days commemorating Kristallnacht, and they have all come to see our performance. Many of them are from the United States, some even from Philadelphia. . . . Afterwards, they surround us. They thank us for having expressed what they would have liked to express themselves: anger, rage, but also gratitude to those who invited them back to Germany after all those years.

Many of us have nightmares. Lisa dreams that she is being persecuted by Nazis who hold red candles in their hands [we use red candles as props]. Erica dreams that she carries the black boots of Goebbels [the boots are props, too]. In her dream, she asks if anyone knows where the boots come from. Although everyone knows, nobody tells her. I dream that we are glued to the stage in Herford and cannot perform.

November 8: Kassel. For the first time, there is family in the audience: my grandmother and two of my cousins are present. Afterwards, my grandmother gives me homemade sweets and some money. She is proud of her grandchildren, she says. She also thinks I am underweight. She does not say anything about the performance, but I think she is touched. The fact that she has come is a statement in itself.

November 9: Bad Homburg. Tonight is the night. It is not only the night commemorating Kristallnacht but also the night when my family and many of my friends come to see the performance. . . .

During rehearsals, the company gets into an argument about rechoreographing a sequence, and I leave the group, hiding in a room backstage. I am nervous and upset. I am also embarrassed about leaving the rehearsal. . . . I suddenly feel tired and have no desire to perform. Nor do I want to participate in our group warm-up. Instead, I hide in a small room and write feverishly in my journal. . . .

At the beginning of tonight's performance, I feel painfully self-conscious. I know that my parents are sitting in the audience and that my father will see my solo about his and his generation's silence. I feel conflicted. I do not want to hurt my parents (who have also helped to advertise the performance), but I definitely want them to see our piece. Fortunately, I get over my self-consciousness. By the time I slip into the Goebbels figure and bellow out antisemitic smears, I am back in my performance mode. When I finally perform my father-piece, I am no longer thinking about my father in the audience. . . . After the performance, my mother walks up to the stage and offers us red roses. It is a nice gesture. [A day later, my parents ask me whether it was my father I intended to portray in the solo. "It wasn't really about your father, was it?" they ask.]

In the discussion in Bad Homburg, a woman in her late fifties says that she does not understand why young Jews are afraid. She would understand it if they lost family in the Holocaust or if they grew up in Israel. But why be afraid as American Jews? Erica responds rather forcefully. Later, the woman approaches Erica and with tears in her eyes and an outpouring of motherly feelings embraces her. She says, "I love you." Is this a true gesture of reconciliation? Erica lets herself be embraced but she is also wonderfully clear about boundaries. "You are doing this more for yourself than for me," she tells the woman. "I can't really forgive you but I want to ask you: Do you talk? Do you talk to your children?"

November 10: Sprendlingen. The performance is excellent. For the first time, people not only applaud but cheer and stamp their feet. It feels good (though I am also suspicious: Is all this enthusiasm pouring out because of these days' commemorating Kristallnacht?). During our discussion, the audience is surprisingly open. I especially remember a 16-year-old boy formulating his fears. "For me," he says, "the worst thing that could happen is if a Jew would not want to become my friend because I am German." The local newspaper picks up on a similar theme: "'I am afraid of you, and you are afraid of me,' is one of the statements during the performance. A long-term concern of this committed ensemble is to reduce this fear of contact and intimacy [*Berührungsangst*]. During their struggles in the ensemble, the performers admit, they experienced for themselves how fear of the other and the stranger can dominate."[11]

November 12: Nuremberg. After the encouraging experience in Sprendlingen, we are in for a big disappointment. In Nuremberg, we get into an argument with the audience after the performance. A harmless discussion in the beginning, it abruptly changes when an older man recounts his teenage fears. When he was sixteen, he says, he had to face American tanks without a weapon in his hands. "I can't say anything about your performance," he concludes, "we were glad that we had survived ourselves." Lisa responds: "There may be pain on your side. But I do not understand why you cannot relate to us today. You are no longer young. How can you be so petty as not to have emotions about our plight?" The man does not respond directly but says later in the discussion: *"Wir müssen ja heute mit Ausländern und Juden leben* [Well, we do have to live with foreigners and Jews today]."

There is again family in the audience. Martin's grandmother and my mother-in-law have come to see us. Martin's grandmother continues the apologetic argumentation. "You young people just don't know what it meant to live through the first and second world wars. I do not feel guilty. You have to consider the historic context." Others continue along this line. But tonight we are no longer willing to take it. It is our next to last performance and we are tired. We are also attuned to each other in miraculous ways. Without prior consultation, all of us take up the challenge. I tell the audience that I find the conversation troubling, especially here in Nuremberg, and suggest that we end the discussion. In response, someone in the audience charges me with overidentifying with the victims. The discussion eventually reaches its peak when a staff person from the theater reproaches us. "Why don't you come in here like normal people?" he asks. "Instead, you come in and provoke this stir." Lisa can't take this. She initially tries to argue with him but eventually owns up to her anger. Stopping in the middle of a sentence, she looks at him and screams, ". . . and by the way, fuck you!" The audience is in an uproar. Everybody talks at the same time, and there is not even a chance to translate any more. When the audience finally calms down, my mother-in-law remarks that neither Jews nor Germans will ever come to terms with the Holocaust. But Brigitte, a German dancer, disagrees fiercely. She angrily asks her and the audience why nobody talks directly to the Jews here on stage. "Instead," Brigitte protests, "everybody beats about the bush and offers explanations [for Germany's past behavior]. Why can't anybody say that we [Germans] are sorry?"

The newspaper writes that "the performance occasionally pushed the mainly young audience, in a simplistic manner, into the role of the accused, which hardly fosters understanding."[12]

The next morning, we go to the *Reichsparteitagsgelände,* the terrain where the Nazis had held their party rallies fifty years ago. It is Sunday morning. The weather is cold and drizzly, and no one is in the streets. When we get near the former Nazi terrain, police block the street and redirect us to a nearby parking place. Police are everywhere, in full gear and with German shepherds on the leash. They protect a small crowd of two or three hundred elderly people who have gathered in front of one of the old Nazi monuments. Wearing loden coats (as is typical for old, conservative Germans) and accompanied by their dachshunds (another sign of a German petty bourgeois), they honor German Veterans Day. It is a bizarre scene. An army honor guard has assembled. Fully equipped with rifles, steel helmets, torches, and the German flag, they pay homage to the dead soldiers. A clergyman delivers a sermon in front of the Nazi monument. We are the only young people present, and wherever we turn, we are not so inconspicuously followed by plainclothes officers. Brigitte says we should do something. Lisa suggests we sing the *Hatikvah*. But the police presence does not exactly invite any wrong moves, and we decide to leave Nuremberg.

November 13: Freiburg. Our last performance. It is a good performance and a productive discussion. But I am so exhausted, like everyone else in the company, that I have a hard time focusing.

We left Germany with conflicting emotions. On the one hand, we were in high spirits about the success of our tour and about the many people we had deeply touched with our performance. On the other hand, we were also troubled by the intensity and resistance with which many audiences had responded, leaving us with a sense of despair. It was at times difficult to find cohesive meaning for the multifarious audience interactions. Many experiences defied clear moral definition and simply pointed to the complexity of the human dimension of reconciliation. But after each performance, something new had been created, and both performers and audiences found themselves in a new place. Communitas inspires! After seeing our performance, a German teenager in Sprendlingen, for example, admitted that he was afraid of not being able to make Jewish friends. A woman in Berlin publicly pledged to search for archival information about her father. A handful of young Germans and German Jews followed the company to three different locations, driving for hours to talk with us again after our performances. These were examples of successful transformative processes between a communitas and the public.

Admittedly, a group like the Jewish-German Dance Theatre will not come into existence very often. But sharing the achievements of a Jewish/German communitas is not limited to the artistic work of a performance group. Other Jewish and German dialogue groups have been established, using a mixture of experiential, cognitive, and therapeutic approaches. For example, Armand Volkas, a child of survivors and a drama therapist, has been working with actors and non-actors on issues of Jewish/German reconciliation since 1989 in San Francisco. This group occasionally presents material from their workshops to the public. Mona Weissmark, a child of survivors, and Ilona Kuphal, a daughter of a SS officer, conducted a joint meeting for children of Nazis and children of Holocaust survivors in Boston in 1992, and so did the German Protestant theologian Wolfgang Bornebusch and the Jewish American therapist Isaac Zieman in May 1992 in New York. Dan Bar-On has also offered programs for Jews and Germans; in 1992, for example, he conducted a meeting between Holocaust survivors and children of victimizers. Most of these programs have remained in a protected therapeutic and group-dynamic environment, reaching out to the public through conferences, publications, and the media. None has focused exclusively on the third generation, like the student programs on the Holocaust, or emphasized performances, like the Jewish-German Dance Theatre; but they all have created forums for Jews and Germans to meet as a communitas.[13]

For third-generation Jews and Germans to share publicly what they experience in intense, experiential processes is often frustrating. Participants in those processes return to a public that is largely unprepared for the new critical awareness they bring to their communities' ethos and discourse. They again must confront old rhetorics, fictionalized images, and claims and counterclaims over the correct way of remembering the past. Participants in reconciliatory practices may realize that the communitas has changed them but that it has not altered society at large. This in part explains why, for example, so many of the American and German students in the summer Holocaust programs found it difficult at first to convey their experiences to family and friends. At semiannual reunions,[14] some students shared their frustrations of not being listened to; others were troubled by their family and friends' reluctance to accept the renewed sense of human bonding they had experienced in the communitas of Jews and German; still others already had decided that no one would understand and therefore kept silent. The responses of students at reunions of the 1993 program demonstrate their situation. Thomas, a West German student, showed slides to his family but raced through the show because he feared that they would only ask superficial questions. Earlier he had talked to his mother about his depression after the program and she responded, "If you do not feel good, you should not have gone on this program." Claudia, an East German, said that her parents felt threatened by her stories but she disregarded their fears and told them anyway. Kolja, another East German, said that his mother was interested in his experiences but refused to talk about antisemitism. Other Germans talked about friends who listened with expressionless faces or countered with statements like "Americans are racist themselves" or "Americans killed the Indians." Some American students did not fare much better. Beth, a very outspoken American Jew, did not talk to anyone about the program the first three months after it ended, not even her parents to whom, as she said, she feels very close. Aviva, another Jewish American, got in a fight with her college roommate about her indifference. "If you want to be a friend," Aviva said, "you have to try to understand me. But you won't understand me if I can't tell you about the program."

These frustrations must be taken into account when facilitating reconciliatory processes. The reunions often helped the students to find a language and the courage to confront the public more forcefully; and many began to share their experiences in imaginative ways. They presented slide shows, published articles, wrote poems, created dramatic skits for their peers, returned to subsequent programs as speakers, went to schools as lecturers, became politically and socially active, or, as in a few cases, changed their career goals.

Interactions between a communitas and the public are reciprocal processes. In spite of frustrations, a Jewish/German communitas can develop enough esprit de corps to motivate a lethargic public. What sometimes are frustrations to people who participated in reconciliatory processes may become inspirations to the public. When a communitas and the public interact, they together can lift their awareness, however slightly, to new levels of honesty, vulnerability, and trust.

A review of a performance of the Jewish-German Dance Theatre, published by a major German regional newspaper, proves this point.[15] I am intrigued by this particular review because the author does not hide her conflicted emotions about her role as a German spectator watching the performance:

"Because She Does Not Want to Speak the German Language"
Hanau. I do not feel guilty. I belong to a generation with a critical mind, for whom the Holocaust is predominantly linked to shame. This explains why I am sometimes bored by moralistic commemorations which evoke the horror, though the latter will always remain unimaginable to me. I am terrified, but I have known this ever since my school days: that images of starvation, humiliation, and torment of people recall a unique and massive crime. That the perfectionism and harshness of Germans are to be blamed for it. That many Germans claim they did not know anything, because they did not want to ask. Yet, for many years, I have also been ashamed of being a German.

A young and beautiful woman, a member of the Jewish-German Dance Theatre, is standing at the edge of the stage. Only a short distance away, she shouts out her fear, her anger. Fear of me. Anger against me. She speaks English because she does not want to speak the German language. She is Jewish. . . .

There is a dance to the poem "Todesfuge" by Paul Celan, a survivor who committed suicide in 1970 in Paris. The writhing bodies, which melt to the floor and rise again, the stamping feet, they say more than words. "Black milk of daybreak, we drink and we drink it. Death is a master from Germany."

I long for rest, for comfort. But there is no mercy. A man talks about a Sunday afternoon: he was reading a book about the death camps. He talks about a prisoner who crawled like a worm on the floor. Suddenly, the stage becomes the death camp, as before, when people staggered against barbed wire. Now a prisoner, [the performer] crawls toward a bowl of warm soup. "Hunger," he whispers, and he drags himself forward with hollow eyes.

In the following scene, [two dancers] meditate over the issue of guilt as they do physical acrobatics. It looks as terrifying and humorous as it is. Is the phrase "Our Father, forgive us our sins," with which the dancers encroach on a praying Jew, a plea for repentance? There were too many nights in which Germans looked the other way when people, as now on stage, were seized in darkness and taken away. I sense how that must have been, and I have a bad conscience. The ability to look the other way has not vanished. Repression as rediscovery. "I have no prejudices, I don't know any Jews anyway," says the man on stage. Me neither.

Germans have forgotten their songs of tenderness. And that is my pain, too: "Talk to me," a son pleads with his father. But the father was too young, did not know anything, carries no guilt, has no time because he has to work and work. . . .

I perceive the anger [of the Jewish woman], which is noticeable even in the conversation afterwards, as unjust if it is directed against me. I feel I would like to rebuff her and am ashamed. Then I accept her anger. "It is not easy," the young [Jewish] woman says when she talks about Jews and Germans confronting the Holocaust together. But there is hope when expressing and reexperiencing the suffering. Will there be a day when I won't be ashamed of being a German?

9   At Auschwitz

Memory and Identity Revisited

Auschwitz is a no-man's-land of the mind.
—**Dan Diner**

To reduce Auschwitz the place to a symbol of unutterable evil
is to avoid the complexity of its human dimension.
—**Kevin Lewis**

Arriving at Auschwitz

Auschwitz, as symbol, means different things to different people. It is hell, a death factory, a place of survival. It is the abyss
of Western civilization. It spurs the imagination of writers and
filmmakers. It is a national symbol for Poles, a cataclysmic
event for Jews, a metaphor of disgrace for Germans. There are
"after-Auschwitz" lessons: theology after Auschwitz; education
after Auschwitz; Adorno's phrase that poetry should not be
written after Auschwitz. There are also "despite-Auschwitz" discourses: despite Auschwitz, Jews survived; despite Auschwitz,
there is hope; despite Auschwitz, the arms race continues. *In
the beginning was Auschwitz,* a recent book title reads (Stern
1991). For some, Auschwitz symbolizes a beginning; for others,
the end.

What about Auschwitz the place? Does the actual site, like
the symbol, mean different things to different people too? Or
do the remains of the death camp speak with such a strong and
unambiguous voice that all visitors hear, see, and learn the same
thing? Visitors, we assume, see the same fences, the same barracks, the same ruins of the crematories. But do all visitors enter
the gas chamber, walk over a field of ashes, touch the rusting
and cold wire? Do they meditate on the evil or do they rush

through the exhibits? Do they cry? Are they silent? Do they talk, whisper, scream?

Thinking of Auschwitz, visitors most often recall images of suitcases, glasses, hair, and shoes piled up in the barracks of the main camp. That camp, Auschwitz I, which between 1939 and 1942 primarily housed Polish political prisoners, is part of the three camps that make up the Auschwitz complex. Nearby is Auschwitz-Birkenau, Auschwitz II, with its four gas chambers and crematories; built in 1942, it was the largest killing center of the Nazis; about 1.3 million Jews perished there. Monowitz, Auschwitz III, was a slave-labor camp for the I. G. Farben corporation, a few miles away from Auschwitz I.

People are shocked by the horror that emanates from the site, especially as they go through the exhibit in the barracks of Auschwitz I. Many are equally appalled by the atmosphere of a tourist attraction, as hundreds of people mill around the barracks each day during the summer months. Polish school classes, American and German travelers, church groups, Japanese visitors, Israeli and French youth groups—they are all guided through Auschwitz the museum. They first watch a movie about the Soviet liberation of the camp and then proceed to the entrance gate, which bears the infamous words ARBEIT MACHT FREI. They are led through barracks in which documents, charts, and photographs are on display. They pass the camp's "hospital," enter the prison and torture chambers, pass the gallows at the roll call place, and see, close by, Rudolf Höss's villa, the residence of the camp commandant and his family. The tour concludes in the crematory. Visitors who still have time and stamina go to Birkenau, the killing center. There, they can be alone. Birkenau is a vast, desolate space slowly being reclaimed by nature. Weeds and flowers cover the remains of the crematories and barracks. Blackberry bushes grow on grounds fertilized by ashes and crushed bones. I saw Polish families picking the berries when I visited in 1989, 1991, and 1993.

What has remained and is preserved of the Auschwitz complex is today a museum, a cemetery, ruins, a memorial, a tourist attraction, a pilgrimage, and, for some, a park (cf. Webber 1992). Depending on the perspectives of those who visit, Auschwitz commemorates the victims, commemorates the possibility of evil, commemorates the strength of survival, or commemorates despair. It commemorates Jews. And Poles. And Polish Jews. And Gypsies. And the Mengele twins. And . . . I hesitate . . . does it also commemorate the perpetrators?

More than any other place, Auschwitz manifests an evil that seems to defy all benign attempts to reconcile Jews and Germans of the third generation. At Auschwitz, the visual and visceral evidence of the genocide is so strong that the term "reconciliation" sounds naive, inept, even offensive. In this death camp, memories clash and identities are questioned and reaffirmed. Auschwitz threatens young Germans because it stains their identity; and it threatens the identity of young Jews because it epitomizes their loss of family, culture, and history. Can young Jews and Germans visit Auschwitz together and comfort each other? Or would they inevitably revert to two separate groups, one affirming the victim, the other rebelling against the victimizer? In this last chapter, we will accompany Jewish and Christian American and East/West German students to Auschwitz, and witness their pain as they grapple with their identities and relations in the face of evil. We will discover that Auschwitz the place subjects a communitas of Jews and Germans to a difficult test; and yet, there were moments in which Jews and Germans are able to accept each other's pain and confusion.

A three-day visit to the camps of Auschwitz was part of the summer programs on the Holocaust. The students dreaded this visit. They were afraid that the evil and pain of this place would overwhelm them. Some feared breaking down, others feared feeling nothing and being judged by their peers. "I don't know how I will react to Auschwitz," students said prior to their arrival in Poland, "and I do not know whether the group is strong enough to give me the support I need." Would the visit harm the friendships they had established over the previous three weeks? As the group approached the day of departure for Oświęcim (the Polish name for the town of Auschwitz), the students were preoccupied by Auschwitz. Other events and experiences were read through the lenses of Auschwitz the symbol. There are "many pairs of children's shoes," Lucia, a German student, wrote in her journal a few days before leaving for Poland. Her entry referred to a visit to the modern Jewish elementary school in Frankfurt, where she saw children's shoes and bags hanging on hooks outside the classrooms. It reminded her of a photograph of the shoes the Nazis had collected from their victims in Auschwitz. "The name tags on their little bags [are] all hung up neatly at the elementary school. Moving in a strange way. The reversal of an experience, so to speak, which we are yet to have. How scared we are of going to Auschwitz" (quoted in Krondorfer and Schmidt 1990:22).

Prior to the groups' leaving Berlin, we conducted a few sessions specifically designed to prepare the students for the death camps. A guest speaker presented a slide show and gave historical background information on Auschwitz, and Jochen Spielmann, a German group counselor, guided the students through an exercise in which they fingerpainted their expectations on large sheets of paper. In these sessions, individual fears were articulated, but the group as a whole remained in a state of dread and apprehension. The students plunged into a crisis the day before departure, acting out their anxieties by getting into fierce arguments. People were hurt, angry, and in tears. They doubted that they could stomach the impending journey. "I don't even know whether I want to go to Auschwitz with this group," some said. "I don't trust the group anymore." But the next morning everyone boarded the bus that would take them to the Youth Center of Oświęcim.

The day before the 1991 group went to Auschwitz, Julie Rubin, a Jewish American student, wrote a poem, "Packing for Auschwitz":

I pack
As they packed
Bound for the same place,
I, like them, think I will return.
They threw together only what was necessary, nothing extra.
They were drawing on a long and illustrious masochistic packing
    tradition
A packing tradition of a people never quite sure when the move
    would come
Maybe tomorrow or the next day
Maybe never in a lifetime—maybe never drawing on the long tra-
    dition
Passed on by their mothers and fathers at the dinner table
Or late at night by the light of a candle.
Nonetheless living portable lives with portable things
Diamonds, not land.

I want to fill my backpack until it bursts at the seams.
Both to prove that I am not them
And to prove that they have gained through me the right to be
    overindulgent packers.

I pack a hairdryer and more tampons than I need
Because they were denied such luxuries.
I carry a bottle of expensive mineral water because they had
     parched mouths.
I demand that the bus be large
2 seats per person
Because they were crammed into cattle cars.
I am armed with rice crackers, peanut butter and chocolate cookies
Because they got only a bowl of watery soup and a dry crust of
     bread
If they were lucky.
. . .
I am going to Auschwitz,
The place where Nazis worked feverishly to prevent my birth
And thus solve this problem of Jewish homelessness
And I go with an overflowing suitcase.[1]

All students came with "overflowing suitcases," packed with expectations
and memories, fears and defenses. When they arrived in Auschwitz, the
students were faced with perhaps their most difficult challenge.

Responding to Auschwitz

On the way to Auschwitz by bus, you pass railroad tracks as you enter the
town of Oświęcim. The tracks did not escape the student's attention.
"Driving through Poland, it was easy to imagine that nothing had
changed in the last fifty years," wrote Steven, a Jew. "Houses were old,
roads were old, and people were old. Our journey culminated with our
entrance to Oswiecim, waiting to cross the ominous railroad tracks"
(Krondorfer and Staffa 1992:82). Catherine, an American Christian student, scribbled the following notes in her journal: "All this trip I enjoyed
myself greatly. Then Stacy began to cry, wailing, 'I don't want to see it,'
and I was reminded of our purpose. It seems unbelievable to me that
we, that I, are going to Auschwitz. We keep passing railroad tracks,
many with parked cargo trains resting on them, and I can only think of
the cattle cars. I thought about it briefly in Germany, but not to the same
extent."

Like the railroad tracks, ordinary objects were charged with emotional and symbolic significance. A student wrote in her journal upon arrival at the Youth Center in Oświęcim: "A beautiful housing facility seemed centered on the view from our large window—a fenced-in area of red bricks and smokestacks which I was sure was 'it,' the concentration camp." But in her imagination she had mistaken an ordinary red brick building for the death camp, which could not be seen from the Youth Center. "I sat in the window," the student continued, "until Annette turned on some Mozart on the radio. As I thought of the SS men who, after a day of death planning, cried when they listened to Beethoven, I too began to cry. Of what use was it to find music beautiful?"

In Auschwitz, every experience acquired special meaning and was read through the lenses of unimaginable evil. Interestingly, though, it was often one's imagination that turned every movement into an act of extraordinary significance. There was no longer a purpose in the beauty of music. People appeared old. Railroad tracks looked ominous. The simple and tasteless food in the Youth Center was tolerated, not so much because of the impoverished Polish economy, but because, as some students said, "people had starved to death in the nearby camps." In 1989, the students complained about the dozens of reporters and film crews roaming Auschwitz in search of stories for the impending fiftieth anniversary of the German occupation of Poland. In 1991, the students were similarly dismayed by the presence of endless columns of Christian youth groups which stopped in Auschwitz on their way to see the Pope, who was visiting Cracow. In 1993, some were annoyed by the efforts at restoring the selection ramp in Auschwitz-Birkenau. The mundane work of the media and the presence of noisy teenagers and of Polish workers were experienced as intrusive. They disturbed the sanctity of the place.

I empathized with the students' initial reactions, for I, too, was dazed when I first visited the camps, overwhelmed by the evil I could see and touch everywhere. There was a concreteness to the place I had not anticipated. And yet, my imagination also played a large a role in how I perceived Auschwitz. Every brick of the barracks seemed to contain the prisoners' screams—but the voices of visitors and guides drowned them. Every flower in Birkenau seemed to be soaked in blood—yet Polish peasants cut them to keep the ruins from being overgrown by weeds. I found the sign SIGHTSEEING TOUR extremely irritating but was glad to get explanations on my way through Birkenau. How did I relate to these grounds? Did I walk through a museum, a memorial, a cemetery? So many taboos had been violated on these grounds that I was cautious not to disturb its perverse sacredness, perhaps fearing some imagined retaliation. I walked through negative sacred space in which everything ordinary turned into something of a precarious nature. Every step seemed to be a statement, every word inadequate, and every experience flooded with symbolic meaning.

"I became obsessed with rescuing a yellow butterfly," remembered Ruth Laibson, executive director of the Philadelphia Interfaith Council on the Holocaust, who accompanied the student groups as an observer. She was standing in one of the remaining barracks in Birkenau, where she saw a butterfly flapping its wings against the inside of the window. "I could concentrate on nothing else but this butterfly throwing itself against the window, flapping its wings, and then pulling away and growing quiet, and then flapping its wings again in this desperate attempt to get beyond the glass." With the help of some students, Ruth tried to rescue the butterfly, but their attempts failed. "By that time," Ruth said, "I had made the determination that I was going to break the glass. The symbolism of the whole thing had gotten too great for me." Eventually, the butterfly was gently pushed out through a small opening in the window panel.

"By some miracle, without injuring the butterfly, we set it loose. It was such a release for me. At that point, I was so totally overwrought that I began to sob uncontrollably and rushed out of the building. I had to separate myself from the group and try to get control of myself. It took me about an hour."

In another incident in Birkenau, a small, shimmering object hidden between weeds next to a crematory attracted the attention of Ben, an American student of Jewish and African descent. He picked it up and was aghast: it was a tooth covered in some silvery metal. "I picked it up," Ben said, "but I didn't want it. I just didn't know what to do with it." This tooth became Ben's personal struggle with a symbolically fraught place. Holding this tiny remnant of an unknown person gassed and burned by the Nazis, Ben was forced to define what Auschwitz-Birkenau meant to him. He was distressed by his options. Keeping the tooth would turn Auschwitz into a tourist attraction vulnerable to souvenir hunters. If Auschwitz was a museum, keeping the tooth would amount to stealing it. On the other hand, leaving the tooth where he found it would define Auschwitz as a memorial, from which nothing could be removed. "I knew that I didn't want anyone else to take it as a souvenir or sell it. It was a silver tooth. So I put it back among the trees." Ben in fact buried the tooth there. He had found and defined his relation to Auschwitz: a burial ground.[2]

Ben and Ruth tried to come to terms with this place of utter evil. The release of the butterfly, of which there were many in Birkenau, became a small miracle, and the tooth became imbued with extraordinary symbolic power. The dilemma Ben faced has also troubled the museum staff at Auschwitz for a long time. What should be done with the remains of the dead? "[A] number of Holocaust survivors have contacted us and asked that their remains be buried at Birkenau," Krystyna Olesky, the deputy director of the Auschwitz museum, has said. "We understand their desire to have their remains interred here. Birkenau is a cemetery, but not a cemetery where you can conduct funerals" (quoted in Ryback 1993:78).

A similarly symbolic event, albeit of a more visceral nature, happened to an American Jewish student in 1993 a few days after we had returned from Auschwitz. Jennifer and a German student were taking the subway to Berlin's center city when a woman entered and without apparent reason sprayed tear gas into the moving train. The passengers flung open doors and windows to get fresh air but Jennifer sat paralyzed, choking on the gas. Something like that could have also happened in New York. But in Berlin's subway, there was only one thought rushing through Jennifer's mind: "Oh my God. Now, they're finally doing it. They're trying to gas me."

If such events acquired so much symbolic weight, we should expect that religious symbols, which have always been vested with passionate convictions, would be especially volatile in Auschwitz. And indeed, the presence of religious symbolism in the death camps has strained Jewish/Christian relations. Since Polish Catholics interpret Auschwitz within their own martyrological tradition, Christian symbols have been erected in and around the camps. Every visitor will see, for example, the basement cell in which Maximilian Kolbe, a Polish priest, died after he had voluntarily taken the place of another prisoner sentenced to death. The martyrological symbolism of the flowers and candles in the dark cell is obvious. It is, however, not generally known, or is rarely acknowledged, that the same priest had been the "editor of a virulently anti-Semitic newspaper" (Roiphe 1988:108) before the German invasion of Poland.

Crosses and stars of David have been erected at the site of pits where corpses had been set ablaze in Auschwitz-Birkenau. At one of those pits, a star of David was nailed to one of the crosses. The students were puzzled about the symbolism, particularly the Jewish American students, who could only see a crucified Jewish star. A few Christian Americans acknowledged the attempt to create a symbol of Jewish/Christian reconciliation. James Young, who studied the significance of Auschwitz as a memorial, reported on the irony of this well-intended reconciliatory gesture: "Young Poles had attempted to create a symbol of solidarity between Jewish and Polish martyrs by nailing Stars of David to the crosses—in effect, crucifying the Jewish star," he wrote. "The memorial volunteers had hoped to perform an egalitarian 'marriage' of Jewish and Christian symbols, but Jewish eyes found an ironic and bitter reference to the martyrdom of Jews at Christian hands" (1992:33).

In the summer of 1989, I witnessed another example of religious conflicts when some of our students decided to participate in a protest staged by survivors from Israel in front of the residence of Carmelite nuns. The nuns lived in a former camp warehouse, where they prayed for the souls of the dead. The warehouse was located outside the gates of Auschwitz I, the main camp, separated from it only by a wall. A huge cross planted next to the warehouse greeted all visitors on their way to the camp's main entrance. To many Jews worldwide, the presence of the nuns and the cross violated religious sensibilities. After all, the vast majority of people killed in Auschwitz were Jews. Earlier protests conducted by Jews in front of the building had already led to confrontations with Poles. Emotions ran high on all sides. On the day when some of our students joined the protest, we witnessed the tensions. A Polish worker inside the warehouse waved menacingly with his hammer, inciting the survivors' hisses in response. Someone threw a bottle over the fence at the building. When a local car drove by and a passenger spat out the window, Isac, one of the Jewish students, ran after the car and might have started a fistfight had the Israeli organizers not reprimanded him.[3]

The railroad tracks, the butterfly, the tooth, the warehouse, the crosses—all these incidents were intense and meaningful to the individuals who experienced them. But the students did not travel alone to

Auschwitz; they visited the camps as a heterogeneous group of Americans, Jews, Christians, and Germans. This introduced a whole new dimension to coming to terms with Auschwitz. As part of a communitas, the students had to realize that they differed in their experiences and perceptions of Auschwitz and that they needed to tolerate and comprehend these differences if they wanted to maintain their friendships. Now that every breath had symbolic weight, the students had to work hard on staying together as a group.

Tensions in the communitas were first acted out over the issue of Poland. Jewish students especially were highly suspicious of Poles and made no secret of it. That our Polish tour guide took us to a field (the same field where Ben had found his tooth) where he dug for bones and teeth with the heels of his shoes did not help to reduce animosities. When the guide explained that we were standing on a field of human ashes from the crematories, a Jewish student almost fainted, and others charged the guide with lack of respect for the dead. As deplorable as the guide's behavior may be, I suspect that he would not have fared much better in the students' judgment had this incident not occurred. Even during our morning tour of the main camp, students were annoyed by his monotonous explanations. "Why doesn't he stop bombarding me with words," Catherine wrote in her journal, expressing a sentiment shared by most. Students later described the guide as cold, detached, insensitive—although, with the exception of the field episode, he did a decent job of introducing visitors to this place and of providing historic information. The guide, I felt, became an easy target for the students' free-floating anger and frustration. James Young similarly reported that, in some cases, "Jewish visitors to the camp had begun to confuse their Polish tour guides for SS guards" (Young 1992:77).[4]

In 1991, the anti-Polish sentiments of Jewish American students almost proved Young's observation. Shortly after arriving at the Youth Center of Oświęcim, even before the students had met any Poles or set foot in the camps, these sentiments spilled over. "With no exception," I wrote in my journal after our first group session in Oświęcim, "the Jewish students shared their feeling of anger toward Poles tonight. They say they are even more angry at Poles than at Germans." (One Jewish student admitted that she was so angry that she "wanted to hit the old [Polish] woman standing in her garden hanging up the laundry.") When my co-facilitator and I asked why, they mentioned Polish antisemitism and the historic animosities between Poles and Jews. Their explanations, however, did not convince the German students, who began to defend Poland. The Germans were conscious about not exhibiting anti-Polish sentiments since Poles had also suffered under the Hitler regime and have been the subject of prejudice and jokes in postwar Germany. They were caught in a bind: they wished to sympathize with their Jewish peers but could not accept their anti-Polish tirades.

The more German students objected to anti-Polish sentiments, the more the Jewish students felt the need to express their strong feelings. The argument peaked when the students accused each other of not listening and of trying to coerce each other into agreeing with their particular perspectives. They parted in frustration: they had just arrived in Auschwitz and were already caught up in an argument. The discussion seemed to prove their earlier apprehensions: as a group, they failed to develop the trust and support they yearned for. My reading of the situation, however, was more optimistic. Since the students got into an argument with each other at the end of the discussion, they had begun to interact directly rather than dumping their frustrations on a third party, the Polish people. The struggle of a communitas of Jews and Germans was set in motion.

Interactions between the students during our three-day stay in Auschwitz were often painful to observe. Especially in the 1989 program, Auschwitz generated extreme anger, distrust, and misunderstandings. At the end of the first day of guided tours through the camps, the students were reluctant to share their experiences and thoughts. "I feel like I'm underwater or in fog—distanced from others," wrote a student in her journal. "I can't find words—truly there is no language for Auschwitz." Students became introverted and distanced themselves from group processes, but gentle prodding eventually encouraged them to verbalize their feelings. Jewish students were the first to speak. They recalled very tangible images and intimate experiences. Jeremy, for example, told the group how he had come across a fallen tree and had discovered layers of earth mixed in with layers of ashes under its trunk. "I had bones in my hand," he said, turning pale. Suzanne recalled in a trembling voice how she had instinctively grabbed her own hair when she stood in front of a display of women's hair in a barrack. German reactions, in contrast, were more detached and vague. "It's still too confusing. I need more time," Lucia told the group. Matthias said, "Strange for me was to see this place as a museum. I didn't feel that much. It was too much like tourism."

The cultural differences in responses to Auschwitz were striking. For Jewish students, it was important to touch the earth, the cold wires, the wooden bunk beds, to walk along the train tracks. They tried to imagine, almost physically, the horrors that had taken place there. The German students, on the other hand, tended to relate to Auschwitz intellectually, at least on the surface. I could see the emotional tensions in their faces, but unlike the Jewish students, they rarely cried. Something prevented them from letting go. They were wary of the "typical American" emotionality, they said. They understood the grief and tears of their Jewish friends but were uncomfortable with what they perceived as exaggerated behavior. To imagine oneself a victim, they said again, trivializes Auschwitz. It is impossible to comprehend the unimaginable evil of this place by touching ashes, burying a tooth, or rescuing a butterfly. "After all, the whole thing is a graveyard," commented Matthias. In a cemetery, one grieves for the dead but does not identify with them.

Although German students objected to showing too much emotion, they were afraid that their more stoic reactions might be misinterpreted as indifference. They described themselves as more critical than Americans, but clearly they were not indifferent. They were as tightly enmeshed in Auschwitz as their Jewish peers. I interpreted their stoicism as an unself-conscious attempt to curb strong and ambivalent feelings. I wondered: Were they stifled by anger and shame because they, as young Germans, identified with the descendants of SS guards? Or did they represent a new generation that was able to lament the loss of Jewish lives and grieve with their new Jewish friends? The German students seemed torn between the equally strong emotions of anger, shame, and grief—and ended up showing none.

Some Germans refrained from talking openly to their Jewish peers in Auschwitz because they were afraid of being judged by them. In 1989, I had a late-night discussion with a small group of German students in the Youth Center, in which they admitted their anger at the Americans. "They have expected so much from Auschwitz," someone said, "and now they are looking for it. It's like a self-fulfilling prophesy." Touching all those objects, the argument continued, is like trying to re-create the prisoners' experience, only "you can never feel like the victims." Another German believed that the group pressured him to feel in a certain way, that people expected a certain emotional response. "We cannot say what we want to say because there is so much group pressure. As Germans, we have to make so many compromises. Jews can just talk. We can't say that we are upset at them. If we do, we are again 'the Germans.'"

During this late-night discussion, I was particularly intrigued by a German student who recounted her experience in a barrack in the main camp, where hundreds of portraits of prisoners were hung on to the walls. The photographs had been taken by the Nazi administration, and the Polish museum staff had arranged them so that visitors would walk through a hallway with faces looking at them from all sides. "I did not feel but was thinking," the student said. "The museum has an agenda and we need to be aware of it. When you walk through this hallway with all the pictures of prisoners staring at you, of course you feel like an SS guard." She suspected that the museum's "hidden agenda" was to make her feel like a victimizer.

I tried to tell her that her identification with an SS guard was not due to any malicious intent on the part of the museum but to her particular perception as a German. Only the children and grandchildren of the society that had produced the perpetrators would feel like SS guards when walking through this hallway. Only they would imagine themselves in uniform and defend themselves against the guilt conjured up by their imagination. If Poles or Jews entered the same barrack, they would not feel a hostile gaze but would relate to the prisoners' portraits in sorrow. They would not see accusers but familiar faces.

That night, this student was unable to hear my argument. She considered herself a person who would not be swept away by feelings but would critically dissect the exhibit's hidden agenda. She did not accept my reasoning that her reactions to the photographs of prisoners were determined by her cultural identity and that her anger was the result of a conflicted inner voice. She insisted on the correctness of her perception: the museum wanted to make her feel guilty. I later imagined that she must have felt terribly exposed and vulnerable to the gaze of prisoners, as if running the gauntlet, and that she experienced this gaze as hostile. Understandably, she reacted defensively and with anger. I again realized how difficult it was to escape the ethos of guilt in which postwar German generations have been raised.

It is possible to interpret the defensiveness, confusion, and fear the German students experienced as a result of unresolved guilt feelings.

Indeed, much of my earlier discussion of the German ethos of guilt would support such an interpretation. However, as I began to reflect on the students' responses, I realized that the vicious cycle of fear, anger, and ensuing guilt disguised another, much stronger feeling: shame. "Guilt is a reaction to a deed, shame a reaction to a mode of being," the psychoanalyst Peer Hultberg writes (1987:85). Third-generation Germans are not guilty of the deeds of their forebears but can still be ashamed of being German, especially at Auschwitz (cf. Krondorfer 1991b). Their intellectual detachment, the fear of being judged, the anger that defends against guilt feelings can actually be read as a giant maneuver against shame. And likewise, the exhaustive discussions of guilt and forgiveness, which have taken up so much space in the post-war German psyche, can be understood as a defense mechanism against this powerful emotion. Young Germans defend themselves against feelings of guilt in order to avoid shame.

In the presence of Jews, the German students, and I myself, became painfully aware of their ambivalent and insecure identities because they were witnessing how they and the descendants of victims approached the death camps differently. Germans were uncomfortable and angry because they feared that their Jewish peers could call them to account for their feelings, or lack of feelings. And even if Jews abstained from doing that, their presence alone put pressure on Germans who felt observed and exposed. Shame, according to some psychologists, is occasioned by an event or object that threatens to expose the discrepancy between an ideal self and a real self. It is based on idealized figures that "become threatening when the I is not as it should be." In the case of guilt, one is punished but "always remains a member of society. . . . In the case of shame [there is] the fear of being banished from the human community" (Hultberg 1987:92). In Auschwitz, the desire of third-generation Germans not to be identified as German was at its strongest, yet the presence of Jewish peers threatened to expose their national identity. Shame surfaced in the widening crack between the desire to be a person free of a noxious history and the realization of one's inheritance from that poisonous past. No wonder the German students became defensive, paralyzed, and helpless.

If the German students felt this way, why take a group of Jews and Germans to Auschwitz? Defensiveness and helplessness can hardly be the goal of a program that wants to foster reconciliation. Here again, the idea of communitas is of help. Third-generation Jews and Germans might temporarily experience disempowerment, but a communitas averts false identifications and transcends the narrow perceptions that often occur in homogeneous groups. Homogeneous groups can easily mistake their particular experience as the only acceptable and valid response to Auschwitz, and, as a result, they might leave the site without being affected. I have heard from a number of young Germans who went to Auschwitz by themselves or only with other Germans that they were not as deeply touched as they had anticipated. They seemed more irritated by the tourist atmosphere of Auschwitz than moved by the actual remains of the death camp. Outsiders watching such German visitors might perceive them as stoic and indifferent. Without the presence of Jews, young Germans were missing out on the perspective of descendants of victims and, in all likelihood, they did not even realize the cultural bias and limitation of their detached and intellectualized "German" perception. In a study of Nazi children's inability to relate to the suffering of Holocaust victims, the psychologists Dan Bar-On and Amalia Gaon write that this inability can "easily be interpreted by others as a lack of interest, a sign of not really caring," which, however, should "not be interpreted as a lack of guilt and shame." Rather, "those who feel shame, guilt, even moral responsibility for their parents' atrocious acts might be incapable of verbalizing their emotions. . . . This phenomenon may even pertain to the third generation" (1991:91). Caught in the conflicting feelings of shame, anger, and guilt, young Germans may appear to be unmoved by Auschwitz, though their identity is shaken.

Young Jews from around the globe are sent to the site of the former camps in the hope that the visit will strengthen their identity as Jews. But as homogeneous groups, they do not transcend the confines of the Jewish ethos. "They leave as Israelis and come back as Jews," said an Israeli who had accompanied such groups to Auschwitz (quoted in Broder 1989; cf. Feldman 1994; Webber 1992). Yet these trips, which have been praised by some and criticized by others, leave some Jewish youngsters untouched. "Their dreams had been peopled by Nazis so long that the ramp left them cold," wrote Susan Neiman about a group of young German Jews in Auschwitz. "[C]ertain sorts of thought-experiments were familiar as mother's milk. 'Would you rather fuck the SS guards, or go to the gas?' called a young man. 'Fuck the guards,' replied the teenage girls, sitting down to try out a barrack bunk" (1992:304).

The indiscriminate indulgence of homogeneous groups in their cultural biases and narrow perceptions can be stopped by traveling to Auschwitz as a communitas of Jews and Germans. What a communitas has to offer is a protective structure in which Jews and Germans can work out their different experiences and perceptions. It is in the nature of Auschwitz that memories and identities clash. But rather than mistake one's own experience as normative and deride other perspectives, in an interactive environment each group is forced to integrate other experiences and realize their own limited views. In the best case, Jews and Germans of the third generation try to comfort each other in Auschwitz, despite the tremendous tensions to which they are exposed. Then, reconciliatory work has been successful. I have witnessed such moments of comfort across cultural and religious differences—but only after a communitas had gone through the inevitable struggles.

I will conclude this book by looking at one specific struggle and its eventual resolution. Faced with the task of creating a commemorative ritual at the end of their three-day visit to Auschwitz, the American and German students plunged into a crisis, only to emerge with a powerful ritual that strengthened the ties between Jews and Germans. After all the conflicts they had endured, the students were able to create a transformative ritual of reconciliation—despite the despair Auschwitz had evoked.

Commemorating Auschwitz

When I returned to Auschwitz with students in 1991, their responses differed from those of the previous group. The 1989 students had struggled intensely with what they had perceived as differences between the "intellectual" Germans and the "emotional" American Jews. This conflict was less visible two years later. It is true that the students of the 1991 program had a fierce argument about Polish people upon their arrival in Oświęcim, but in general they were less reluctant to share their experiences and better able to comfort each other. The larger contingent of American Christians and the presence of East Germans, who were not included previously, accounted in part for these changes. Like their German peers, the Christian American students, for example, were afraid that Auschwitz might not affect them. "I don't know what to expect," said Jennifer during a preliminary session in Berlin, "but I know I am not afraid of Auschwitz itself. I'm scared that I may not be affected by it. What if I alone am untouched?" The East Germans, on the other hand, were willing to imagine the victimization that had taken place in the camps, perhaps because they had felt oppressed by the old East German government. "In the exhibit, I saw the same type of glasses I am wearing," said Katharina, the daughter of an East German Protestant minister. And Torsten, an East German medical student, identified with "a man's face in the gallery who had my birthday." The gallery Torsten referred to is the same place where, two years earlier, a West German woman had felt like a SS guard.

I was pleased with this situation: there was less overt resistance to the emotional impact of Auschwitz among German students and more cohesion in the group as a whole owing to their willingness to listen to each other. But differences between Jewish and German responses still existed, more subtle perhaps, and I wondered when they would surface and create conflicts. In her essay "Encountering Auschwitz," Catherine, a Christian American student, noticed these differences as well:

> "I've been there before," she said. "I'm more afraid of going this time because I'm with you and the Jewish American students. I'm afraid of what you'll think of us." So spoke my German friend when I asked her about going to Auschwitz. "Don't be silly," I replied quickly with all the confidence bravado brings. "My feelings for you won't change at all." And so I believed before the visit that wrenched my soul and tried the bonds of our group.
>
> Surely our group must have been unique among all the others we saw at Auschwitz and Birkenau. Catholic youth groups with banners blazing in the sunshine (the Pope had been in nearby Cracow). French families, Italian tourists, a few couples passing through. And then there was us, the twenty Christian, American, Jewish, and East and West German students. We had spent nearly three weeks dealing with the dynamics of this mix, individual personalities aside, when we headed for Poland from Berlin. Certainly our identities as, and within, this particular group were integral to our days at the camps. . . .
>
> As I walked with my friends through the exhibits showing the different aspects of this insanity, I was oblivious to the fine distinctions of our group make-up. All was lost in a feeling of such intense and

profound pain at what human beings had set out to do to others. Had I stopped to think of my German peers whose families might have been involved in some way with this outrage, I would have marveled at their courage, trying to grapple openly with this past, attempting to break the silence of denial.

Yes, we tended to divide along national lines when the group splintered into smaller ones during our walk through the camps. But I would not jump to any dramatic conclusions or look for hidden significance of our behavior. I expected that we would seek the most comfortable and supportive companions during an experience as wrenching as a visit to the camps, if only because of the language.

Now, as I write this essay, I wonder if my initial impression results from my naivete, my desire to see only the positive. Were the Germans really less emotionally affected than the Americans? For that matter, were the Christian Americans less affected than the Jewish Americans? Were the Germans burdened by an unshakeable guilt, and did the presence of the Jewish Americans contribute to this feeling? (Quoted in Krondorfer and Staffa 1992:67–68)

Tensions finally came to the fore on our last day in Auschwitz. The students had assembled in the afternoon with the task of planning a commemorative ritual. My co-facilitator, Christian Staffa, and I had suggested this idea to mark our visit to Auschwitz as a special event and to strengthen the ties among the students. To our surprise, the preparation of the ritual reopened a schism: the American students, both Christian and Jewish, welcomed the opportunity to create a common ritual, while the East and West German students were skeptical of the event. As facilitators, we posed three questions designed to help students prepare the commemoration: Why do you want to create a commemorative ritual? Where do you want it to take place? How should it unfold? We figured that "why," "where," and "how" addressed three components—intention, location, and procedure—that were necessary to a meaningful ritual.

The first question prompted very different responses. American students were able to give precise reasons for their wish for a commemoration. The following remarks by Catherine and Steven represent their reasoning:

Catherine (American Christian): I feel the need to have a service . . . because I want us to "leave a mark" as a group and as individuals. I

also want to ritualize and sanctify my vow to be committed to the
lessons of the Holocaust, to learn and to teach. I also feel it brings a
sense of closure to our time here. It also brings our time here to a
level one step higher, to pay respect, not just to gawk and stare, but to
explicitly show acknowledgement . . . of what happened [here] and
how it connects with what we're doing.

Steven (Jewish American): The commemoration is, first, for the dead,
for the people, although I don't know what they get out of it—perhaps that they didn't die in vain. Second, it is for us as individuals
and a group, to find a moment of closure and to say farewell. Third,
it is a public statement. It shows others a different kind of approach
to Auschwitz. And on a fourth level, it is spiritual. It is not just historical but deeper, like God or faith.

German students had difficulties in answering the same question. They
remained evasive and ambiguous and attached certain conditions to their
responses. A commemoration would be acceptable if it took place in
silence and in Birkenau, a German said. "Otherwise, I am not interested."
From the "why" we moved on to the "where," the ritual location.
During this part of the discussion, tensions increased because the group
was unable to agree on a place. They quickly reached consensus about
Birkenau as the general area, rather than the crowded main camp, but
they could not agree on a specific location. Several places were suggested: the field of ashes and bones next to the crematory; the crematory itself; beneath the famous watchtower at the entrance gate; inside
one of the women's barracks; the end of the train tracks, where a memorial sculpture had been erected; the selection ramp; the barrack where
Ed Gastfriend, who had talked to the students in America, had been
imprisoned; the small pond where ashes had been dumped. Each place
triggered a long debate since each held special meaning for those who
suggested it. Ed's barrack, for example, offered a personal link between
the camp and the students; but others argued that a single barrack
would ignore the totality of evil. The train tracks were a good location,
some students suggested, because they represented the border between
life and death; also, in reverse direction, the tracks would lead back to
Germany. The pond was quickly rejected because of mosquitos; the
women's barrack was rejected because it kept nature outside; and the
crematory was dismissed because it represented pure evil without any

glimpse of hope. Finally, someone suggested that we think of the ritual not as a fixed location but as a journey. In that way, several places could be connected and different rituals created for each.

This proposal broke the deadlock of the discussion, and we were able to move on to the last question: How should the ritual unfold? A list of components was quickly compiled: candles; flowers; prayers (especially Kaddish); silence; sharing journal entries; reading poems; time to go to one's special place individually; a group pledge; reading names of people who perished in the camp. Many creative ideas were tossed around, but group tensions made it impossible to put them in any kind of order. Frustration spread. The Americans adopted a pragmatic approach to resolve the conflict, while most Germans became annoyed and refused to participate. It all came to a head when Kay and Michael, two East German students, walked out of the room.

I interfered and asked how the group felt about Kay's and Michael's departure. The American students expressed their anger and disappointment over the German refusal to help in creating the ritual. "In my notes on the ensuing conversation, it seems that only three Germans actively took part in crafting the commemoration service," Catherine recalled in her journal. Most of the German students denied that there was any significance to their indifference and nonparticipation. When I suggested that Kay's and Michael's withdrawal was a statement in itself, a German quickly objected: "We should not overinterpret it." Another added: "It's not a statement, they are just bored."

"The German students don't want to discuss the commemoration service," wrote Jennifer, a Christian American, in her journal. "Why can't they deal with it? Are they so scared of anything spiritual?" Indeed, part of the problem was a difference in how Germans and Americans related to religion. As practicing Christians and Jews, many of the Americans had previously organized religious gatherings. Most Germans, by contrast, did not define themselves by religious affiliation or were, as in the case of many East Germans, unfamiliar with religious services. "This is too much like a church, like liturgy," Germans complained. Rather than structure the ritual in advance, they wanted to get together in Birkenau and rely on what people would come up with spontaneously. Kay wrote in his journal: "I had a bad feeling about the discussion. Especially the Americans were struggling for hours(!) about the place, if we [should] take candles, read poems. . . . It was like preparing a worship."

A year later, I received a letter from Kay in which he explained again why he had left the room:

> That I finally left the room had to do with the fact that I really had a headache and that I wanted to prepare myself for "the service" alone and in peace. It really wasn't meant as a protest, and I certainly did not want to offend anyone.
>
> The situation changed because Michael also left the room. It looked as if we had agreed on leaving together, as a protest. Maybe, this was Michael's intention. I don't want to apologize for what I did. . . . but it hurt me that my excuse [the headache] was not accepted. Furthermore, I am not surprised that Michael escaped [since] the discussion was so pragmatic and somehow not appropriate for a commemoration service. This is why I do not accept Jennifer's question whether we Germans are scared of anything spiritual. . . . I had no problems with commemorating the victims at this place, to somehow identify with their suffering, perhaps because I am an East German and do not identify with Germany of either past or present. [But] I had difficulties with the trivial squabbling over location, procedure, etc. As if we had to prepare a liturgy, stifled and predetermined (which, of course, eliminates potentially "disturbing spontaneity"). I got the impression that the Americans wanted to conduct an "inter-faith service," which would have excluded religiously unaffiliated people.

Although the students cited religious upbringing as the primary reason for their adverse views of the commemoration, I believe that other forces were also fueling the conflict. It was Auschwitz itself that thwarted the smooth progression of the planning process for the ritual. The fact that German students were reluctant to organize a commemorative ritual was, I believe, intimately linked to the threat Auschwitz posed to their identity. If it is true that Germans feel shame and want to escape their "Germanness" in Auschwitz, who and what would be the subject of their remembrance? Would they commemorate the victims or the victimizers? Would they identify with the grief and anger of their Jewish friends or with the denial and silence of their own families? Would the ritual be intended to reconcile them with their Jewish peers or with their country's past? The American students, on the other hand, did not have to struggle with this kind of ambiguity. Certainly, the Jewish ethos of remembrance had prepared the Jewish students to partake in a commemorative ritual. The Christian American students, on the other hand, were comfortable with the event because they had prior experience with religious gatherings. My co-facilitator and I wondered, however, why the Christian Americans were so eager to create a commemoration, for they, too, could have been seriously troubled by the legacy of Christian antisemitism. Since they were not, we asked ourselves whether their pragmatic approach served to protect them from questioning more deeply their Christian identity in the light of the Shoah.

The struggle over the commemorative ritual maintained its intensity for four hours. The Germans resisted any imposition of "liturgical" structures and opted for "spontaneity"; the Americans kept tossing ideas around and attempted to create a ritual order agreeable to everyone.

Thanks to the pragmatic skills of the American students, the group eventually agreed on a ritual structure. Based on the idea of a journey, the ritual would allow alternate times for individual and group activities, for silent meditation and "liturgical" moments. At dusk, we would drive to Birkenau and, for half an hour, wander around individually, going back to places most meaningful to each of us. We would then gather as a group between the two crematories, at the end of the railroad tracks. In silence, we would walk down the road along the tracks toward the entrance gate, toward liberation. Halfway down the road, at the selection ramp, we would form a circle, put flowers and stones in the middle, and light candles. We would share poems, prayers, thoughts, individual pledges, names of the dead and names of people we had met during our program. After another moment of silence, we would walk out of the camp—for the last time.

A Ritual at the Selection Ramp

In the twilight, Birkenau appeared an even more desolate space than it did during the day. All other visitors had left. The students dispersed and soon disappeared in the vast camp. I was alone now. It was quiet. Walking along the road toward the crematory, parallel to the railroad tracks, I could only hear the crunch of the gravel under my feet. The silence was soothing. The last days had taken their emotional toll on me. Facilitating the various crises and struggles of the students did not allow much time for myself. I had cried only once, when I was alone in the dark rooms of a barrack commemorating Jewish victims.

I had been afraid of revisiting Auschwitz, afraid of becoming a "Holocaust professional" who could lecture on the Shoah but no longer feel the pain. I was wrong. Auschwitz greeted me like an unwanted acquaintance. I was again moved by it and developed a keener sense for details. I spent some time in the public archives and read documents. Every winter the SS had collected money among themselves for the Red Cross; a soldier got special leave for having prevented an escape; a memo reprimanded SS men to respect SS women; the children of SS families were invited to watch the film *Der gestiefelte Kater;*[5] I found the article about the slave-labor camp of Blechhammer, where Ed Gastfriend had been imprisoned (and which my father would read six months later). The details gave me a chilling insight into the daily routine of administering evil.

"I do not go back to the camp very often," I recalled Sophia Boharecka's remarks. Sophia had talked to the students the night before about her experience in Auschwitz as a Polish political prisoner. After her liberation, she had settled in the town of Oświęcim, within walking distance of the camp. "I now smell the flowers and trees," Sophia had said, "but I still have the stench of the crematories in me." For me, it was just the opposite. Walking alone toward the ruins of the crematories I could not imagine the stench. I was strangely comforted by the stillness and smells of a late summer night. Nature had begun to reclaim the killing center, overgrowing human evil with weeds and flowers. What remained of the gas chambers and crematories were loose bricks, bent steel poles, and large slabs of concrete from collapsed ceilings. A suffocating peacefulness emanated from these ruins, and it was there that I waited for the return of the students. Of the many locations in Auschwitz-Birkenau, the ruins did not leave the deepest impression on me. But I decided not to return to those places where I had felt most vulnerable. I wanted to part from the death camp rather than reexperience its pain.

One by one, the students gathered at the ruins of the crematories in silence. We watched the sun disappear behind the evening clouds. The camp stretched out in front of us, turning gray as clouds rapidly moved in. Unexpectedly, it began to rain. A cold wind picked up force and the drizzle quickly changed to a summer storm. Patiently, we waited for the last student to arrive. We were not prepared for bad weather, but no one broke the silence or suggested that we seek the safety of the bus in front of the gate. Despite the tensions in the afternoon, the students now were so well attuned to each other that we proceeded with the ritual despite the storm. Still in silence, we walked down the road back to the selection ramp, where German doctors had decided over life and death. There we formed a circle, placed stones and flowers in the middle, and held hands. We were soaked by cold rain and mercilessly bitten by mosquitos.

Our discomfort intensified the pain and rage we had felt the previous days. It was a befitting change. The August sun no longer warmed our bodies. Only the black contours of watch towers and fences stood out against a drab horizon. Mosquitos and rain now replaced the flowers and butterflies of the day. I was proud of the students who, drenched to the bone and covered with mosquito bites, withstood the cold and continued with the commemoration. Stacy read a poem she had drafted overnight; Sam read a passage from Walt Whitman; Hermann read a poem in German; Steven recited names of survivors and the dead and said Kaddish. As I listened to their voices, I thought about my earlier objections to the selection ramp as the main location for the ritual. The American students had argued in favor of the ramp because they wanted to reclaim it and remind us of our option to affirm life. But I, like some of the German students, was conflicted about this site, where my countrymen had made decisions over life and death as newly arriving Jews were lined up for selection. I had no desire to crawl into the minds of the SS doctors. Nor had my grandparents been among those who had been hurried out of the cattle cars and ordered to go to the left or right. Whom would I remember at the selection ramp? The victims? The victimizers? I wanted to place myself in history, for otherwise remembrance in Auschwitz would remain empty and meaningless. Where, then, was my place? I looked into the wet faces of the students who had worked so hard to understand each other, the Shoah, this camp. My place, I suddenly realized, was in the ritual circle, in this communitas of young Jews and Germans, at least for the moment.

"We walked in the rain, hand in hand, silently," wrote Jim, an American student preparing himself for the Christian ministry. "I felt so powerful! It was as if we were standing up against all the Nazi power that had once unveiled itself here." Kay later said, "I realized that Birkenau will always be there. Seeing the barracks and towers in the twilight made me feel very small." Catherine, an American student, "made a vow in this darkening, rainy, stormy night, on the site of Mengele's selections: that I would never forget what happened." Anna, another American, wished that "the rain would wash everything clean." And Volker, a West German, dreamed that night that Torsten, the East German medical student, stood at the ramp making selections.

The rain eased off and we tried to light the candles. They sputtered nervously in the dark. After everything was said, we remained quiet for a few more minutes. Night had caught up with us. It was pitch dark when we ended the ritual. As we walked slowly out of the camp, we placed the burning candles along the railroad tracks. The flickering lights grew smaller and smaller until they were barely visible—a frail glimmer engulfed in darkness.

Suddenly, a howling scream pierced the night, coming from the entrance gate: "WHY?" The scream lingered over this wasteland long after it had died away. "Why" had been on everyone's mind—but who had had the courage to cry out her despair so forcefully? Jennifer stood under the gate sobbing. She was the Christian American student who had been afraid that she alone would not be affected by Auschwitz. Now, at the end of the journey, she alone dared to hurl WHY back into the dark open space.

Black milk of daybreak, we drink and we drink it.

Epilogue

Memory is something terrifying.
—**St. Augustine**

Is memory something we have, or something we have lost?
—**Woody Allen,** *Another Woman*

My book ends in Auschwitz, but Auschwitz is not the end. The summer programs did not end there either. For the children and grandchildren of survivors, rescuers, bystanders, accomplices, and perpetrators, life continues: the students returned to Berlin and evaluated their experiences. In the death camps, their identities and relationships were profoundly challenged; but as a group of third-generation Jews and Germans, they were able to continue their work toward reconciliation.

We all left Auschwitz with mixed feelings of despair, relief, and strength. Despair, because our efforts seemed so small compared to the overwhelming evil, trauma, and pain that the Holocaust left us as a heritage. Living with the memory of the Holocaust is living with a curse. It is difficult to tolerate the ominous presence of pain and the latent and open anger that burden Jewish/German relations. Pain and anger are among and between the generations, among and between victims and victimizers, among and between third-generation American Jews and non-Jewish Germans. Pain and anger have no single voice but speak in many tongues. They can be denied, ridiculed, endured, or coped with. Holocaust memory is terrifying because it does not disappear but always poses more questions than it is capable of answering.

But post-Shoah generations can always leave Auschwitz. They may react viscerally and intellectually to the camps, identify with the victims, imagine the horror and the pain, or recoil from such identifications. But in the end, they can return to their families and homes. This is their privilege. Even after visiting Auschwitz, young Jews and Germans can look into each other's eyes with awareness and compassion. This is the strength of a communitas in which people divided by an antagonistic past are allowed to be angry and hurt so that hostility disappears and genuine human bonding emerges. Reconciliation is not something that we possess but something that requires our struggle. The collective work of remembering is healing (cf. Heimannsberg 1993:166). Reconciliation is a journey, a kind of cultural therapy, saturated with a great deal of hurt, hope, and experimentation.

As I have tried to show in the first part of the book, "Memory and Identity," Jews and Germans have exhibited in the public discourses of previous decades a desire to arrange an uneasy truce that does not challenge the deeply felt beliefs each group holds about the other. But we can equally observe the desire among some members of the third generation to risk new relationships that triumph over the so-called negative symbiosis. These two desires are real and strong and reflect a pattern of attraction and rejection that is one of the many paradoxes that afflict post-Shoah Jewish/German relations.

Where do we go from here? The third generation will shape the discourse on Jewish/German relations in the near future. That the Wall crumbled on the night of 9 November 1989, precisely fifty-one years after Kristallnacht, is just another irony of history. Some Germans have already begun to move from a "postwar" to a "post-Wall" discourse. No doubt, the newly unified country will affect the self-understanding of young Germans. With the Wall, another reminder of the dire consequences of Germany's fascist past disappeared. Not surprisingly, many Jews were skeptical about German unification, fearing a surge of German pride and nationalism at the expense of remembering the Holocaust. But as long as young generations do not take a "post-Wall identity" to mean an attitude of "I have heard enough about the past" or "I don't care about the Holocaust and Jews," it is a chance for young Germans to struggle constructively with their past and present.

It is too soon to predict how unification will influence the identity of third-generation Germans in relation to Holocaust memory. The new visibility and militancy of right-wing radicals is certainly a warning sign, but we need to remember that they are only a marginal movement. The willingness among youth to commit violence is not just a German problem. In the last five years, 224 children under the age of eighteen have been killed in Washington, D.C., alone. What is frightening about violence in American urban areas is its randomness and its origins in a sociopolitical climate that does not care about the poor and minorities. What is frightening about violence in Germany is its political roots and motivations and the fact that it is always directed against marginal people—foreigners, Jews, the disabled, homosexuals, and the homeless.

Third-generation American Jews have their own struggle with relating to Holocaust memory in the future. They have to be careful not to be flooded with Holocaust imagery (as, for example, through Holocaust museums), which tempt them to define themselves only as victims or to prove the opposite and join militant movements (as, for example, the Jewish Defense League or new settlements in the West Banks). Young American Jews do not have to follow a specific victimology. They are a post-Shoah generation—but they can also move toward a "post-victim" discourse and ethos without betraying the memory of the Holocaust.

When hearing about projects in which Jews and Germans confront the Holocaust together, some people have said that these are fueled by German masochism and Jewish self-hate and attempt to either exonerate Germans or conform to a specific Jewish interpretation of the Holocaust. I hope that this book has shown otherwise. Reconciliatory practices attempt to mend the wounds between Jews and Germans by confronting a divisive past together. In a world fearfully divided by ethnic, national, and religious strife, such encounters bring some hope.

Notes

Introduction

1. For my use of the term "Jewish/German relations," see p. 12.

2. In the last three decades, there has been a concentrated effort by Jews and Christians to talk to each other and build bridges of understanding and communication. These efforts have become known as Jewish-Christian dialogue. See, for example, Charlesworth 1990 and Eckardt 1973.

3. The summer programs were organized by the Interfaith Council on the Holocaust, Philadelphia, and the Evangelische Akademie Berlin (a church-related adult-education center). The programs were offered as extracurricular activities for college and university students who wished to learn about the Holocaust and its effects on post-Shoah generations. The Philadelphia Interfaith Council has also organized Holocaust curricula for the public school system and organized conferences, programs, and exhibitions centered around the lessons of the Holocaust for American society.

4. My co-facilitator in 1991 and 1993 was Christian Staffa; a Protestant theologian and adult educator in Berlin, he was responsible for the German half of the program. Ruth Laibson, executive director of the Interfaith Council on the Holocaust, was responsible for the logistics of the American half and accompanied the groups as an observer. Jon Schmidt, then an American volunteer working for the Evangelische Akademie in Berlin, was the co-facilitator of the 1989 program.

5. Jews who live in Germany have pointed out that phrases like "Jewish/German relations" ignore the fact that they belong to both the Jewish and German communities. But they do not agree on how to call themselves. Some prefer to be called "German Jews" (insisting on their right to German citizenship), others "Jews living in Germany" (indicating the precarious situation of living in a country that tried to annihilate them). In this book, I will use these two phrases indiscriminately when referring to the Jewish community in Germany.

6. Lisa Green (1992) outlines the history and aesthetic vision of the Jewish-German Dance Theatre. Esther Röhr (1989) sensitively describes the performance from a German perspective. Elsewhere, I have written about the use of experimental theater for Jewish/German reconciliation (Krondorfer 1988) and for the academic teaching of the Holocaust (Krondorfer 1989).

Part I: Memory and Identity

1. Tense moments in the history of post-Shoah Jewish/German relations which have gained international attention include the dispute over reparation payments; the debate over the statute of limitations; the trial of Adolf Eichmann; the attempted performance of Rainer Maria Fassbinder's antisemitic play *Der Müll, die Stadt und der Tod* in Frankfurt; German chancellor Helmut Kohl's infamous reference to the "grace of late birth," by which he tried to exonerate himself during a visit to Israel; Kohl and U.S. president Ronald Reagan's visit to a military cemetery at Bitburg; Phillip Jenninger's hapless speech on the fiftieth anniversary of Kristallnacht in 1988, which

resulted in his resignation as president of the German parliament; and German complicity in Iraqi production of chemical weapons (cf. Henningsen 1988; Stern 1991).

2. I often use the terms "German society" and "Jewish community" to indicate the sociopolitical differences between a nation-state (Germany) and the diaspora communities of Jews in America and elsewhere. I am fully aware that neither the "German society" nor the "Jewish community" (or "communities") is a monolithic unit or speaks with one voice. I use these terms to indicate the differences between dominant German and Jewish voices, much the same way as I use discursive practices (see Introduction).

Chapter 1: Discourse: Victim and Victimizer

1. This book cannot provide a historiographic survey of the development of Jewish/German relations since 1945, but I encourage the reader to consult other sources, such as Anson Rabinbach and Jack Zipe's anthology *Germans and Jews since the Holocaust* (1986) and Fritz Stern's assessment of Jewish-German relations, *Dreams and Delusions* (1987). For more theoretical perspectives, see Charles Maier's historical-political approach (1988) and James Young's literary-hermeneutic approach (1990). The German literature is extensive. For a perspective from the political left, see Henryk Broder (1986) and the anthology *Solidarität und deutsche Geschichte* (Schneider and Simon 1984). For a conservative view, see Julius Schoeps (1990) and Michael Wolff-sohn (1988).

2. Reagan's remarks are reprinted in Hartman 1986:239f. See also Miller 1990:228.

3. Speeches that were delivered before, during, and after the Bitburg events are reprinted in Hartman 1986. See also Hans-Ulrich Wehler's (1988) essay on the career and thought of Michael Stürmer, a German historian who became Helmut Kohl's ghostwriter.

4. Wiesel gave this speech on 19 April 1985 (reprinted in Hartman 1986:241f).

5. Judith Miller lists strategies of comparison, distortion, and inversion (1990:40–45). See also Henningsen 1988, 1989, who writes about Germany's "politics of memory" as a "politics of symbolic evasion"; the essays of Jean-Paul Bier and Jeffrey Herf, in Rabinbach and Zipes 1986; and Adorno, "What Does Coming to Terms with the Past Mean?" in Hartman 1986.

6. On the impact of the television movie *Holocaust*, see the essays of Bier, Herf, Markovits, and Zielinski in Rabinbach and Zipes 1986.

7. I thank Josey Fisher for making me aware of a study of Jewish Holocaust education that she conducted in 1992. Looking at a cross-section of Philadelphia Jewish schools, she found very uneven patterns with respect to the content and methodology of Holocaust education. "We are just beginning to question our denial (within the Jewish community) that the Jewish educational system is challenged to evaluate the best and most developmentally appropriate way to present the [Holocaust] material to our students, and that certain issues are idiosyncratic to an all-Jewish population. This includes . . . putting this experience within the context of the richness of Jewish tradition and culture, and not reinforcing a Jewish identity as 'victim'" (personal correspondence).

8. The survey consisted of telephone interviews with 885 randomly sampled

American adults, less than 3 percent of whom were Jewish. News Release of ADL-USHMC, 9 January 1991.

9. Wolffsohn has called this kind of discourse "political biologism" (1988:53). Cf. Haas 1988:2.

10. In German, Arendt's difficult sentence reads, "und wir Juden sind mit Millionen Unschuldiger belastet, aufgrund deren sich heute jeder Jude gleichsam wie die personifizierte Unschuld vorkommt" (quoted in Diner 1986:246).

11. The continuing debate over the integrity of the *Judenräte*, or councils of Jewish elders, is one example. The *Judenräte* were appointed by the Nazis to administer the Jewish ghettos in occupied Poland, and the ongoing dispute is to what degree they could have used their limited power to subvert the smooth functioning of the Nazi killing machine. Different *Judenräte* tried different tactics—all, ultimately, to no avail (cf. Bauer 1982:157ff).

12. For further discussion of literary testimony of survivors, see Langer 1991, Young 1990, Rosenfeld 1980, Roskies 1984. Oral Holocaust testimonies often contain more complex and individualized stories of survival than written memoirs and other literary expressions (cf. Fisher 1991).

13. One has to be careful in making general assumptions about survivors' reactions to Nazi Germany and to young Germans today. The place and length of imprisonment by the Nazis, the severity of treatment, the circumstances of escape or liberation, the loss of family members, individual psychological makeup, and other such factors still have had an impact on their outlook on postwar Germany. In my experience, Jews who lived in Germany before the war feel more disposed to reach out to the young German generation. Jews from Eastern Europe, on the other hand, especially if they had not had much contact with Germans before 1939, are less inclined to reach out to young Germans. But for each generalization, I could name exceptions. For a reporter's view on different reactions, see Miller 1990:13–32. For further discussion of survivors coping with their trauma, see Klein 1983, Hoppe 1971, Bergmann and Jucovy 1990, Grubrich-Simitis 1984, and Langer 1991.

Chapter 2: Ethos: Remembrance and Guilt

1. For more information on psychoanalytic perspectives, see Luel and Marcus 1984. On the centrality of the Holocaust, see Michael Berenbaum's dialogues with A. J. Wolf and D. W. Weiss (Berenbaum 1990:43–60).

2. Whether West Germany's policy of *Wiedergutmachung* ("making amends"; the term connotes both reparations and atonement) should be considered sincere and effective or shallow and inadequate depends largely on one's perspective. Giordano 1990 and Broder 1986 present a negative analysis; Wolffsohn 1988 compares West German efforts to Austria's and East Germany's policies and arrives at a more positive assessment. Without doubt, the issue of financial compensation had an agonizing impact on individual survivors. Not only did they have qualms about accepting money from Germany but they often experienced the German bureaucratic process as flawed and humiliating. See Kestenberg 1990 and Eissler 1984.

3. Quoted in Simon Wiesenthal's *The Sunflower* (1976:198), a collection of responses to Wiesenthal's question about forgiveness, to which people from different religious, national, and political backgrounds contributed.

4. The sermon was broadcast on 8 May 1985 over West German radio WDR. Quoted in Friedländer 1986:35.

5. From the film *Now . . . After All These Years*. For more information about the film, see chapter 4.

6. Political motives cannot be discounted since President Von Weizsäcker gave the speech only three days after Bitburg. Aware of Bitburg's negative effect on Germany's international reputability, the German president may have designed the speech, at least in part, to contain the damage. But Von Weizsäcker, like Kohl and Reagan, included sentences ("Today we mourn all the dead of the war and the tyranny") that inflated the term "victim" (quoted in Hartman 1986:263).

7. Rafael Seligmann, a German Jewish writer, describes a similar experience. After he talked to a German high-school audience about Jewish/German relations, he was confronted with a litany of hostile questions: "Why should we be responsible for what happened before our time? - Why should we be responsible for the Jews and not for Native Americans? - Do you think that the attitude of Israelis toward Palestinians is better than ours toward Jews? . . . Why should we be distressed over a few Russian Jews? What do we have to do with them?" (1991:174f).

8. Since the mid-1980s, some German students have been exposed to stories of Jewish survivors. Many of these survivors came back as guests of German city governments, which had invited them as a gesture of reconciliation, and some went to talk in schools. See, for example, Judith Miller's report on a survivor reunion in Fulda (1990:13ff).

9. Quoted in *Der USA-Besuch hat tiefe Eindrücke hinterlassen*, Dokumentation der Studien- und Begegnungreisen der ESG im Rheinland, Bonn 1987.

10. In 1991 and 1993, the groups consisted of five Jewish Americans, five Christian Americans, five West Germans, and five East Germans. The 1989 group consisted of eight American Jews and three Christian Americans and West Germans only (except for a Dutch student). Participants had different religious ties: they followed the Jewish orthodox, conservative, and reform movements and the Catholic, Quaker, and various Protestant faith traditions; some were assimilated Jews, others unaffiliated Christians. Germans, in general, did not define themselves along religious lines as strongly as their American counterparts. Attempts to recruit Jewish Germans into the program failed. The American group was not balanced with respect to gender, because women applied in considerably higher numbers; the reverse was true for the German group. The students were not restricted to specific academic disciplines but had to be between 18–25 years of age. Since the programs were funded by a variety of foundations, organizations, and private contributions, the students were on scholarships.

11. This letter was written in January 1990 and sent out in German and English. Because the German version is more frank than the students' own translation, I translated directly from the German original.

Chapter 3: Communitas: Envisioning Transformation

1. The quotation is from Scholem's article "Against the Myth of the German-Jewish Dialogue," collected with two other essays on Jewish/German relations in *On Jews and Judaism in Crisis: Selected Essays* (1976:63). For a brief discussion of Scholem's ideas, see Rabinbach 1986:3ff.

2. Before Broder, Jean-Paul Sartre and the Austrian writer Hermann Bahr had already observed that a passionate investment is a defining feature of antisemites. At the turn of the century Bahr wrote that "an antisemite is a person who longs for the frenzy and euphoria of a passion. . . . If there weren't any Jews, the antisemites would have to invent them" (quoted in Seligmann 1991:49). Fifty years later, Sartre's study of antisemitism (1965; first published in 1946) used almost the exact wording. Broder 1986 lists countless incidents of passionate, albeit often unself-conscious, expressions of antisemitism in German culture.

3. Julius Beeke, "Die Zärtlichkeit nicht gespürt?" *Frankfurter Rundschau,* 15 November 1988, is a response to a review by Roland Langer, "Alle verharrten in schweigender Betroffenheit," *Frankfurter Rundschau,* 12 November 1988.

4. Quoted in a report by Peter Ross Range on a Washington symposium, "German-Jewish Reconciliation? Facing the Past and Looking to the Future," 15–17 December 1991 (AICGS Seminar Papers, a publication of the American Institute for Contemporary German Studies, Washington, D.C.).

5. In Germany, dialogues with Jews are perceived foremost as programs between Germans and Israelis—not unlike Adorno, who spoke only of "encounters between young Germans and young Israelis" (1986:127f). The concept of negative symbiosis must be applied broadly to include other diaspora communities as well as the Jewish youth in Germany itself. Karlheinz Schneider wrote that it would be erroneous to replace the German/Jewish dialogue with a German/Israeli dialogue, since the latter would most likely deteriorate into a debate about Israeli politics and Zionism. I agree with his observation, but he also does not extend his invitation to the American Jewish as well as East European Jewish communities (Schneider and Simon 1984:121–128).

6. *Webster's Second New Riverside University Dictionary* (Boston: Houghton Mifflin, 1984).

7. For a good overview of the literature on the problems of survivor families, see Hass 1990, who avoids the limitation of a psychoanalytic framework. See also the Bergmann and Jucovy 1990, Luel and Marcus 1984, Epstein 1979, Grubrich-Simitis 1984, Hoppe 1971, Klein 1983, Heller 1982.

8. The survivor syndrome was first identified and treated in the early 1960s by William Niederland (1964; cf. Hass 1990:8).

9. Even Robert Jay Lifton's work on Nazi doctors (1986), which tries to understand the perpetrators' behavior in psychological terms, is not derived from therapeutic treatment but from archival materials and interviews.

10. To my knowledge, this volume is to date alone in examining the intergenerational transmission of Nazi ideology and Holocaust memory in German families of perpetrators. Our knowledge about the personality of victimizers stems mostly from psychohistorical, social, and literary works. For case studies of children of German perpetrators, see Rosenthal and Bar-On 1992, Posner 1991, Bar-On 1990, Eickhoff 1986, Lohmann 1984, and Rosenkötter, Eckstaedt, and Hardtmann in Bergmann and Jucovy 1990.

11. The issue of countertransference is not limited to German therapeutic settings; it also applies to the treatment of survivors. See Danieli 1980:366.

12. For three brief and interesting case studies, see Salm 1993.

13. According to Von Westernhagen (1987:101f), children of Nazi parents had to stabilize the crippled self-esteem of their parents, who, with the loss of the war, had

lost fantasies of omnipotence and power and were now afraid of retribution. Ensuing guilt made the parents rigid and emotionally unavailable to their children. Their children, in turn, used the past as a weapon to cut ties to their families. As a result, neither parents nor children could become emotionally vulnerable in their families.

14. Other groups have also worked in cross-cultural settings, but they have focused mostly on the second generation. Cf. Heimannsberg 1993:231; and chapter 8.

Chapter 4: Skeletons in the Closet: German Family Histories

1. Dan Bar-On (1989) called this repression of memory a "legacy of silence." Heimannsberg and Schmidt (1993) called it "collective silence" and a "legacy of shame." In a psychoanalytic essay on Nazi persecutors, Erich Siemenauer writes that "silence is inevitably practiced so as to let sleeping dogs lie. The analyst cannot but adjust in varying degrees to the social constraints of the surrounding world—to the conspiracy of silence" (1990:175). In case studies on second-generation Germans, Anita Eckstaedt (1990) and Gertrud Hardtmann (1990) speak of the silence of German parents and society. The psychoanalyst Judith Kestenberg, who has worked with the Jewish second generation, speaks of "the conspiracy of silence in survivors, persecutors, and their children" (1990:162).

2. For three case studies on reconstructing German family histories, see Hecker 1993.

3. Cf. Glaser's comprehensive work on West Germany's cultural history (1990). Lothar Baier (1987) claims that second-generation Germans benefited from guilt feelings. See also Schneider 1987, Greiner 1988, and Krondorfer 1994 on German generations and identity conflicts.

4. The 1990 findings of the American Jewish Committee (Jodice 1991) and a 1985 German poll (cf. Friedländer 1986) corroborate this observation. There are indications, however, that after unification young people reject the past more aggressively.

5. For the use of family history in individual psychotherapy and family therapy, see Salm 1993 and Hecker 1993.

6. Despite the centrality of the Holocaust in Jewish American families, many children of survivors, according to Hass (1990), also lack detailed historic knowledge about their parents' lives during the Shoah. But if the rapid increase of Holocaust courses at universities is any indication, third-generation American Jews (and non-Jews) show an ongoing interest in the history and meaning of the Holocaust.

7. The film was produced in 1981 for German television (*Hessische Rundfunk*) by Pavel Schnabel and Harald Lüders and is distributed in the United States by Arthur Cantor.

8. Heimannsberg and Schmidt 1993, Bar-On 1989, Sichrovksy 1985, 1988, and Von Westernhagen 1987 contain the best collections of interviews with Germans of the second and third generations. Other autobiographical accounts include works by Sabine Reichel (1989), Wolf (1980), Ruth Rehmann (1979), Christoph Meckel (1980), Hanns-Josef Ortheil (1992); and there are autobiographical elements in the literary works of such better-known authors as Günther Grass, Heinrich Böll, Rolf Hochhuth, Siegfried Lenz, and Peter Weiss (cf. Bosmajian 1986; Friedländer 1986:38). Lerke Gravenhorst and Camen Tatschmurat's *Töchter-Fragen: NS-Frauen-*

Geschichte (Daughter-Questions: Women's Nazi History; 1990) is an anthology of feminist writers who have begun to question their mothers.

9. For more information on West German trials of Nazi war criminals, see Friedrich 1985, Lichtenstein 1986, and Just-Dahlmann and Just 1988.

10. For other stories about father-son relations in post-Shoah Germany, see Krondorfer 1994.

Chapter 5: From Generation to Generation

1. The epigraphs are from Bar-On (1989:224) and Hass (1990:51).

2. The fear that Holocaust memory is contagious is also described by Yael Danieli (1980:360), but there in the context of Jewish Holocaust survivors and their therapists.

3. Quoted from "ADL Gives Hard Lesson," *Forward,* 9 August 1992.

4. Ibid.

Chapter 6: Whose History Is It Anyway?

1. For a more detailed analysis, see Young 1993, 1990:172–189, Spielmann 1988, and Maier 1988:121–172.

2. Cf. Ronald Grimes (1990:63–88), who discusses the relation of museums and rituals in more detail, although from a different angle. A special form of ritualized commemoration is the official invitations extended to Jews by their former hometowns in Germany. A sense of "spontaneous communitas" can develop among the visiting survivors, as is evident, for example, in Judith Miller's report on former Jewish residents visiting Fulda (1990:13–32).

3. For more information on Holocaust museums, see Wieseltier 1993, Gourevitch 1993, Norden 1993, Krondorfer 1993, Berenbaum 1981, 1990, Miller 1990, and Alter 1981.

4. Quoted in Marc Fisher, "Germany's Holocaust Fears," *Washington Post,* 30 March 1993.

5. Some of the German students argued in favor of the "human touch," in favor of humanizing the victims. The discussion was dominated, however, by those who argued that identification with victims is impossible.

6. The philosopher Susan Neiman responded similarly to an exhibit in Berlin, where she saw a postcard written in 1942 by a young Berliner to his brother. "A note in the glass case," Neiman described, "explained that this was the last word ever heard from the sender. Tears filled my eyes and ran down my face. . . . I felt my fists clenching in rage" (1992:81).

Chapter 7: Memory Embodied

1. *Jewish Week,* 27 October 1989. Wolfgang Bornebusch, the Protestant minister of Schermbeck who helped to organize this commemoration, told me in a conversation in March 1994 that the man's death could be interpreted this way, although it would be impossible to prove a direct link between his death and his admitting his role as perpetrator. The Gestalt therapist Richard Picker (1993:28) reports a similar story of an Austrian man who, upon sharing his memory with his daughter,

"promptly died, as if he had only wanted to live until the time when the Nazi past . . . had been witnessed, noted, and preserved in memory." This man, however, was not a perpetrator: he had withstood the Nazi pressure to divorce his half-Jewish wife and had kept her out of concentration camps through bribery.

2. The core group consisted of Lisa Green (co-founder), Brigitte Heusinger, Erica Kaufman, Björn Krondorfer (co-founder), Sheila Zagar, and Martin Zeidler. Steve Marcucci was our musician until spring 1988, and Tony Miceli from 1988 onwards.

3. At the end of the war, with the advance of the Soviet army, the Nazis evacuated the concentration camps and marched the remaining prisoners to other camps located farther west. Thousands died on these marches.

4. Sociodrama is a derivative of psychodrama, shifting the latter's therapeutic focus from individuals to social crises.

Chapter 8: Reconciliation on Stage: The Public Responds

1. The Jewish-German Dance Theatre's original production, "But What About the Holocaust?" gradually consolidated over months of rehearsals. We did not follow a preformulated aesthetic vision but collaboratively developed a blend of movements, sounds, short stories, rhythms, and improvised music woven into a sequence of symbolic and narrative pieces. For the interested reader, a collection of material, including videotapes and reviews, is available at the Library of the Performing Arts, Lincoln Center, New York City.

2. Judith Miller (1990:288n2) reports that there were so many commemoration ceremonies throughout the Federal Republic that the German Information Center in New York City could not maintain a complete list.

3. Many other performances on the Holocaust have been produced and shown in postwar Germany: plays on the Holocaust by German authors (e.g., Peter Weiss, Rolf Hochhuth), adaptations of Jewish playwrights (e.g., Joshua Sobol, Eli Wiesel); guest ensembles from Israel or the United States (e.g., A Traveling Jewish Theatre); and works by Jews living in Germany (e.g., Andrea Morein's solo performance on her Jewish German identity [Morein 1989], or the ensemble work of the Jüdisches Theater in Deutschland). In contrast to these and other performances, the collaborative effort of the Jewish-German Dance Theatre emphasized direct encounters between post-Shoah Jews and Germans. For other experimental performances on the Holocaust, see Krondorfer 1988:231–236.

4. Dietmar Danner, "Vom Umgang mit dem Holocaust," *Schwäbische Zeitung*, 25 Oct. 1988.

5. Dieter Kleibauer, "Der Tod ist ein Meister aus Deutschland," *Schramberger Zeitung*, 25 October 1988.

6. Anna Görler, "Nie wieder nach Deutschland," *Marburger Allgemeine Zeitung*, 24 October 1988.

7. The letter is entitled "A Few Thoughts about the Guest Performance of the Jewish-German Dance Theatre in the State Theater of Tübingen on 25 October 1988" and is signed by Jürgen Moltmann, Carmen Krieg, and Thomas Kucharz.

8. Since the taxes for the churches are collected by the state, Germans are registered as church members.

9. "Begegnung and Erinnerung in Gestik und ausdrucksvollem Tanz," *Westfälische Nachrichten,* 3 November 1988.

10. The *Einsatzgruppen* were mobile killing units following the regular army in Poland and the Soviet Union. They were responsible for the mass shootings of Jews and political opponents.

11. "Die Nazi-Greuel tänzerisch aufgearbeitet," *Dreieich Stadtanzeiger,* 14 November 1988.

12. C. H., "An der Grenze," *Nürnberger Zeitung,* 15 November 1988.

13. Armand Volkas's group is called Acts of Reconciliation. The four-day conference organized by Weissmark and Kuphal in 1992 was attended by eleven children of Nazis and eleven children of Holocaust survivors; it was sponsored by the Medical School's Department of Psychiatry at Cambridge Hospital, Massachusetts (cf. Weissmark, Giacomo, and Kuphal 1993). Bornebusch and Zieman have worked together since 1987; the 1992 conference was held at the Anti-Defamation League in New York (cf. Bornebusch 1993). See also Bar-On 1993. For a partial listing of Jewish/German groups, see Harris 1993:231.

14. The American and German students of the summer programs had separate reunions, in which they worked through some unresolved issues and tried to put their experiences into a larger context.

15. Regine Schlett, "Weil sie die deutsche Sprache nicht sprechen will," *Frankfurter Rundschau,* 29 October 1988.

Chapter 9: At Auschwitz: Memory and Identity Revisited

1. This is a shortened version of the original poem.

2. Ben's and Ruth's stories are also cited in Robert Leiter, "Facing the Holocaust: German, U.S. Youths Confront History," *Jewish Exponent,* 6 October 1989.

3. After long negotiations between Jewish communities, the Polish church, and the Vatican, the conflict has now been settled. The Carmelite nuns have moved to a new building farther from the camp.

4. For other reports on Polish-Jewish animosities at Auschwitz, see Roiphe 1988:106–121 and Lewis 1991.

5. *Der gestiefelte Kater* (Puss-in-Boots) was a widely read children's book in Germany. I, too, read it in my childhood.

References

Adorno, Theodor W. 1966. *Negative Dialektik*. Frankfurt: Suhrkamp.

———. 1986. "What Does Coming to Terms with the Past Mean?" In *Bitburg in Moral and Political Perspective*, ed. Geoffrey Hartman. Bloomington: Indiana University Press.

Alexander, Bobby. 1991. *Victor Turner Revisited: Ritual as Social Change*. Atlanta, Ga: Scholars Press.

Alter, Robert. 1981. "Deformations of the Holocaust." *Commentary*, February:48–54.

Anhalt, Irene. 1993. "Farewell to My Father." In *The Collective Silence*, ed. Barbara Heimannsberg and Christoph Schmidt. San Francisco: Jossey-Bass.

Arendt, Hannah. 1963. *Eichmann in Jerusalem: A Report on the Banality of Evil*. New York: Penguin.

Baier, Lothar. 1987. "Selig sind die Schuldigen: Wie den Deutschen ihr schlechtes Gewissen zum Vorteil ausschlug." *Die Zeit* 39 (September 18).

Bar-On, Dan. 1989. *Legacy of Silence: Encounters with Children of the Third Reich*. Cambridge, Mass.: Harvard University Press.

———. 1990. "Children of Perpetrators of the Holocaust: Working Through One's Own Moral Self." *Psychiatry* 53, August:229–245.

———. 1993. "Holocaust Perpetrators and Their Children: A Paradoxical Morality." In *The Collective Silence*, ed. Barbara Heimannsberg and Christoph Schmidt. San Francisco: Jossey-Bass.

Bar-On, Dan, and Amalia Gaon. 1991. "'We Suffered Too': Nazi Children's Inability to Relate to the Suffering of the Victims of the Holocaust." *Journal of Humanistic Psychology* 3/4, Fall:77–95.

Bauer, Yehuda. 1982. *A History of the Holocaust*. New York: Franklin Watts.

Behrendt, Waltraud. 1993. "Unwilling to Admit, Unable to See: Therapeutic Experiences with the National Socialist 'Complex.'" In *The Collective Silence*, ed. Barbara Heimannsberg and Christoph Schmidt. San Francisco: Jossey-Bass.

Berenbaum, Michael. 1981/2. "On the Politics of Public Commemoration of the Holocaust." *Shoah*, Fall/Winter:6–9, 37.

———. 1990. *After Tragedy and Triumph: Essays in Modern Jewish Thought and the American Experience*. New York: Cambridge University Press.

Bergmann, Martin S., and Milton E. Jucovy, eds. 1990. *Generations of the Holocaust*. New York: Columbia University Press.

Bier, Jean-Paul. 1986. "The Holocaust, West Germany, and Strategies of Oblivion, 1947–1979." In *Germans and Jews since the Holocaust*, ed. Anson Rabinbach and Jack Zipes. New York: Holmes & Meier.

Bole, William. 1986. "Bitburg: The American Scene." In *Bitburg in Moral and Political Perspective*, ed. Geoffrey Hartman. Bloomington: Indiana University Press.

Bornebusch, Wolfgang. 1993. "'How Can I Develop on a Mountain of Corpses?' Observations from a Theme-Centered Interaction Seminar with Isaac Zieman." In *The Collective Silence*, ed. Barbara Heimannsberg and Christoph Schmidt. San Francisco: Jossey-Bass.

Bosmajian, Hamida. 1986. "German Literature about the Holocaust— A Literature of Limitations." *Modern Language Studies* 16, no. 1 (Winter):51–61.

References

Brook, Peter. 1984. *The Empty Space*. New York: Atheneum.

Broder, Henryk. 1986. *Der Ewige Antisemit: Über Sinn und Funktion eines beständigen Gefühls*. Frankfurt: Fischer Taschenbuch.

———. 1989. "Die Opfer der Opfer." *Die Zeit*, July 14.

———. 1993. "Das Shoah-Business: Henryk M. Broder über die Amerikanisierung des Holocaust." *Der Spiegel* 16:248–256.

Brumlik, Micha. 1991. "The Situation of the Jews in Today's Germany." Bloomington: Jewish Studies Program, Indiana University.

Brumlik, Micha, et al., eds. 1986. *Jüdisches Leben in Deutschland seit 1945*. Frankfurt: Athenäum.

Chaikin, Joseph. 1980. *The Presence of the Actor*. New York: Atheneum.

Charlesworth, James, ed. 1990. *Jews and Christians: Exploring the Past, Present, and Future*. New York: Crossroad.

Claussen, Detlev. 1986. "In the House of the Hangman." In *Germans and Jews since the Holocaust*, ed. Anson Rabinbach and Jack Zipes. New York: Holmes & Meier.

Danieli, Yael. 1980. "Countertransference in the Treatment and Study of Nazi Holocaust Survivors and Their Children." *Victimology: An International Journal* 5 (2–4):355–367.

Darsa, Jan. 1987. "Confronting Germany and Its History." *Facing History and Ourselves*, Spring:10.

Diner, Dan. 1986. "Negative Symbiose—Deutsche und Juden nach Auschwitz." In *Jüdisches Leben in Deutschland seit 1945*, ed. Michael Brumlik et al. Frankfurt: Athenäum.

———. 1987. "Zwischen Aporie und Apologie." In *Ist der Nationalsozialismus Geschichte? Zu Historisierung und Historikerstreit*, ed. Dan Diner. Frankfurt: Fischer.

Driver, Tom. 1991. *The Magic of Ritual: Our Need for Liberating Rites that Transform Our Lives and Our Communities*. San Francisco: Harper San Francisco.

Eckardt, Roy. 1973. *Elder and Younger Brothers: The Encounter of Jews and Christians*. New York: Schocken Books.

Eckstaedt, Anita. 1990. "A Victim of the Other Side." In *Generations of the Holocaust*. ed. Martin Bergmann and Milton Jucovy. New York: Columbia University Press.

Eickhoff, F. W. 1986. "Identification and Its Vicissitudes in the Context of the Nazi Phenomenon." *International Journal of Psycho-Analysis* 67:35–44.

Eissler, K. R. 1984. "Die Ermordung von wievielen seiner Kinder muß ein Mensch symptomfrei ertragen können, um eine normale Konstitution zu haben?" In *Psychoanalyse und Nationalsozialismus*, ed. Hans-Martin Lohmann. Frankfurt: Fischer.

Epstein, Helen. 1979. *Children of the Holocaust: Conversations with Sons and Daughters of Survivors*. New York: Putnam.

Fackenheim, Emil. 1975. "Sachsenhausen 1938: Groundwork for Auschwitz." *Midstream* 21 (April):27–31.

———. 1989. "The 614th Commandment." In *Holocaust: Religious and Philosophical Implications*, ed. John K. Roth and Michael Berenbaum. New York: Paragon House.

Fein, Leonard. 1988. *Where Are We? The Inner Life of America's Jews*. New York: Harper & Row.

Feldman, Jackie. 1994. "'It Is My Brother Whom I Am Seeking': Israeli Youth's Pilgrimage to Poland of the Shoah." Paper presented at the Remembering for the Future II Conference, March, Berlin.

Fichter, Tilman. 1984. "Der Staat Israel und die neue Linke in Deutschland." In *Solidarität und deutsche Geschichte*, ed. Karlheinz Schneider and Nikolaus Simon. Berlin: Schriftenband 9 des DIAK.

Fisher, Josey, ed. 1991. *The Persistence of Youth: Oral Testimonies of the Holocaust*. New York: Greenwood Press.

Foucault, Michel. 1972. *The Archaeology of Knowledge and the Discourse on Language*. Trans. A. M. Sheridan Smith. New York: Pantheon Books.

Friedländer, Saul. 1986. "Some German Struggles with Memory." In *Bitburg in Moral and Political Perspective*, ed. Geoffrey Hartman. Bloomington: Indiana University Press.

Friedrich, Jörg. 1985. *Die kalte Amnestie: NS-Täter in der Bundesrepublik*. Frankfurt: Fischer.

Geertz, Clifford. 1973. *The Interpretation of Cultures*. New York: Basic Books.

Giordano, Ralph. 1990. *Die zweite Schuld oder Von der Last Deutscher zu sein*. Munich: Knaur.

Glaser, Hermann. 1990. *Die Kulturgeschichte der Bundesrepublik Deutschland: Zwischen Protest und Anpassung 1968–1989*. Vol. 3. Frankfurt: Fischer.

Gourevitch, Philip. 1993. "Behold Now Behemoth: The Holocaust Memorial Museum: One More American Theme Park." *Harper's Magazine*, July:55–62.

Gravenhorst, Lerke, and Camen Tatschmurat, eds. 1990. *Töchter-Fragen. NS-Frauen-Geschichte*. Freiburg: Kore.

Green, Lisa. 1992. "The Jewish/German Dance Theatre." In *Contact Quarterly* 17 (Winter):26–28. In German: 1989. "Jewish German Dance Theatre: Jenseits der Sprachlosigkeit." *Tanz Aktuell* 6:20–21.

Greiner, Ulrich. 1988. "Söhne und ihre Väter: Die Revolte der Nachgeborenen war auch eine Revolte gegen die Täter von Auschwitz." *Die Zeit*, April 29.

Grimes, Ronald. 1990. *Ritual Criticism: Case Studies in Its Practice, Essays on Its Theory*. Columbia: University of South Carolina Press.

———. 1992. "Reinventing Ritual." *Soundings* 75 (Spring):21–41.

Grotowski, Jerzy. 1968. *Towards a Poor Theatre*. New York: Simon and Schuster.

Grubrich-Simitis, Ilse. 1984. "Extremtraumatisierung als kumulatives Trauma. Psychoanalytische Studien über seelische Nachwirkungen der Konzentrationslagerhaft bei Überlebenden und ihren Kindern." In *Psychoanalyse und Nationalsozialismus*, ed. Hans-Martin Lohmann. Frankfurt: Fischer.

Haas, Peter J. 1988. *Morality after Auschwitz: The Radical Challenge of the Nazi Ethic*. Philadelphia: Fortress Press.

Hardtmann, Gertrud. 1990. "The Shadows of the Past." In *Generations of the Holocaust*, ed. Martin Bergmann and Milton Jucovy. New York: Columbia University Press.

Harris, Cynthia Oudejans. 1993. "Translator's Afterword." In *The Collective Silence*, ed. Barbara Heimannsberg and Christoph Schmidt. San Francisco: Jossey-Bass.

Hartman, Geoffrey, ed. 1986. *Bitburg in Moral and Political Perspective*. Bloomington: Indiana University Press.

Hass, Aaron. 1990. *In the Shadow of the Holocaust: The Second Generation*. Ithaca: Cornell University Press.

Hecker, Margarete. 1993. "Family Reconstruction in Germany: An Attempt to Confront the Past." In *The Collective Silence*, ed. Barbara Heimannsberg and Christoph Schmidt. San Francisco: Jossey-Bass.

Heimannsberg, Barbara. 1993. "The Work of Remembering: A Psychodynamic View of the Nazi Past as It Exists in Germany Today." In *The Collective Silence,* ed. Barbara Heimannsberg and Christoph Schmidt. San Francisco: Jossey-Bass.

Heimannsberg, Barbara, and Christoph Schmidt, eds. 1993. *The Collective Silence: German Identity and the Legacy of Shame.* Trans. Cynthia Oudejans Harris and Gordon Wheeler. San Francisco: Jossey-Bass.

Heller, David. 1982. "Themes of Culture and Ancestry among Children of Concentration Camp Survivors." *Psychiatry* 45 (August):247–261.

Helmreich, William B. 1992. *Against All Odds: Holocaust Survivors and the Successful Lives They Made in America.* New York: Simon & Schuster.

Henningsen, Manfred. 1988. "The Politics of Symbolic Evasion: Germany and the Aftermath of the Holocaust." In *Echoes from the Holocaust,* ed. Alan Rosenberg and Gerald E. Myers. Philadelphia: Temple University Press.

———. 1989. "The Politics of Memory: Holocaust and Legitimacy in Post-Nazi Germany." In *Remembering for the Future,* ed. Yehuda Bauer et al. Oxford: Pergamon Press.

Herf, Jeffrey. 1986. "The 'Holocaust' Reception in West Germany: Right, Center, and Left." In *Germans and Jews since the Holocaust,* ed. Anson Rabinbach and Jack Zipes. New York: Holmes & Meier.

Hoppe, K. D. 1971. "The Aftermath of Nazi Persecution Reflected in Recent Psychiatric Literature." In *Psychic Traumatization: Aftereffects in Individuals and Communities,* ed. H. Krystal and W. G. Niederland. Boston: Little, Brown.

Hultberg, Peer. 1987. "Scham—eine überschattete Emotion." *Analytische Psychologie* 18:84–104.

Jodice, David A. 1991. *United Germany and Jewish Concerns: Attitudes toward Jews, Israel, and the Holocaust.* Working Papers on Contemprary Anti-Semitism. Publication of the American Jewish Committee, New York.

Just-Dahlmann, Barbara, and Helmut Just. 1988. *Die Gehilfen: NS-Verbrechen und die Justiz nach 1945.* Frankfurt: Athenäum.

Katz, Steven T. 1983. *Post-Holocaust Dialogues: Critical Studies in Modern Jewish Thought.* New York: New York University Press.

Kertzer, David I. 1988. *Ritual, Politics, and Power.* New Haven: Yale University Press.

Kestenberg, Judith. 1990. "The Persecutor's Children: Introduction." In *Generations of the Holocaust.* ed. Martin Bergmann and Milton Jucovy. New York: Columbia University Press.

Kestenberg, Milton. 1990. "Discriminatory Aspects of the German Indemnification Policy: A Continuation of Persecution." In *Generations of the Holocaust.* ed. Martin Bergmann and Milton Jucovy. New York: Columbia University Press.

Klein, Hillel. 1983. "The Meaning of the Holocaust." *Israel Journal of Psychiatry and Related Sciences* 20:119–128.

Krondorfer, Björn. 1986. "Holocaust Photography: Innocence, Corruption, Holocaust." *Christianity and Crisis* 46 (August):276-277.

———. 1988. "Experimental Drama and the Holocaust: The Work of the Jewish-German Dance Theatre and Its Application to the Teaching of the Holocaust." In *Methodology in the Academic Teaching of the Holocaust,* ed. Zev Garber et al. Lanham: University Press of America.

———. 1989. "Embodied Testimonies: Experimental Drama as a Device for Confronting the Holocaust." In *Remembering for the Future,* ed. Yehuda Bauer et al. Oxford: Pergamon Press.

———. 1991a. "Ist die deutsche Kultur antisemitisch? Gedanken zur (Fremd-) Bestimmung des Judentums." *Tribüne* 117:131–143.

———. 1991b. "Gefühle der Schuld und Abwehr: Begegnungen zwischen Nachkriegs-Deutschen und Juden der Nach-Shoah." *Tribüne* 119:130–139.

———. 1992a. "The Agony of Reconciling: Reflections on a Summer Program for Jewish/American and East/West German Undergraduate Students." In *The Future of Nontraditional/Interdisciplinary Programs: Margin or Mainstream?* Selected Papers from the Tenth Annual Conference on Nontraditional/Interdisciplinary Programs, ed. Sally Reithlingshoefer. George Mason University, Fairfax, Va.

———. 1992b. "Bodily Knowing, Ritual Embodiment, and Experimental Drama: From Regression to Transgression." *Journal of Ritual Studies* 6 (Summer):27–38.

———. 1993. "Kulturgut 'Holocaust': Gedanken zum neuen U.S. Holocaust Memorial Museum in Washington." *Tribüne* 127:91–104.

———. 1994. "Our Soul Has Not Suffered: Intimacy and Hostility between Fathers and Sons in Post-Shoah Germany." *Journal of Men's Studies* 2, no. 3 (February):157–169.

Krondorfer, Björn, and Jon Schmidt, eds. 1990. *A Journal of a German/American Student Exchange Program: Encountering the Holocaust as a Third Generation.* Berlin: Evangelisches Bildungswerk. Dokumentation 73/90.

Krondorfer, Björn, and Christian Staffa, eds. 1992. *The Third Generation after the Shoah between Remembering, Repressing and Commemorating.* American/Jewish and East/West German Student Exchange Program. Berlin: Evangelisches Bildungswerk. Dokumentation 88/92.

———. 1994. *Living in a Post-Shoah World: Reflections of American, German, Jewish and Christian Students.* Berlin: Evangelisches Bildungswerk.

Krystal, H., ed. 1968. *Massive Psychic Trauma.* New York: International Universities Press.

Langer, Lawrence L. 1991. *Holocaust Testimonies: The Ruins of Memory.* New Haven: Yale University Press.

Lanzmann, Claude. 1985. *Shoah: An Oral History of the Holocaust.* New York: Pantheon Books.

Laub, Dori, and Nanette C. Auerhahn. 1984. "Reverberations of Genocide: Its Expresssion in the Conscious and Unconscious of Post-Holocaust Generations." In *Psychoanalytic Reflections on the Holocaust,* ed. Steven A. Luel and Paul Marcus. New York: KTAV Publishing House.

Lewis, Kevin. 1991. "The Auschwitz Museum and the Clash of Memories." *Christian Century,* January:75–77.

Lichtenstein, Heiner. 1986. "NS-Prozesse: Ein Kapitel deutscher Vergangenheit und Geschichte." In *Jüdisches Leben in Deutschland seit 1945,* ed. Micha Brumlik et al. Frankfurt: Athenäum.

Lifton, Robert Jay. 1986. *The Nazi Doctors: Medical Killing and the Psychology of Genocide.* New York: Basic Books.

Linenthal, Edward. 1993. "Contested Memories, Contested Space: The Holocaust Museum." *Moment,* June:46–53, 78.

Lohmann, Hans-Martin, ed. 1984. *Psychoanalyse und Nationalsozialismus: Beiträge zur Bearbeitung eines unbewältigten Traumas.* Frankfurt: Fischer.

Luel, Steven A. 1984. "Living with the Holocaust: Thoughts on Revitalization." In *Psychoanalytic Reflections on the Holocaust,* ed. Steven A. Luel and Paul Marcus. New York: KTAV Publishing House.

References

Luel, Steven A., and Paul Marcus, eds. 1984. *Psychoanalytic Reflections on the Holocaust: Selected Essays*. Holocaust Awareness Institute, Center for Judaic Studies, University of Denver. New York: KTAV Publishing House.

Maier, Charles. 1988. *The Unmasterable Past: History, Holocaust, and German National Identity*. Cambridge, Mass.: Harvard University Press.

Meckel, Christoph. 1980. *Suchbild: Über meinen Vater*. Düsseldorf: Claassen.

Miller, Judith. 1990. *One, by One, by One: Facing the Holocaust*. New York: Simon and Schuster.

Mitscherlich, Alexander and Margarete Mitscherlich. 1975. *The Inability to Mourn*. New York: Grove Press. German: 1967. *Die Unfähigkeit zu Trauern*. Munich: Piper.

Mitscherlich-Nielsen, Margarete. 1984. "Die Notwendigkeit zu trauern." In *Psychoanalyse und Nationalsozialismus*, ed. Hans-Martin Lohmann. Frankfurt: Fischer.

Morein, Andrea. 1989. *Das Magische Leben der Steine*. Berlin: Transit.

Neiman, Susan. 1992. *Slow Fire: Jewish Notes from Berlin*. New York: Schocken Books.

Norden, Edward. 1993. "Yes and No to the Holocaust Museum." *Commentary* 96, no. 2 (August):23–32.

Ophir, Adi. 1987. "On Sanctifying the Holocaust: An Anti-Theological Treatise." *Tikkun* 2, no. 1:61–66.

Ortheil, Hans-Josef. 1992. *Abschied von den Kriegsteilnehmern*. Munich: Pieper.

Ozick, Cynthia. 1976. "A Liberal's Auschwitz." In *The Pushcart Press: Best of Small Presses*, ed. Bill Henderson. Yonkers: Pushcart Book Press.

Piper, Franciszek. 1967. "Das Nebenlager 'Blechhammer.'" *Hefte von Auschwitz* 10:19–39.

Posner, Gerald. 1991. *Hitler's Children: Sons and Daughters of Leaders of the Third Reich Talk about Their Fathers and Themselves*. New York: Random House.

Rabinbach, Anson. 1986. "Reflections on Germans and Jews since Auschwitz." In *Germans and Jews since the Holocaust*, eds. Anson Rabinbach and Jack Zipes. New York: Holmes & Meier.

Rabinbach, Anson, and Jack Zipes, eds. 1986. *Germans and Jews since the Holocaust: The Changing Situation in West Germany*. New York: Holmes & Meier.

Rehmann, Ruth. 1979. *Der Mann auf der Kanzel. Fragen an einen Vater*. Munich: Hanser.

Reichel, Sabine. 1989. *What Did You Do in the War, Daddy? Growing Up German*. New York: Hill and Wang.

Renn, Walter F. 1987. "The Treatment of the Holocaust in Textbooks." In *Social Science Monograph*, ed. Randolph L. Braham. Social Science Monographs, Boulder, Co., and Institute for Holocaust Studies, City University of New York.

Röhr, Esther. 1989. "Steine sind wie Zeit: Das Jewish-German Dance Theatre." *Religion Heute* 3, no. 4:255–257.

Roiphe, Anne. 1988. *A Season for Healing: Reflections on the Holocaust*. New York: Summit.

Rosenberg, Alan. 1988. "The Crisis in Knowing and Understanding the Holocaust." In *Echoes from the Holocaust*, ed. Alan Rosenberg and Gerald E. Myers. Philadelphia: Temple University Press.

Rosenberg, Alan, and Gerald E. Myers, eds. 1988. *Echoes from the Holocaust: Philosophical Reflections on a Dark Time*. Philadelphia: Temple University Press.

Rosenfeld, Alvin H. 1980. *A Double Dying: Reflections on Holocaust Literature*. Bloomington: Indiana University Press.

———. 1986. "Another Revisionism: Popular Culture and the Changing Image of the

Holocaust." In *Bitburg in Moral and Political Perspective,* ed. Geoffrey Hartman. Bloomington: Indiana University Press.

Rosenkötter, Lutz. 1984. "Schatten der Zeitgeschichte auf psychoanalytischen Behandlungen." In *Psychoanalyse und Nationalsozialismus,* ed. Hans-Martin Lohmann. Frankfurt: Fischer. An abbreviated English version: 1990. "The Formation of Ideals in the Succession of Generations." In *Generations of the Holocaust,* ed. Martin Bergmann and Milton Jucovy. New York: Columbia University Press.

Rosenthal, Abigail. 1988. "The Right Way to Act: Indicting the Victims." In *Echoes from the Holocaust,* ed. Alan Rosenberg and Gerald E. Myers. Philadelphia: Temple University Press.

Rosenthal, Gabriele, and Dan Bar-On. 1992. "A Biographical Case Study of a Victimizer's Daughter's Strategy: Pseudo-Identification with the Victims of the Holocaust." *Journal of Narrative and Life History* 2, no. 2:105–127.

Roskies, David G. 1984. *Against the Apocalypse: Responses to the Catastrophe in Modern Jewish Culture.* Cambridge, Mass.: Harvard University Press.

Rubinstein, Richard L. 1966. *After Auschwitz: Radical Theology and Contemporary Judaism.* New York: Bobbs-Merrill.

Ryback, Timothy. 1993. "Evidence of Evil." *The New Yorker,* November 15:68–81.

Salm, Heidi. 1993. "I Took Part: Confrontations with One's Own History in Family Therapy." In *The Collective Silence,* ed. Barbara Heimannsberg and Christoph Schmidt. San Francisco: Jossey-Bass.

Sartre, Jean-Paul. [1946] 1965. *Anti-Semite and Jew.* Trans. George J. Becker. New York: Schocken Books.

Schechner, Richard. 1977. *Essays on Performance Theory, 1970–1976.* New York: Drama Book Specialists.

Schneider, Karlheinz, and Nikolaus Simon, eds. 1984. *Solidarität und deutsche Geschichte: Die Linke zwischen Antisemitismus und Israelkritik.* Berlin: Schriftenband 9 des DIAK.

Schneider, Peter. 1983. *The Wall Jumper.* Trans. Leigh Hafrey. New York: Pantheon. German: 1984. *Der Mauerspringer.* Darmstadt: Luchterhand.

———. 1987. "Im Todeskreis der Schuld." *Die Zeit* 14 (March 27). A similar version in English: 1987. "Hitler's Shadow: On Being a Self-Conscious German." *Harper's Magazine* (September):49–54.

Schoeps, Julius H. 1990. *Leiden an Deutschland: Vom antisemitischen Wahn und der Last der Erinnerung.* Munich: Piper.

Scholem, Gershom. 1976. *On Jews and Judaism in Crisis: Selected Essays.* New York: Schocken.

Seligmann, Rafael. 1991. *Mit Beschränkter Hoffnung: Juden, Deutsche, Israelis.* Hamburg: Hoffmann und Campe.

Sereny, Gitta. 1990. "Children of the Reich." *Vanity Fair,* July:76–81, 127–130.

Sichrovsky, Peter. 1985. *Wir wissen nicht was morgen wird, wir wissen wohl was gestern war: Junge Juden in Deutschland und Österreich.* Cologne: Kiepenheuer & Witsch.

———. 1988. *Born Guilty: Children of Nazi Families.* Trans. Jean Steinberg. New York: Basic Books. German: 1987. *Schuldig geboren: Kinder aus Nazifamilien.* Cologne: Kiepenheuer & Witsch.

Siemenauer, Erich. 1990. "The Return of the Persecutor." In *Generations of the Holocaust,* ed. Martin Bergmann and Milton Jucovy. New York: Columbia University Press.

Speier, Sammy. 1986. "Von der Pubertät zum Erwachsenendasein—Bericht einer

Bewußtwerdung." In *Jüdisches Leben in Deutschland seit 1945,* ed. Micha Brumlik et al. Frankfurt: Athenäum.

———. 1993. "The Psychoanalyst without a Face: Psychoanalysis without a History." In *The Collective Silence,* ed. Barbara Heimannsberg and Christoph Schmidt. San Francisco: Jossey-Bass.

Spielmann, Jochen. 1988. "Steine des Anstoßes—Denkmale in Erinnerung an den Nationalsozialismus in der Bundesrepublik Deutschland." *Kritische Berichte* 3:5–16.

Stern, Frank. 1991. *Im Anfang war Auschwitz: Antisemitismus und Philosemitismus im deutschen Nachkrieg.* Gerlingen: Bleicher Verlag.

Stern, Fritz. 1987. *Dreams and Delusions: The Drama of German History.* New York: Knopf.

Stierlin, Helm. 1993. "The Dialogue between the Generations about the Nazi Era." In *The Collective Silence,* ed. Barbara Heimannsberg and Christoph Schmidt. San Francisco: Jossey-Bass. First published in 1981 as "The Parent's Nazi Past and the Dialogue between the Generations." *Family Process* 20:379–390.

Turner, Victor. 1982. *From Ritual to Theatre: The Human Seriousness of Play.* New York: PAJ Publications.

Von Kellenbach, Katharina. 1990. "Anti-Judaism in Christian-Rooted Feminist Writings: An Analysis of Major U.S. American and West German Feminist Theologians." Ph.D thesis, Temple University. Ann Arbor: UMI.

Von Westernhagen, Dötte. 1987. *Die Kinder der Täter: Das Dritte Reich und die Generation danach.* Munich: Kösel.

Webber, Jonathan. 1992. *Die Zukunft von Auschwitz.* Materialien Nr. 6. Trans. Josefine Raab and Annette Winkelmann. Frankfurt: Frankfurter Lern- und Dokumentationszentrum des Holocaust.

Wehler, Hans-Ulrich. 1988. *Entsorgung der deutschen Vergangenheit? Ein politischer Essay zum 'Historikerstreit'.* Munich: C. H. Beck.

Weissmark, Mona S., Daniel A. Giacomo, and Ilona Kuphal. 1993. "Common Threads in the Lives of Children of Survivors and Nazis." *Journal of Narrative and Life History* 3, no. 4:319–335.

Wieseltier, Leon. 1993. "After Memory." *The New Republic,* May 3:16–26.

Wiesenthal, Simon. 1976. *The Sunflower.* New York: Schocken.

Wolf, Christa. 1980. *A Model Childhood.* Trans. Ursule Molinaro and Hedwig Rappolt. London: Virago Press. German: 1979. *Kindheitsmuster.* Darmstadt: Luchterhand.

Wolffsohn, Michael. 1988. *Ewige Schuld? 40 Jahre Deutsch-Jüdisch-Israelische Beziehungen.* Munich: Piper.

Wyschograd, Michael. 1971. "Faith and the Holocaust." *Judaism* 20, no. 3 (Summer):286–294.

Young, James E. 1990. *Writing and Rewriting the Holocaust: Narrative and the Consequences of Interpretation.* Bloomington: Indiana University Press.

———. 1992. "The Future of Auschwitz." *Tikkun* 7 (November/December):31-33, 77.

———. 1993. *The Texture of Memory: Holocaust Memorials and Meaning in Europe, Israel, and America.* New Haven: Yale University Press.

Index

Index

Index

Holocaust memory: bodily reactions to, 54, 164–65; coming to terms with, 96, 163, 177, 184, 233; as curse, 231; emotional, 34, 49, 53, 63, 67; and identity, 21, 47, 166; as intergenerational transmission of motifs, 83–85, 88; manipulation of, 180; and museum, 145, 153; scars of, 81, 129; and therapy, 84, 88. *See also* Memory, injurious
Holocaust museums. *See* Museums, Holocaust
Holocaust survivors: adjustment of, 82–83; and anger, 43, 81; anguish of, 133; children of, 14, 43–44, 51, 53–55, 76, 81–84, 129–30, 132, 137, 143, 183, 201; experiences of, 12, 14; gathering of, 3–4, 50; German, 10, 141–42; and Germans, 6, 43–44, 65, 131–38, 140, 142, 183, 237n13; going back to Germany, 34; in Israel, 83, 87; joy of, 51; in Rhina, 110; in *Shoah* (film), 117; stories of, 123, 133, 136; and therapy, 81–84, 87, 129–30; and Yom Ha-Shoah, 41, 183. *See also* Amery, Jean; Celan, Paul; Gastfriend, Ed; Levi, Primo; Millman, Edith
Holocaust (television series), 33
Homogeneous groups, 67, 96, 177, 219–20
Hultberg, Peer, 218

Identification: with biases, 48; with enemies of Israel, 36; false, 176, 219; (of author) with father, 178; with Hitler 177; lack of positive, 52; symbolic, 175. *See also* Victim, identification with; Victimizer, identification with
Identity: Christian, 186, 191, 226; collective, 11, 24, 27, 47, 91; cultural, 21, 26–27, 31, 88, 91, 95, 138, 144, 179, 217; formation of, 22; German, 5, 37, 45, 48, 62, 65, 87, 160, 175, 190, 207, 218–19, 225, 232; Jewish, 5, 39, 45, 48, 186, 207, 219; national, 5, 10, 16, 21–22, 26–27, 30, 47, 88, 101, 144–46, 218; post-Wall, 232; religious, 10, 180
Improvisation, 166–68, 172–73, 184
Indifference: to Auschwitz, 216; to commemoration, 224; toward Jews, 59;

toward past, 103, 155; toward Shoah, 59; to summer program, 202; of young, 101
Interfaith Council on the Holocaust (Philadelphia), 8, 63, 134, 211
Intergenerational: bonds, 129; conflict, 7; dysfunctions, 130; patterns, 101
Intermarriage, 38, 67, 170
Intimacy, 6, 27, 70, 77, 87, 126, 130, 169, 171, 176, 199
Israel, 3, 11–12, 24, 36, 51, 56, 60, 73, 83, 87, 139, 174, 188, 198, 213

Jewish-Christian: dialogue, 2–3, 75, 165, 235n2; reconciliation, 213; relations, 189, 212
Jewish Defense League, 28, 233
Jewish-German Dance Theatre: 59–63, 68, 135, 137, 155, 164, 168, 177, 180, 182, 185–86; as communitas, 90, 166, 178, 184, 192, 201; history, 6, 166, 242n1; performances, 59–60, 73–74, 166–67, 179, 183–4; rehearsals and workshops, 166–71, 180, 198
Jewish-German symbiosis. *See* Symbiosis
Jewish resistance. *See* Resistance, Jewish
Jews: absence of, 5–6, 34, 75, 104, 155–156, 158; annihilation of, 31, 33, 40, 44, 47; conspiracy of, 35, 42, 174; innocence of, 35–36, 41–43; reincarnated, 176. *See also* Family history, Jewish; Identity, Jewish
Jucovy, Milton, 85, 130
Judenrat, 42, 237n11

Kassel, 197
Kertzer, David, 26
Kestenberg, Judith, 71, 84, 130
Klein, Hillel, 83, 88
Kohl, Helmut, 23–24, 26–27, 57
Kolbe, Maximilian, 212
Königsberg (Kaliningrad), 2
Kristallnacht, 155, 157, 164, 166, 182, 185, 197–98, 232
Kuphal, Ilona, 201

Laibson, Ruth, 211, 235n4
Langer, Lawrence, 42, 81, 118, 133, 163
Lanzmann, Claude, 81, 117–18, 163, 167

Index